Data Mashup with Microsoft Excel Using Power Query and M

Finding, Transforming, and Loading Data from External Sources

Adam Aspin

Apress®

Data Mashup with Microsoft Excel Using Power Query and M: Finding,
Transforming, and Loading Data from External Sources

Adam Aspin
Stafford, UK

ISBN-13 (pbk): 978-1-4842-6017-3   ISBN-13 (electronic): 978-1-4842-6018-0
https://doi.org/10.1007/978-1-4842-6018-0

Managing Director, Apress Media LLC: Welmoed Spahr
Acquisitions Editor: Jonathan Gennick
Development Editor: Laura Berendson
Coordinating Editor: Jill Balzano

Cover image designed by Freepik (www.freepik.com)

Distributed to the book trade worldwide by Springer Science+Business Media New York, 233 Spring Street, 6th Floor, New York, NY 10013. Phone 1-800-SPRINGER, fax (201) 348-4505, e-mail orders-ny@springer-sbm.com, or visit www.springeronline.com. Apress Media, LLC is a California LLC and the sole member (owner) is Springer Science + Business Media Finance Inc (SSBM Finance Inc). SSBM Finance Inc is a **Delaware** corporation.

For information on translations, please e-mail rights@apress.com, or visit http://www.apress.com/rights-permissions.

Apress titles may be purchased in bulk for academic, corporate, or promotional use. eBook versions and licenses are also available for most titles. For more information, reference our Print and eBook Bulk Sales web page at http://www.apress.com/bulk-sales.

Any source code or other supplementary material referenced by the author in this book is available to readers on GitHub via the book's product page, located at www.apress.com/9781484260173. For more detailed information, please visit http://www.apress.com/source-code.

Printed on acid-free paper

Table of Contents

About the Author

Adam Aspin is an independent business intelligence consultant based in the United Kingdom. He has worked with SQL Server for over 25 years. During this time, he has developed several dozen reporting and analytical systems based on the Microsoft Analytics Stack.

Business intelligence has been Adam's principal focus for the last 20 years. He has applied his skills for a variety of clients in a range of industry sectors. He is the author of Apress books: *SQL Server 2012 Data Integration Recipes*, *Pro Power BI Desktop* (now in its third edition), *Business Intelligence with SQL Server Reporting Services*, and *High Impact Data Visualization* in Excel with Power View, 3D Maps, Get & Transform and Power BI.

A graduate of Oxford University, Adam began his career in publishing before moving into IT. Databases soon became a passion, and his experience in this arena ranges from dBase to Oracle, and Access to MySQL, with occasional sorties into the world of DB2. He is, however, most at home in the Microsoft universe when using SQL Server Analysis Services, SQL Server Reporting Services, SQL Server Integration Services, and Power BI—both on-premises and in Azure.

A fluent French speaker, Adam has worked in France and Switzerland for many years.

About the Technical Reviewer

Karine Aspin is a principal consultant with Calidra Ltd., a UK-based data and analytics consultancy. A mathematics graduate of the Swiss Federal Institute of Technology, Karine has worked at a range of IT companies including IBM Global Services.

Acknowledgments

Writing a technical book can be a lonely occupation. So I am all the more grateful for all the help and encouragement that I have received from so many fabulous friends and colleagues.

First, my considerable thanks go to Jonathan Gennick, the commissioning editor of this book. Throughout the publication process, Jonathan has been both a tower of strength and an exemplary mentor. He has always been available to share his vast experience selflessly and courteously.

Heartfelt thanks go to Jill Balzano, the Apress coordinating editor, for calmly managing this book through the production process. She succeeded—once again—in the well-nigh impossible task of making a potentially stress-filled trek into a pleasant journey filled with light and humor. Her team also deserves much praise for their efficiency under pressure.

I also owe a debt of gratitude to my wife, Karine, for her time and effort spent reviewing this book. Being a technical reviewer is a thankless task, but I want to say a heartfelt "thank you" to her for the range and depth of her comments and for picking up so much that otherwise would have gone unnoticed. The book is a better one thanks to her efforts.

My thanks also go to Ann Gemer Tuballa for her tireless and subtle work editing and polishing the prose and to the team at SPi Global for the hours spent preparing the book for publishing.

Introduction

Analytics has become one of the buzzwords that define an age. Managers want their staff to deliver meaningful insight in seconds; users just want to do their jobs quickly and well. Everyone wants to produce clear, telling, and accurate analysis with tools that are intuitive and easy to use.

Microsoft recognized these trends and needs a few short years ago when they extended Excel with an add-in called Power Query. Once a mere optional extension to the world's leading spreadsheet, Power Query is now a fundamental pillar of the Excel toolkit. It allows a user to take data from a wide range of sources and transform them into the base data that they can build on to add metrics, instant analyses, and KPIs to project their insights.

With Power Query, the era of self-service data access and transformation has finally arrived.

What Is Power Query?

Power Query is a tool that is used to carry out ETL. This acronym stands for **Extract, Transform, Load**. This is the sequential process that covers

- Connecting to source data outside the current Excel workbook (or file if you prefer) and accessing all or part of the data that you need to bring into Excel. This is the *extract* phase of ETL.

- Reshaping the data (the "data mashup" process) so that the resulting data is in a form that can be used by Excel. Essentially, this means ensuring that the data is in a coherent, structured, and complete tabular format. This is the *transform* phase of ETL.

- Returning the data into Excel as a table in a worksheet or into the Excel/Power Pivot data model. This is the *load* phase of ETL.

These three phases make up the data ingestion process. So it is worth taking a short look at what makes up each one of them.

Connecting to Source Data

Gone are the days when you manually entered all the data you needed into a spreadsheet. Today's data are available in a multitude of locations and formats—and are too voluminous to rekey.

This is where Power Query's ability to connect instantly to 40-odd standard data sources is simply invaluable. Is your accounting data in MS Dynamics? Just connect. Is your CRM data in Salesforce? Just connect. Is your organization using a Data Lake?...you can guess the reply.

Yet this is only a small part of what Power Query can do to help simplify your analyses. For not only can it connect to a multitude of data sources (many of which are outlined in Chapters 1 through 5), it does this via a unified interface that makes connecting to data sources brilliantly simple. On top of this, you can use Power Query to preview the source data and ensure that you are loading exactly what you need. Finally, to top it all, the same interface is used for just about all of the available source data connections. This means that once you have learned to set up *one* connection, you have learned how to *connect to virtually all of the available data sources*.

In essence, part of Power Query is just another connection to external data. However, its unified data access interface, range of available data sources, and sheer simplicity will probably induce you to replace any data connections made using older technologies pretty quickly.

Data Transformation

Once you have established a connection to a data source, you may need to tweak the data in some way. Indeed, you may even need to reshape it entirely. This is the data mashup process—and it is the area where Power Query shines.

Power Query can carry out the simplest data transformation tasks to the most complex data restructuring challenges in a few clicks. You can

- Filter source data so that you only load exactly the rows and columns you need

- Extend the source data with calculations or data extracted from existing columns of data

- Cleanse and rationalize the data easily and quickly in a multitude of ways

- Join or split source tables to prepare a logical set of data tables for each specific analytical requirement

- Group and aggregate source data to reduce the quantity of data loaded into Excel

- Prepare source data tables to become a usable data model

This list merely scratches the surface of all that Power Query can do to mash up your data. It is, without hyperbole, unbelievably powerful at transforming source data. Indeed, it can carry out data ingestion and transformation tasks that used to be the preserve of expensive products that required complex programming skills and powerful servers.

All of this can now be done using a code-free interface that assists you in taking the messiest source data and delivering it to Excel as limpid tables of information ready to work with. If you wish to become a Power Query super-user, then you can extend its possibilities using the built-in M language.

Loading into a Worksheet or the Data Model

This final phase is the easiest by far. It is simply a question of telling Power Query where to land the data. This can be one—or both—of

- *A worksheet*: Power Query can place the data from each source query into a separate worksheet. Once in a worksheet, it is perfectly "normal" Excel data. From here on you can do what you want to the data in Excel just as you normally would using all the Excel techniques that you have learned over the years.

- *The data model*: Also referred to, often, as the *Power Pivot data model* (which is the term that I prefer to use), this is an in-memory data store. It can handle many more rows of data than Excel—tens of millions in some cases—and is normally the basis for pivot table output in Excel. When dealing with large source datasets, it is often the ideal destination for data that you have accessed using Power Query, as it is compressed in memory (and consequently takes up less space when saved to disk) and can easily exceed the 1,048,576 row limit of Excel worksheets.

The data model and Power Pivot are extensive subjects in their own right, and this book will not be looking at either of them in detail.

Integrating Power Query into Daily Workflows

Power Query is completely integrated into the latest versions of Excel. This means that you can use it seamlessly as part of your daily routines when ingesting and analyzing data. Put simply:

- Data source connections, transformation routines, and data loading into Excel are created once and can be reused whenever suits you.

- You can trigger manual data refreshes at any time—and these can be total refreshes of every source connection in a workbook or refreshes of a single source if you prefer.

- Data sources can be reused across different Excel workbooks.

- Power Query processes can be copied between different Excel files.

- Power Query processes (called queries) can be managed and extended with interactive parameters to create immensely powerful ETL processes.

- Power Query–based data flows can be customized and extended using the built-in M language.

So, as is the case for nearly all your Excel-based work, you are likely to build once and use often.

The Evolution of Power Query

Power Query has evolved considerably over the years since it was first made available as a downloadable add-in for Excel 2010. It was still optional for Excel 2013 and only attained the status of being completely integrated into Excel by the 2016 version. Indeed, it suffered a name change at that point and was accessed under the heading "Get & Transform."

Since around 2017—and since the Excel 2019 version—it has reverted to being Power Query once again. *This is the version that is the subject of this book.* This does not mean that you cannot use the techniques described in these pages with earlier versions of the product. However, it will mean that certain aspects of the Excel interface that you use to launch Power Query will be slightly different from those described in Chapters 1 through 5. These differences are essentially minor and should not present any difficulties to experienced Excel users.

This is made possible due to the fact that Power Query is accessed using a separate interface. It is called from inside Excel, but exists in its own parallel universe. This ensures a consistent look and feel whatever the version of Excel that you are using. The entry point into Power Query may change with Excel versions—but the product itself remains the same. Just remember that the range of available data sources will depend on the version of Excel that you are using. Some of the "enterprise-level" data sources are only available in Pro and Enterprise subscriptions to Excel.

How to Use This Book

If you wish, you can read this book from start to finish as it is designed to be a progressive tutorial that will help you to learn Power Query. However, as Power Query is composed of four main areas, this book is broken down into four sets of chapters that focus on the various key areas of the product. It follows that you can, if you prefer, focus on individual topics in Power Query without having to take a linear approach to reading this book.

- Chapters 1 through 5 show you how to connect to a range of varied data sources and bring this data into Excel using Power Query. Depending on the source data that you need to use, you may only need to dip into parts of these chapters to find guidance on how to use a specific source data type.

- Chapters 6 through 9 explain how to transform and clean data so that you can use it for analysis. These data transformations range from the extremely simple to the potentially complex. Indeed, they are as potentially vast as data itself. You may never need to apply all of the extensive range of data modification and cleansing techniques that Power Query can deliver—but just about everything that it can do is explained in detail in these chapters.

- Chapters 10 and 11 explain how to tame the real world of data loading and transformation. Here you will learn how to organize and manage your queries, as well as how to add parameters to make them more interactive and resilient.

- Chapter 12 introduces you to M—the language that Power Query uses to transform your data. Using M you can push your data ingestion and transformation routines to new heights that are simply not possible using just the Power Query interface.

On to Learning Power Query

This book comes with a small set of sample data that are used to create the examples that are used throughout the book. I realize that it may seem paradoxical to use a tiny dataset for a product that can handle tens of millions of rows of data, but I prefer to use a comprehensible set of source data so that the reader can concentrate on what is being learned, rather than the data itself.

It is inevitable that not every question can be anticipated and answered in one book. Nonetheless, I hope that I have answered many of the data ingestion and transformation questions that you might encounter and—more importantly—have given you the approaches and the confidence to resolve most of the Power Query challenges that you might meet when applying this product to solve real-world problems.

As a final point, the information on "pure" Power Query in Chapters 6–12 is independent of Excel. So if you are learning Power Query in Power BI, SQL Server Integration Services, or the Power BI Service, you can find a wealth of relevant information to assist you in your data transformation projects.

I wish you good luck in using Power Query, and I sincerely hope that you have as much fun using it as I did in writing this book.

CHAPTER 1

Using Power Query to Discover and Load Data into Excel

If you are reading this book, it is most likely because you need to use data. More specifically, it may be that you need to take a journey from data to insight in which you have to take quantities of facts and figures, shape them into comprehensible information, and add the analysis that delivers clear meaning. More to the point, you want to do all this using the spreadsheet that you know and trust—Microsoft Excel.

This book is all about that journey. It covers the many ways that you, an Excel user, can transform external raw data into the information structures that enable you to deliver high-impact analyses. This fresh approach presumes that you are not dependent on central IT to help you to load data from external sources, nor do you need their help on a regular basis. It is based on enabling the user to handle industrial-strength quantities of source data using the world's most popular spreadsheet in the shortest possible time frame.

The keywords in this universe are

- Fast

- Decentralized

- Intuitive

- Interactive

- Delivery

© Adam Aspin 2020
A. Aspin, *Data Mashup with Microsoft Excel Using Power Query and M*,
https://doi.org/10.1007/978-1-4842-6018-0_1

Using the techniques described in this book, you can discover and load data from a multitude of external sources. You can then, quickly and intuitively, transform and cleanse this raw data to make it structured and usable. Once ready for use, you can load it into either Excel worksheets or the Power Pivot data model in Excel and start using the tool you already know so well—Excel—to provide detailed analytics.

It follows that this book is written from the perspective of the user. Essentially it is all about *empowerment*—letting users define their own requirements and satisfy their own needs simply and efficiently by building on their existing skills. The amazing thing is that you can do all of this using Excel without needing any other tools or utilities. Your sources could be in many places and in many formats. Nonetheless, you need to access them, sample them, select them, and, if necessary, transform or cleanse them in order to deliver your analyses. All of this is enabled by Power Query.

Power Query

Power Query is one of the most recent additions to the Excel toolkit. Now fully integrated into Excel, it allows you to discover, access, and consolidate information from varied sources. Once your data is selected, cleansed, and transformed into a coherent table, you can then place it in an Excel worksheet for detailed analysis or load it directly into Power Pivot (the Excel data model), which is a natural repository for data when you want to "slice and dice" it interactively.

Power Query allows you to do many things with source data, but the four main steps are likely to be

- *Import* data from a wide variety of sources. This covers corporate databases to files and social media to big data.

- *Merge* data from multiple sources into a coherent structure.

- *Shape* data into the columns and records that suit your use cases.

- *Cleanse* your data to make it reliable and easy to use.

There was a time when these processes required dedicated teams of IT specialists. Well, not any more. With Power Query, you can mash up your own data so that it is the way you want it and is ready to use as part of your self-service solution.

This is because discovering, loading, cleansing, restructuring, and modifying source data are what Power Query is designed to do. It allows you to accomplish the following:

- *Data discovery*: Find and connect to a myriad of data sources containing potentially useful data. This can be from both public and private data sources. This is the subject of Chapters 1 through 5.

- *Data loading*: Select the data you have examined and load a subset into Power Query for shaping.

- *Data modification*: Modify the structure of each dataset that you have imported.

- *Filter and clean the data itself.*

Although I have outlined these three steps as if they are completely separate and sequential, the reality is that they often blend into a single process. Indeed, there could be many occasions when you will examine the data *after* it has been loaded into Excel—or clean datasets *before* you load them. The core objective will, however, always remain the same: find some data and then sample it in Power Query where you can tweak, clean, and shape it before loading it into Excel.

This process could be described simplistically as "First, catch your data." In the world of data warehousing, the specialists call it ETL, which is short for **E**xtract, **T**ransform, and **L**oad. Despite the reassuring confidence that the acronym brings, this process is rarely a smooth, logical progression through a clear-cut series of steps. The reality is often far messier. You may often find yourself importing some data, cleaning it, importing some more data from another source, combining the second dataset with the first one, removing some rows and columns, and then repeating these operations, as well as many others, several times over.

In this and the following few chapters, I will try to show you how the process can work in practice using Power Query. I hope that this will make the various steps that comprise an ETL process clearer. All I am asking is that you remain aware that the range of options that Power Query includes make it a multifaceted and tremendously capable tool. The science is to know *which* options to use. The art is to know *when* to use them.

The Data Load Process

Let's begin with a rapid overview of what you need to do to get some data into Excel (assuming that you have downloaded the sample data that accompanies this book from the Apress website—this is explained in Appendix A). The following steps explain what you have to do to load data from a source that you know well already—Excel itself. Yes, I know that you can copy and paste data between workbooks, but that would be to miss the point and miss out on all the incredible extra facets of data mashup that Power Query can offer. In this initial case, the actual source of the data is irrelevant. It could come from any of a few dozen available sources. Excel is simply an example of potential source data.

1. Open a new, blank workbook in Excel.

2. Click Data in the menu to switch to the Data ribbon.

3. Click Get Data. The Get Data popup menu will appear, as shown in Figure 1-1.

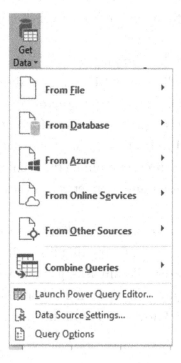

Figure 1-1. *The Get Data popup menu*

4. Click From File.

5. Click From Workbook. The Import Data dialog will appear.

6. Click the file C:\DataMashupWithExcelSamples\
   BrilliantBritishCars.xlsx. The Import Data dialog will look like the
   one in Figure 1-2.

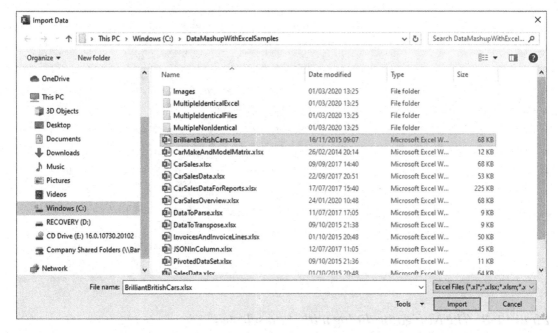

Figure 1-2. *The Import Data dialog when loading data from an Excel workbook*

7. Click the Import button. The Navigator dialog will appear.

8. You will see that the BrilliantBritishCars.xlsx file appears on
   the left of the Navigator dialog and that any workbooks, named
   ranges, or data tables that it contains are also listed under the file.

9. Click the BaseData worksheet name that is on the left. The
   contents of this workbook will appear in the data pane on the
   right of the Navigator dialog. The Navigator dialog should look like
   Figure 1-3.

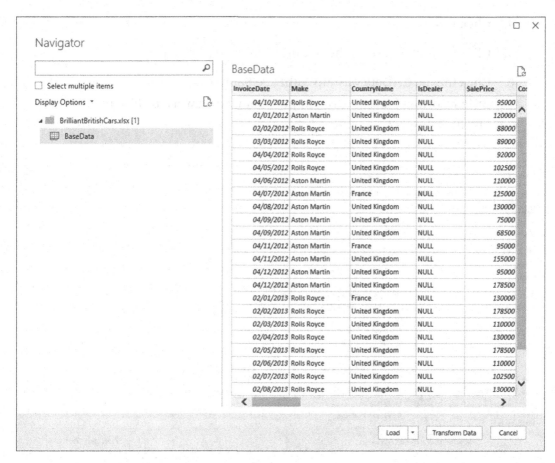

Figure 1-3. *The Navigator dialog with data selected*

10.   Click Load. The data will be loaded from the external Excel
workbook into a new worksheet inside the current workbook.

You will see the Excel window, like the one shown in Figure 1-4. The external data is
now an Excel table (named BaseData, as this was the name of the source data table). You
can see that the connection to the external workbook now appears on the right of the
Excel spreadsheet data in the new Queries & Connections pane. I will explain this new
element in a couple of pages once I have explained exactly why Power Query is such a
cool solution to data ingestion challenges.

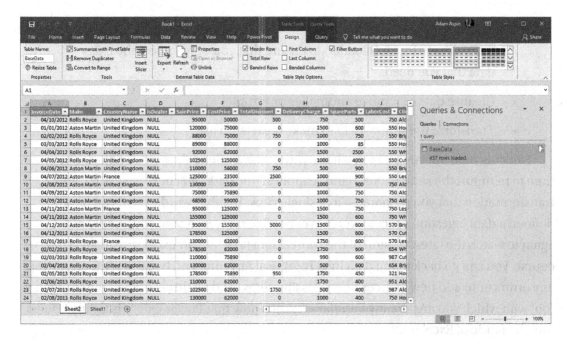

Figure 1-4. *Data available in Excel*

I imagine that loading this data took a few seconds at most. Yet you now have a complete set of external data in Excel that is ready to be used for analysis and reporting. However, for the moment, I would like to pause and explain exactly what you have seen so far.

Why Use Power Query?

What you have just done is to open up Excel to become the preferred analysis and MI/BI (Management Information and Business Intelligence) tool when it comes to connecting to the information held in dozens of external data sources. What you just saw was that Excel can now connect to multiple sources of data and bring them into spreadsheets for further analysis in a few clicks.

However, it is vital to understand that you have so far only scratched the surface of Power Query and all that it can do to facilitate data ingestion. This is because viewing and loading data are just the start. As well, you can use it to

- Import data from multiple different data sources
- Import multiple datasets from external data sources at the same time

- Join datasets from multiple different types of source data systems

- Filter data before it is loaded to ensure that you only import the exact data that you need

- Cleanse data to remove anomalies or errors

- Transform the source data to make it easier to use

Not only that, but you can refresh the process and reload the source data at any time to reimport the source data—and reapply all the data selection, cleansing, and transformation that you prepared—in a single click. In other words, once you have defined a data ingestion process, you never need to create it again, you simply run it again to watch the latest version of the source data flow into an Excel spreadsheet. Of course, you can go back to the data load routine at any time and tweak it either to correct any errors or to add new sources or processing steps. And all this is carried out using the tool with which you are already familiar—Excel—now that Power Query is tightly bound into the fabric of Excel itself.

The Queries & Connections Pane

The first really new aspect of using Power Query inside Excel is the Queries & Connections pane. Put simply, this window displays all the Power Query connections that you have made to external data sources. It is your point of entry into Power Query data ingestion processes, and allows you to

- List all active connections

- Refresh the data delivered by a Power Query connection

- Display a sample of the source data

- Move to the destination worksheet where the data is imported

- Delete the connection

- Modify the connection and any aspect of the data transformation process

- Manage connections

As the Queries & Connections pane is your gateway to the world of Power Query, it is worth familiarizing yourself with a couple of its key aspects from the start. As you progress through this book, you will be using more and more of its possibilities to unlock the immense capabilities of Power Query, so I will only attempt to demystify it now—the detail will come later.

Displaying the Queries & Connections Pane

To display (or hide) the Queries & Connections pane

1. Click Data in the menu to switch to the Data ribbon.

2. In the Data ribbon, click Queries & Connections. The Queries & Connections pane will be displayed (or hidden if it is already visible).

The main elements of the Queries & Connections pane are outlined in Figure 1-5.

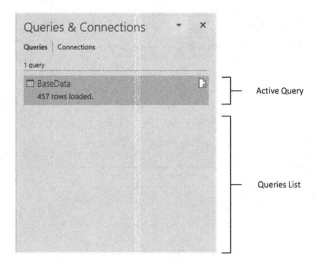

Figure 1-5. *The Queries & Connections pane*

The Peek Window

The Queries & Connections pane lets you take a glimpse of the data that is returned by a query. This can be extremely useful when you have added dozens of connections to an Excel file and cannot remember which connection returns which dataset.

To display the Peek window

1. Hover the mouse pointer over the query in the Queries & Connections pane whose data you want to view. If you have followed the previous examples in this chapter, it will be the query named BaseData.

The Peek window will appear showing some of the data as well as the key properties of the source data connection. You can see the Peek window explained in Figure 1-6.

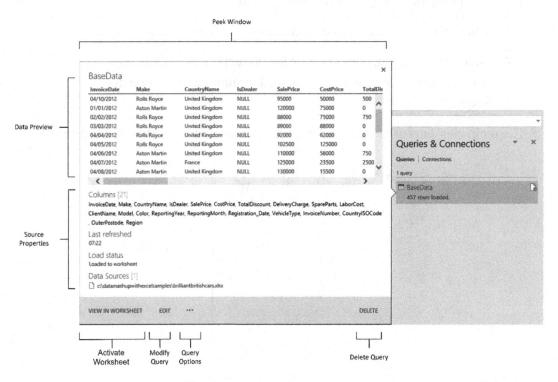

Figure 1-6. *The Peek window*

Peek Window Options

The key information that the Peek window makes available is outlined in Table 1-1.

Table 1-1. *The Peek Window*

Element	Description
Query or Connection Name	The name of each query or connection to a data source
Data Preview	A quick overview of a sample of the data
Column List	The column output from a query
Refresh Date	The last date that the data was refreshed
View in Worksheet	Activate the worksheet containing the data output from the query (if the data has been output this way)
Edit	Modify the query in Power Query
Query Menu	A subset of query modification options
Delete	Remove the query from the workbook file

View in Worksheet

The Peek window lets you move directly to the imported data in the destination worksheet (assuming that the data has not been padded into the Power Pivot data model).

To "jump" to the worksheet containing the data

1. Click the query in the Queries & Connections pane whose data you want to view.

The worksheet containing the imported data will be activated.

Inversely, you can click inside a worksheet that contains the data output from a query, and the query name will be highlighted in the Queries & Connections pane.

Note   Another (but slightly more complicated) way to activate the worksheet containing the data loaded from the query is to hover the pointer over the query in the Queries & Connections pane and then click View in Worksheet in the Peek window.

Deleting a Query

To complete this initial high-level overview of queries and connections using Power Query, let's see how to delete a connection that you have created:

1. Hover over the query in the Queries & Connections pane that you want to delete. The Peek window will appear.

2. In the Peek window, click Delete. The status bar of the Peek window will display a confirmation message as shown in Figure 1-7.

Figure 1-7. *Delete confirmation in the Peek window*

3. Click Delete. The connection will be deleted.

Note   This action does not delete the data that has been imported into a worksheet, only the connection to the source data and any processing steps that you have applied. If you want to remove the data, then simply delete the worksheet as you would normally. Deleting a query does, however, prevent any future data refresh.

Understanding Data Load

What you have seen so far is an extremely rapid dash through a Power Query data load scenario. In reality, this process can range from the blindingly simple (as you just saw) to the more complex where you join, filter, and modify multiple datasets from different sources (which you will discover in Chapters 6 through 12). However, loading data will always be the first step in any data analysis scenario when you are using Power Query to load data into Excel.

In this short example, you nonetheless saw many of the key elements of the data load process. These included

- Accessing data that is available in any of the source formats that Power Query can read

- Taking a first look at the data before loading it into Excel

What you did not see here is how Power Query can add an intermediate step to the data load process and edit the source data in Power Query Editor. This aspect of data manipulation—data mashup—is covered extensively in later chapters.

The Navigator Dialog

One key aspect of the data load process is using the Navigator dialog correctly. You saw this dialog in Figure 1-3. The Navigator window appears when connecting to nearly all data sources. It allows you to

- Take a quick look at the available data tables in the source data

- Filter multiple data elements that are available in a single data source

- Look at the data held in individual tables in the source application

- Select one or more data tables to load into Excel

Note   One of the really impressive aspects of Power Query (and the Navigator) is that in most cases you do not need client software installed on your PC to access the data. This means that you can access data in, for example, SQL Server or Salesforce directly from Excel.

Depending on the data source to which you have connected, you might see only a few data tables in the Navigator window, or hundreds of them. In any case, what you can see are the structured datasets that Power Query can recognize and is confident that it can import. Equally dependent on the data source is the level of complexity of what you will see in the Navigator window. If you are looking at a database server, for instance, then you may start out with a list of databases, and you may need to dig deeper into the arborescence of the data by expanding databases to list the available data tables and views. If you are connecting to an Excel file, you may only see a handful of tables of data.

The more you work with Power Query, the more you will use the Navigator dialog. It seems appropriate, therefore, to explain at this early juncture some of the tricks and techniques that you can apply to make your life easier when delving into a plethora of potential sources of data.

Let's start by taking a closer look at the available options. I will use the Navigator dialog that you first saw in Figure 1-3 when loading data from the Excel file BrilliantBritishCars.xlsx. The available options are outlined in Figure 1-8.

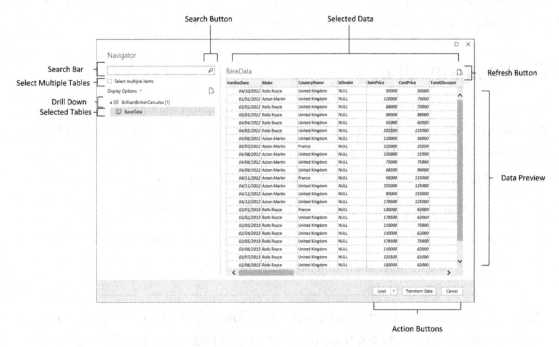

Figure 1-8. *The Navigator dialog*

The Navigator dialog is essentially in two parts:

- *On the left*: The hierarchy of available data sources. These can consist of a single dataset or multiple datasets, possibly organized into one or many folders.

- *On the right*: A preview of the data in the selected element.

The various Navigator dialog options are explained in the following sections.

Select Multiple Source Tables

Power Query lets you select and load more than one source data table from the same connection at once. Let's see an example of this.

1. In the Data ribbon, click Get Data ➤ From File ➤ From Workbook.

2. Navigate to the Excel file C:\DataMashupWithExcelSamples\
    CarSales.xlsx and click Import.

3. In the Navigator dialog, check the Select multiple items check box.
    This is shown in Figure 1-9.

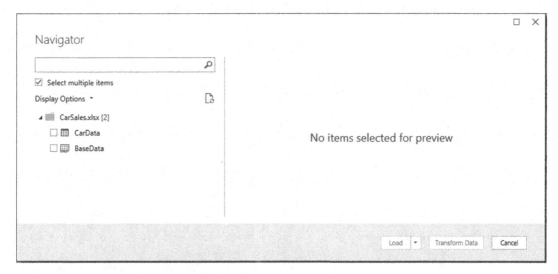

Figure 1-9.   *Selecting multiple source items*

This will cause a check box to appear to the left of each source data item (or table or dataset if you prefer). You can then check the box for each source element that you want to load as part of this query.

Searching for Datasets

You will, inevitably, come across cases where the data source that you are connecting to will contain hundreds of datasets. This is especially true for databases. Fortunately, Power Query lets you filter the datasets that are displayed extremely easily.

1. In the Navigator dialog, click inside the Search box.

2. Enter a part of a dataset name that you want to isolate. In this example, I have entered "li".

3. The list of available datasets will be filtered to show only those containing the text that you entered. You can see this in Figure 1-10 for the Excel source file CarSalesDataForQueries. xlsx (also in the directory C:\DataMashupWithExcelSamples).

Figure 1-10. *Dataset search in the Navigator dialog*

To remove the filter, simply click the cross at the right of the Search box. Navigator will clear the filter and display all the datasets in the data source.

Note   You must expand the hierarchy (or hierarchies) containing the items that you want to filter datasets on *before* using the Navigator Search function.

Navigator Display Options

Clicking Display Options in the Navigator dialog will show a popup menu with two options:

- Only selected items

- Enable data previews

You can see this in Figure 1-11.

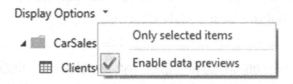

Figure 1-11. *Navigator display options*

Only Selected Items

Selecting this option will prevent any datasets that you have not selected from appearing in the data source pane.

Enable Data Previews

Selecting this option will show a small subset of the data available in the selected dataset. You could choose to disable data previews if the connection to the source data is slow.

Refresh

If you need to, you can refresh either or both of the following:

- The source data

- The data preview

Source Data Refresh

Clicking the preview button under the search bar will refresh the list of source data tables displayed in the source data pane.

Data Preview Refresh

Clicking the preview button on the top right of the Navigator dialog will refresh the preview data visible on the right for the selected table.

Select Related Tables

Clicking the Select Related Tables button is only valid for database sources, such as Microsoft SQL Server or Oracle. If the source database has been designed correctly to include joins between tables, then this option will automatically select all tables that are linked to any tables that you have already selected.

Note In a database source, some tables can be related to other tables that are, themselves, related to other tables. This hierarchy of connections is not discovered in its entirety when you click Select Related Tables. In other words, you might have to select several tables and click this button repeatedly to select all the tables that you need.

This is the end of our whirlwind tour of the Navigator. However, you will see much, much more of the Navigator window in the following four chapters as you learn how to connect to a wide range of data sources.

The Navigator Data Preview

The Navigator Data Preview pane (on the right) is, as its name implies, a preview of the data in a data source. It provides

- A brief overview of the *top few records* in any of the datasets that you want to look at. Given that the data you are previewing could be hundreds of columns wide and hundreds of rows deep, there could be scroll bars for the data table visible inside the Navigator Data Preview. Remember, however, that you are not examining *all* the available data and are only seeing a *small sample of the available records*.

- A list of the available columns in the data table. These are shown at the bottom of the Navigator Data Preview.

Power Query can preview and load data from several different sources. Indeed (as you can see from the list of possible data sources in the Get Data popup menu), it can read most of the commonly available enterprise data sources as well as many, many others. What is important to appreciate is that Power Query applies a common interface to the art and science of loading data, whatever the source. So whether you are examining a SQL Server or an Oracle database, an XML file or a text file, a web page or a big data source, you will always be using a standardized approach to examining and loading the data. This makes the Power Query data experience infinitely simpler—and extremely reassuring. It means that you spend less time worrying about technical aspects of connecting to data sources and that you are free to focus, instead, on the data itself.

Note   The Navigator Data Preview is a brilliant data discovery tool. Without having to load any data, you can take a quick look at the data source and any data that it contains that can (probably) be loaded by Power Query. You can then decide if it is worth loading. This way you do not waste time on a data load that could be superfluous to your needs.

Modifying Data

Once you have one or more queries in Power Query that can connect to data sources and bring the data into this environment, you can start thinking about the next step—transforming the data so that it is ready for use. Depending on the number of data sources that you are handling and the extent of any modifications that are required, this could vary from the simple to the complex. To give a process some structure, I advise that you try to break down any steps into the following main threads:

- *Shape the dataset*: This covers filtering out records to reduce the size of the dataset, as well as removing any extraneous columns. It may also involve adding columns that you create by splitting existing columns, creating calculated columns, or even joining queries.

- *Cleanse and modify the data*: This is also known as *data transformation* (the *T* in ETL). It encompasses the process of converting text data to uppercase and lowercase, as well as (for

19

instance) removing nonprinting characters. Rounding numbers and extracting date parts from date data are also possible (among the many dozens of other available transformations).

For the moment, however, it is only important to understand that Power Query can do all of this if you need it to. Transforming data is explained in detail in Chapters 6 through 12.

The Power Query Editor

In the previous example, you loaded data directly into Excel. In the course of this book, you will also learn how to extend this approach with an additional step—because you also have the option of loading data into the Power Query Editor *before* adding it to the data model. This "detour" is the part of the process that allows you to cleanse and transform the data *before* it is added to the data model. Of course, if your data is perfect, then you can add it straight into the data model and start analyzing just as you did previously. However, if your data needs any adjustment at all, then the Power Query Editor will likely soon become a trusted tool. Consequently, it is probably worth reading Chapters 1 through 5 that describe how to load data from a range of possible sources and then Chapters 6 through 12 to shape, modify, and structure your data so that it becomes a clear source of new and valuable insights.

Data Sources

Now that you have seen how quickly and easily you can load data into Excel, it is time to take a wider look at the *types* of data that Power Query can ingest and manipulate.

As the sheer wealth of possible data sources can seem overwhelming at first, Power Query groups potential data sources into the following categories:

- *File*: Includes Excel files, CSV (comma-separated values) files, text files, JSON files, and XML files. Power Query can even load entire folders full of files.

- *Database*: A comprehensive collection of relational databases that are currently in the workplace and in the cloud, including (among others) MS Access, SQL Server, and Oracle. The full list of those available when this book went to press is given in Chapter 3.

- *Azure*: This option lets you see a wide range of data types that is hosted in the Microsoft Cloud. This covers data formats from SQL Server through to big data sources. You can see how a few of these are used with Power Query in Chapter 4.

- *Online services*: These sources range from SharePoint lists to Salesforce, Dynamics 365 to Facebook—and many, many others. Some of these are examined in Chapter 4.

- *Other*: A considerable and ever-growing range of data sources, from Hadoop to Microsoft Exchange. Some of these will be touched on in the course of Chapters 2 through 5.

The list of possible data sources is changing all the time, and you need to be aware that you have to look at the version of Excel that you are using if you want an exhaustive list of all the available data sources that you can use. Indeed, I expect that more will have been added by the time that you read this book.

You can also list the contents of folders on any available local disk, network share, or even in the cloud and then leverage this to import several files at once. Similarly (if you have the necessary permissions), you can list the databases and data available on the database servers you connect to. This way, Power Query can provide not only the data but also the *metadata*—or data about data—that can help you to take a quick look at potential sources of data and only choose those that you really need.

Unfortunately, the sheer range of data sources from which Power Query can read data is such that we do not have space in a few chapters to examine the minutiae of every one individually. Consequently, we will take a rapid tour of *some* of the most frequently used data sources in this and the next few chapters. Fortunately, most of the data sources that Power Query can read are used in a similar way. This is because the Power Query interface does a wonderful job of making the arcane connection details as unobtrusive as possible. So even if you are faced with a data source that is not described in these chapters, you will nonetheless see a variety of techniques that can be applied to virtually any of the data sources that Power Query can connect to.

Note   The list of data sources that Power Query can access is growing all the time. Consequently, when you read this book, you will probably find even more sources than those described in this and the next four chapters.

Source Data Properties

Excel allows you to tweak a handful of options relating to the Power Query connection to an external data source.

1. Click inside the table containing data inserted into a worksheet by Power Query.

2. Click Properties in the Data ribbon. The External Data Properties dialog will appear. You can see this in Figure 1-12.

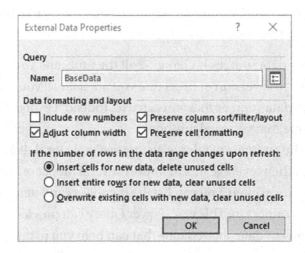

Figure 1-12. *The External Data Properties dialog*

These options are explained in Table 1-2.

Table 1-2. *External Data Properties Options*

Element	Description
Query Name	The name of the query or connection
Include row numbers	Adds an automatically increasing row number to the left of the data
Adjust column width	Adjusts the width of each column to display the data fully
Preserve column sort/filter/ layout	Keeps filters and sorting from the source query and not from the output in Excel
Preserve cell formatting	Keeps formatting (if any) from the source query and not from the output in Excel

Note   You will only see the result of any changes that you make to these options when the query is refreshed.

Query Properties

Excel has always proposed a series of query options when connecting to external data sources—even when older connection techniques were used. Fortunately, these options are also available when using Power Query.

1. Click inside the table containing data inserted into a worksheet by Power Query. I will use the initial query named BaseData that you created earlier in this chapter using the file BrilliantBritishCars. xlsx.

2. Click the small triangle at the bottom right of the Refresh All button. The Refresh popup menu will appear, as shown in Figure 1-13.

Figure 1-13. *The Refresh popup menu*

3. Click Connection Properties in the popup menu. You will see the Query Properties dialog as shown in Figure 1-14.

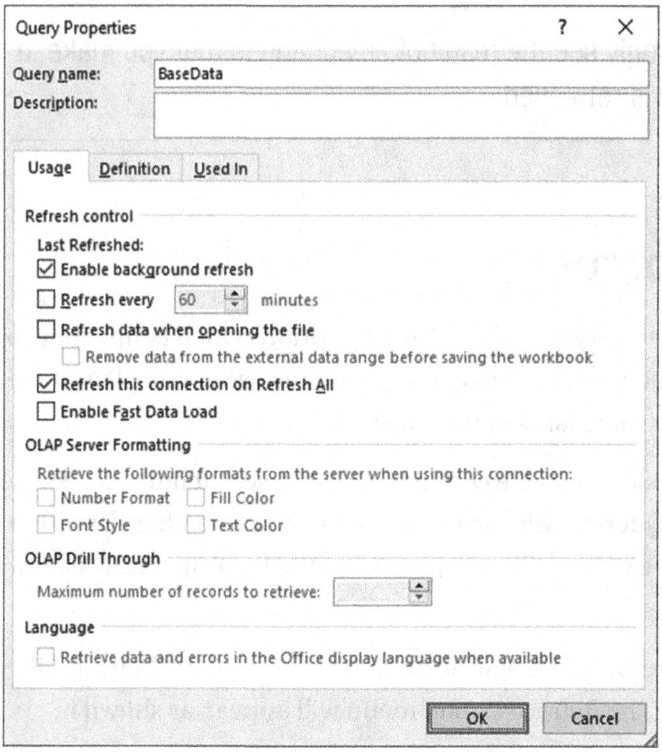

Figure 1-14. *The Query Properties dialog*

These options are explained in Table 1-3.

Table 1-3. *Query Properties Options*

Element	Description
Query name	The name of the query or connection
Description	Any comments that you wish to add
Enable background refresh	Allows the refresh to take place while working in Excel at the same time
Refresh every "N" minutes	Schedules an automated refresh
Refresh data when opening the file	Runs the query to refresh the data each time the Excel file is opened
Refresh this connection on Refresh All	Allows you to exclude a query from an overall refresh
Enable Fast Data Load	Loads the data as fast as possible—even if this causes Excel to appear to "hang"

Load Destinations

I mentioned at the start of this chapter that Power Query allows you a choice of load destinations once you have finished preparing the source data. The default load option is to place the output data directly in a new worksheet in the current Excel file. However there are several variations on this theme that are available. They are

- Load into an Excel named table (the default)

- Load into a pivot table based on the source data

- Load into a pivot chart based on the source data

- Only create a connection to the data, but do not load it yet

On top of this, you have the choice whether you want to

- Create the table of data, pivot table, or pivot chart in the current worksheet.

- Create the table of data, pivot table, or pivot chart in a new worksheet.

- Optionally, add the data to the Power Pivot data model. Queries added to the data model can be joined and extended separately to provide a complete and powerful source of analytical data.

Note   It is perfectly possible to load data to both the data model *and* to a worksheet table.

Assuming that you have connected to a data source and can view the required source data in the Navigator (as shown in Figure 1-3):

1. Click the small triangle at the right of the Load button in the Home menu. The popup menu will appear. You can see this in Figure 1-15.

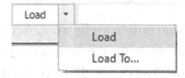

Figure 1-15. *Load options*

2. Select Load To.... The Import Data dialog appears, as shown in Figure 1-16.

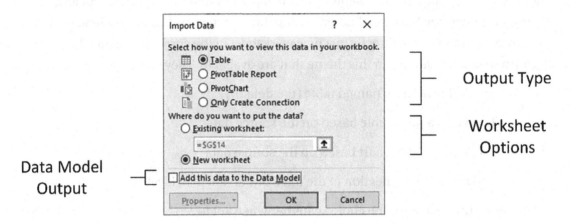

Figure 1-16. *Load destination options*

3. Select the Table radio button.

4. Select New worksheet as the data destination.

5. Leave the Add this data to the Data Model check box unchecked.

6. Click OK.

The connection—and data load if you opted for this outcome—will be created according to the options that you specified. If you followed the steps exactly as defined earlier, then you should obtain a new worksheet containing the data from the data source.

Note   Selecting the Only Create Connection radio button prevents you from choosing an output destination. This is useful when you want to prepare a data load process, but might not yet be sure how and where to output the final data.

Repurposing an Existing Connection

On some occasions, you may want only to set up a connection to source data, but not actually import the data. As you saw in the previous section, choosing the option Only Create Connection in the Import Data dialog allows you to do this.

There could be a variety of reasons for choosing this solution:

- You want to "pause" the work on a data transformation and load process and come back to it later—without losing the work that you have already carried out and without loading the data (which could be, potentially, voluminous and time-consuming).

- This query will not be used to access data directly, but used as an intermediate step in a more complex process. You will learn more about this approach in Chapter 9.

- The data will be loaded into the Power Pivot data model and not used directly in a table or Power Pivot table or chart.

Equally, it is worth knowing that if you delete a worksheet that contains the data output from a query, then the source query will become a connection only and will not load the data until you redefine an output destination.

It follows from this that you also need to know how to take a connection and apply a data destination. Here is how:

1. In the Queries & Connections pane, hover over the connection that you want to repurpose. The Peek window will appear.

2. Click the ellipses in the menu bar at the bottom of the Peek window. The menu that is shown in Figure 1-17 will appear.

Figure 1-17. *Peek window options*

3. Select Load To... and choose the options that you require from the Import Data dialog that you saw in Figure 1-16.

Note   You cannot simply redefine a new destination for an existing data load. You have first to remove the current load destination (by deleting the Excel table or the destination worksheet, e.g., or by removing the data table from the Power Pivot data model) and then reapply a new destination.

Load to Excel

Loading data into Excel is not only the default option, it is probably the preferred choice of many users. There are a multitude of valid reasons for choosing this data destination:

- It is the simplest option.

- The data is instantly available and ready to use.

- You can apply the techniques and functions that you are used to using directly in Excel to analyze the data.

You need to be aware, however, that this approach does have a few limitations:

- Large data loads will hit the 1,000,000 row limit in Excel.

- Large data loads can mean huge Excel file sizes.

In these latter cases, loading data into the Power Pivot data model is probably a wiser choice, as the data will be compressed and can contain, potentially, many millions of rows of data.

Load to the Data Model

As this is fundamental to the practice of self-service BI using Excel and Power Query, you really need to understand what this data model is and how it helps you to create valid analyses.

The data model is a collection of one or more tables of data that are loaded into Power Pivot and then joined together in a coherent fashion. The data can come via Power Query, be obtained from existing Excel tables or worksheets, or be imported from a variety of sources. There can only be a single data model per Excel file.

Admittedly, you can place all your data in a single "flat" table in Excel and use that as the basis for analytical output. However, it is highly likely that you will want to develop a data model using Power Pivot if you intend to use datasets of any complexity. There are occasions when building a good data model can take a while to get right, but there are many valid justifications for spending the time required to build a coherent data model using Power Pivot. The reasons for this investment include

- You can go way beyond the million-row limit of an Excel worksheet if you are using the Excel data model in Power Pivot. Indeed, in Power Pivot tables of tens of millions of rows are not unknown.

- A coherent data model makes understanding and visualizing your data easier.

- A well-thought-out data model means less redundant information stored in a single table when it can be referenced from another table rather than repeated endlessly.

- Power Pivot saves space on disk and in memory because it uses a highly efficient data compression algorithm to store the data in the data model. This means that a workbook using a dataset will take up considerably less space than storing data in Excel worksheets.

- Since a dataset is loaded entirely into the PC's memory, calculations are faster.

- A data model can be prepared for data output.

- A data model can contain certain calculations (some of which can get fairly complex) that are designed to ensure that the correct results are returned when slicing and filtering data in Excel.

- A data model can contain hierarchies and KPIs.

- A data model can be used to create complex pivot tables in Excel.

- A data model can be the basis, or the proof of concept, for a fully fledged SSAS (SQL Server Analysis Services) tabular data warehouse.

- A data model can avoid you having to implement complex VLOOKUP( ) functions in Excel.

As this is not a book on Power Pivot, I will not be describing how to create and use Power Pivot data models to carry out data analysis. I will merely point out that you can specify that the Power Pivot data model can be the destination for data imported using Power Query.

There are many excellent books and web resources on Power Pivot and the Power Pivot data model, and I encourage you to look at these for detailed explanations on using this amazing tool. If you want a short introduction, you can find this in my book *High Impact Data Visualization with Power View, Power Map, and Power BI* (2nd Edition Apress 2016.)

Conclusion

In this chapter, you have seen how Power Query can be used to connect to any of a wide range of data sources. You have seen that as long as you know what kind of data you want to load—and that Power Query has an available connector to this data—you can preview and load the data into either an Excel worksheet or the built-in Power Pivot data model.

Now it is time to delve deeper into the details of some of the various data sources that you can use with Power Query. The next chapter will start on your journey by introducing many of the file-based data types that you can use as sources of your data.

CHAPTER 2

Discovering and Loading File-Based Data with Power Query

Sending files across networks and over the Internet or via email has become second nature to most of us. As long as the files that you have obtained conform to some of the widely recognized standards currently in use (of which you will learn more later), you should have little difficulty loading them into Power Query.

As the first part of your journey through the data mashup process, this chapter will show you how to find and load data from a variety of file-based sources. These kinds of data are typically those that you can either locate on a shared network drive, download from the Internet, receive as an email attachment, or copy to your computer's local drive. The files that are used in the examples in this chapter are available on the Apress website. If you have followed the download instructions in Appendix A, then these files will be in the C:\DataMashupWithExcelSamples folder.

File Sources

In this chapter we will be looking at how to import file-based data from

- CSV files

- Text files

- XML files

- Excel files

- Access databases

31

© Adam Aspin 2020
A. Aspin, *Data Mashup with Microsoft Excel Using Power Query and M*,
https://doi.org/10.1007/978-1-4842-6018-0_2

The file sources that Power Query can currently read and from which it can load data are given in Table 2-1.

Table 2-1. *File Sources*

File Source	Comments
Excel	Allows you to read Microsoft Excel files (versions 97 to 2019) and load worksheets, named ranges, and tables
CSV	Lets you load text files that conform to the CSV (comma-separated values) format
XML	Allows you to load data from XML files
Text	Lets you load text files using a variety of column separators
Folder	Lets you load the information about all the files in a folder
SharePoint folder	Allows you to list the files in a SharePoint folder
Access database	Lets you connect to a Microsoft Access file on your network and load queries and tables
JSON	Helps you to load data from JSON files

More advanced techniques (such as importing the contents of entire folders of text or Excel files or importing *complex* XML files and JSON files) are described in Chapter 10. I prefer to handle these separately as they require more advanced knowledge of data transformation techniques—and you need to learn these first.

Note   I realize that Power Query considers MS Access to be a database and not a "file" data type. While I completely agree with this classification, I prefer nonetheless to treat Access as if it were a file-based data source, given that all the data resides in a single file that can be copied and emailed, and not in a database on a distant server. For this reason, we will look at MS Access in this chapter, and not the next one that deals with corporate data sources.

Loading Data from Files

It is time to start looking at the heavy-lifting aspect of Power Query and how you can use it to load data from a variety of different sources. I will begin on the bunny slopes (or "nursery" slopes as we say in the UK) with a simple example of loading data from a text file. Then, given the plethora of available data sources, and to give the process a clearer structure, we will load data from several of the ubiquitous file-based data sources that are found in most workplaces. These data sources are the basis of the data that you will learn to tweak and "mash up" in Chapters 6 through 12.

CSV Files

The scenario is as follows: you have been given a CSV file containing some useful information that you need to load into Excel for further analysis. You now want to use Power Query to look at the data and consider what (if anything) needs to be done to make it usable. On this occasion you have decided to load the data into Power Query first—and load the data into Excel once you have made any necessary modifications to the source data structure.

First, you need an idea of the data that you want to load. If you open the source file C:\DataMashupWithExcelSamples\Countries.csv with a text editor, such as Notepad (by right-clicking the file in the Windows Explorer and selecting Open With ➤ Notepad), you can view its contents. This is what you can see in Figure 2-1.

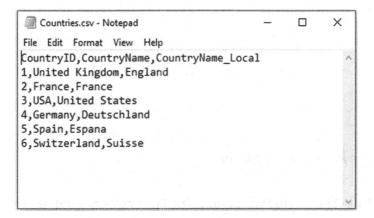

Figure 2-1. *The contents of the Countries.csv file*

The following steps explain what you have to do to load the contents of this file into Power Query:

1. In Excel click Data.

2. Click the Get Data button.

3. Click From Text/CSV. The Import Data dialog will appear.

4. Navigate to the folder containing the file that you want to load and select it (C:\DataMashupWithExcelSamples\Countries.csv, in this example).

5. Click Import. A dialog will display the initial contents of the file, as shown in Figure 2-2.

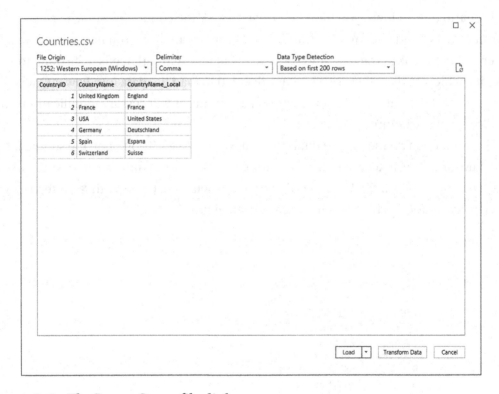

Figure 2-2.   *The Power Query file dialog*

6. Click the Transform Data button. The Power Query window appears; it contains a sample of the contents of the CSV file—or possibly the entire file if it is not too large. You can see this in Figure 2-3.

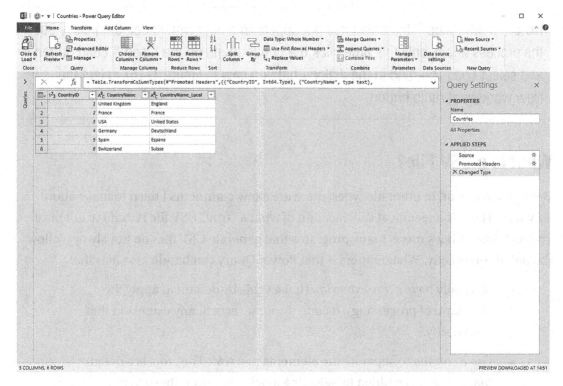

Figure 2-3. *The Power Query window with the contents of a CSV file loaded*

7. Click the Close & Load button in the Power Query window (you
    can see this at the top left of Figure 2-3). The Power Query Editor
    will close and return to Excel. The source data will be loaded into
    a new worksheet.

Tip   In step 7, make sure that you click the top part of the Close & Load button.
Otherwise, you will see a popup menu appear containing a couple of options. If you
do see the popup menu, just click Close & Load.

And that, for the moment, is that. You have loaded the data from the source file into
Excel in a matter of a few clicks, and it is ready for further analysis. In later chapters, you
will learn how to shape this data. For the moment, however, let's continue looking at
some other file-based data sources.

Note   If after step 7 the data does not appear in a new worksheet, then carry out the process again, only this time click the popup menu on the Close & Load button and select Load To—and in the dialog (that you saw in Figure 1-16), select the New worksheet radio button.

What Is a CSV File?

Before we move on to other file types, there are a few comments I need to make about CSV files. There is a technical specification of what a "true" CSV file is, but I won't bore you with that. What's more, many programs that generate CSV files do not always follow the definition exactly. What matters is that Power Query can handle text files that

- Normally have a *.csv extension* (it uses this by default to apply the right kind of processing). It can, of course, accept any extension that you specify.

- Use a *comma* to separate the elements in a row. This, too, is a default that can be overridden by selecting a delimiter from those in the dialog shown in Figure 2-2.

- End with a *line feed, carriage return, or line feed/carriage return.*

- Can, optionally, *contain double quotes to encapsulate fields.* These will be stripped out as part of the data load process. If there are double quotes, they do not have to appear for every field nor even for every record in a field that can have occasionally inconsistent double quotes.

- Can contain "irregular" records, that is, rows that do not have every element found in a standard record. However, the first row (whether or not it contains titles) must cover every element found in all the remaining records in the list. Put simply, any other record can be shorter than the first one but cannot be longer.

- Do not contain anything other than the data itself. If the file contains header rows or footer rows that are not part of the data, then Power Query cannot load the dataset without further work. There are workarounds to this all-too-frequent problem; one is given in Chapter 8.

Text Files

If you followed the process for loading a CSV file in the previous section, then you will find that loading a text file is virtually identical. This is not surprising. Both are text-based files and both should contain a single list of data. The following are the core differences:

- A text file can have something *other* than a comma to separate the elements in a list. You can specify the delimiter when defining the load step.

- A text file should normally have the extension .txt (though this, too, can be overridden).

- A text file *must* be perfectly formed; that is, every record (row) must have the same number of elements as every other record.

- A text file, too, *must not* contain anything other than the dataset if you want a flawless data load the first time.

- If a text file encounters difficulties, it should import the data as a single column that you can then try and split up into multiple columns, as described in Chapter 8.

Here, then, is how to load a text file into Power Query:

1. Open a new, blank Excel file.

2. In the Data ribbon, click From Text/CSV. The Import dialog will be displayed.

3. Navigate to the folder containing the file and select the file (C:\ DataMashupWithExcelSamples\CountryList.txt, in this example).

4. Click Import. A dialog will display the initial contents of the file (this dialog is essentially identical to the one that you saw for CSV files in Figure 2-2.). You can, of course, double-click the file name rather than click Open.

5. Click the Cancel button (because after a quick look at the contents of the file, you have decided that you do not really need it).

Where Power Query is really clever is that it can make a very educated guess as to how the text file is structured; that is, it can nearly always guess the field separator (the character that isolates each element in a list from the other elements). And so not only will it break the list into columns, but it will also avoid importing the column separator. If it does not guess correctly, then don't despair. You will learn how to correct this in Chapter 8.

Looking at the contents of a file and then deciding not to use it is part and parcel of the *data discovery* process that you will find yourself using when you work with Power Query. The point of this exercise is to show you how easy it is to glance inside potential data sources and then decide whether to import them into the data model or not. Moreover, it can be easier to see the first few rows of large text or CSV files directly in the Load dialog of Power Query than it is to open the whole file in a text editor.

Tip   At the risk of stating the obvious, you can press Enter to accept a default choice in a dialog and press Esc to cancel out of the dialog.

Text and CSV Options

You can see in Figure 2-3 that there are few options available that you can tweak when loading text or CSV files. Most of the time Power Query will guess the correct settings for you. However, there could be times when you will need to adjust these parameters slightly. The potential options that you can modify are

- File Origin
- Delimiter
- Data Type Detection

File Origin

This option defines the character encoding in which the file is stored. Different character sets can handle different ranges of characters, such as accents and other diacritics. Normally this information is correctly interpreted by Power Query, and you should only need to select a different character set (file origin) on very rare occasions.

Delimiter

Power Query will try and guess the special character that is used in a text or CSV file to separate the "columns" of data. Should you wish to override the chosen delimiter, you have the choice of

- Colon

- Comma

- Equals sign

- Semicolon

- Space

- Tab character

You can also decide to enter a custom delimiter such as the pipe (|) character or even specify that every field has a fixed width. Choosing either of these options will display another entry field where you can type in the required delimiter.

Data Type Detection

Power Query will make an educated guess at the data encoding and data type that are used in a text or CSV file. By default, to save time, it will only read the first 200 records. However, you can choose from any of the following three options:

- Read the first 200 rows

- Read the entire file

- No data type detection

Note   Be warned that reading a large file in its entirety can take quite a while. However, without accurate data type detection, you risk seeing badly formed columns in the output data.

Fixed-Width Text Files

Another form of text file that you might occasionally encounter is a fixed-width file. This kind of source data ensures that each column contains exactly the same number of characters. An example of what this can look like is shown in Figure 2-4.

```
CountryID CountryName        CountryName_Local
1         United Kingdom     England
2         France             France
3         USA                United States
4         Germany            Deutschland
5         Spain              Espana
6         Switzerland        Suisse
```

Figure 2-4. *Fixed-width text source data*

To load data like this

1. In the Data menu, click Get Data ➤ From File ➤ From Text/CSV. You will see something like Figure 2-5.

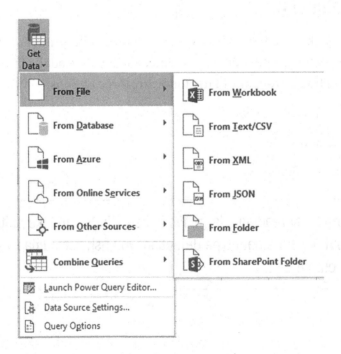

Figure 2-5. *The file data connectors in Power Query*

2. Select the file Countries.prn from the folder C:\
    DataMashupWithExcelSamples.

3. Click Open. The dialog displayed in Figure 2-6 will appear.

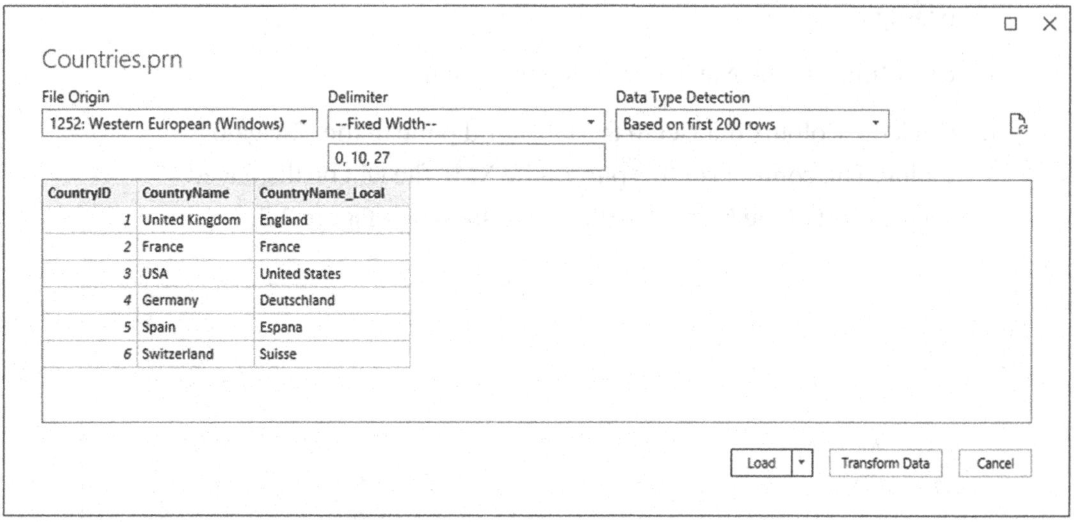

Figure 2-6. The fixed-width text file import dialog

4. Click Load. The source data will be loaded into a new worksheet.

You can see from Figure 2-6 that Power Query gives you a certain amount of information about fixed-width files. Specifically it calculates the length of each column and provides the required column lengths under the delimiter popup. You can alter this, but hopefully you will never need to.

As was the case with text and CSV files, you can force Power Query to sample the entire source file if you consider this necessary by selecting Based on entire dataset from the Data Type Detection popup menu.

Simple XML Files

XML, or Extensible Markup Language, is a standard means of sending data between IT systems. Consequently, you likely will need to load an XML file one day. Although an XML file is just text, it is text that has been formatted in a very specific way, as you can see if you ever open an XML file in a text editor such as Notepad. Do the following to load an XML file:

1. In the Data ribbon, click the Get Data button, and then click From File and From XML. The Import Data dialog will appear.

2. Navigate to the folder containing the file and select the file (C:\DataMashupWithExcelSamples\ColoursTable.xml, in this example).

3. Click Import. The Navigator dialog will open.

4. Click the Colours dataset in the left-hand pane of the Navigator dialog. The contents of this part of the XML file will be displayed on the right of the Navigator dialog, as shown in Figure 2-7.

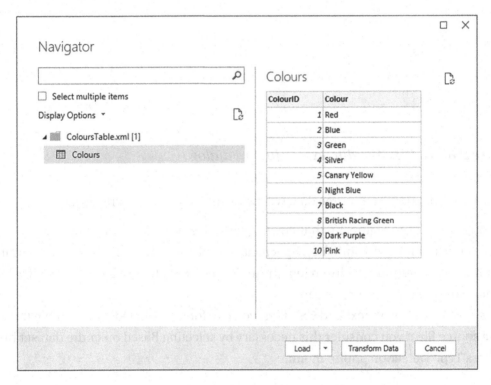

Figure 2-7. *The Navigator dialog before loading an XML file*

5. Click the Transform Data button. The Power Query Data window will display the contents of the XML file.

6. Click the Close & Load button in the Power Query Data window. The list of colors will be loaded into a new worksheet.

The actual internal format of an XML file can get extremely complex. Sometimes an XML file will contain only one dataset; sometimes it will contain many separate datasets. On other occasions, it will contain one dataset whose records contain nested levels of data that you need to handle by expanding a hierarchy of elements. You will see how the Navigator dialog handles nested hierarchies of XML data in Chapter 10—once you have learned some of the required data transformation techniques.

Note   Certain types of data source allow you to load multiple sets of data simultaneously. XML files (unlike CSV and text files) *can* contain multiple independent datasets. You can load several datasets simultaneously in the Navigator window if you first select the Select multiple items check box and then select the check box to the left of each dataset that you want to load from the XML file.

Excel Files

You are probably already a major Excel user and have many, many spreadsheets full of data that you want to rationalize and use for analysis and presentation in Power Query. Moreover, you saw how to load a single worksheet from an Excel file in the previous chapter. So, let's see how to load a couple of worksheets at once from an Excel file this time. This exercise will allow you to appreciate the whole process in detail from start to finish.

1. In the Excel Data ribbon, click Get Data ➤ From File ➤ From Workbook. The Import Data dialog will appear.

2. Navigate to the directory containing the file that you want to look at (C:\DataMashupWithExcelSamples, in this example).

3. Select the source file (InvoicesAndInvoiceLines.xlsx, in this example) and click Import. The Navigator dialog will appear, showing the worksheets, tables, and ranges in the workbook file.

4. Click one of the datasets listed on the left of the Navigator dialog. The top few rows of the selected spreadsheet will appear on the right of the dialog to show you what the data in the chosen dataset looks like.

5. Ensure the Select multiple items check box is selected.

6. Click the check boxes to the left of the Invoices and InvoiceLines datasets on the left. The Navigator dialog will look like the one shown in Figure 2-8.

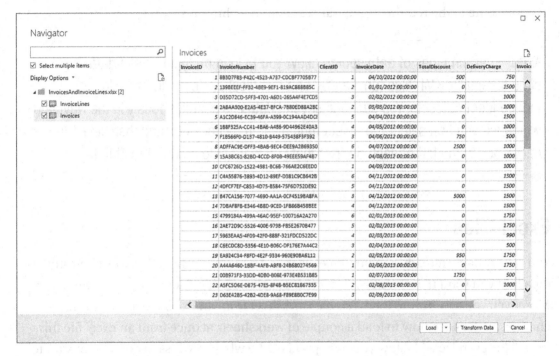

Figure 2-8. *The Navigator dialog before loading data from an Excel workbook*

7. Click the popup arrow at the right of the Load button.

8. Select Load To. The Processing Queries dialog will appear, briefly. You can see this in Figure 2-9.

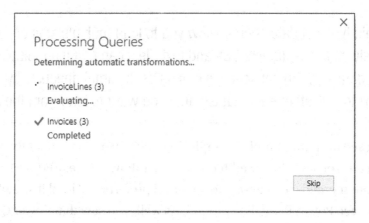

Figure 2-9. *The Processing Queries dialog*

9. This Import Data dialog will now appear. Ensure that Add this
    data to the Data Model is unchecked and leave the Table and New
    worksheet radio buttons selected. You can see how this looks in
    Figure 2-10.

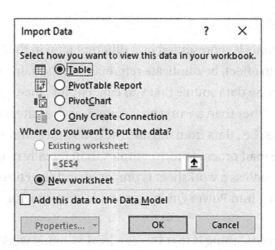

Figure 2-10. *The Import Data dialog*

10. Click OK. The selected source datasets will be loaded into
    separate Excel worksheets.

Note   Certain types of data source allow you to load multiple sets of data simultaneously. XML files (unlike CSV and text files) can contain multiple independent datasets. You can load several datasets simultaneously by selecting the check box to the left of each dataset that you want to load from the XML file.

As you can see from this simple example, having Power Query read Excel data is really not difficult. You could have edited this data in Power Query Editor before loading it, but as the data seemed clean and ready to use, I preferred to load it straight into Excel (or rather the Excel/Power Pivot data model). As well, you saw that Power Query can load multiple datasets at the same time from a single data source. However, you might still be wondering about a couple of things that you saw during this process, so here are some anticipatory comments:

The Navigator dialog displays

- Worksheets (Invoices and InvoiceLines like in Figure 2-8)

- Named ranges

- Named tables

Each of these elements is represented by a different icon in the Navigator dialog. Sometimes these can, in effect, be duplicate references to the same data, so you should really use the most precise data source that you can. For instance, I advise using a named table or a range name rather than a worksheet source, as the latter could easily end up containing "noise" data (i.e., data from outside the rows and columns that interest you), which would make the load process more complex than it really needs to be—or even cause it to fail. Indeed, unless a worksheet is prepared and structured in a simple tabular format, ready for loading into Power Query, you could end up with superfluous data in your data model.

However, the really cool thing is that you can load as many worksheets, tables, or ranges as you want at the same time from a single Excel workbook. You do not need to load each source dataset individually.

Note   Power Query will list and use data connections to external data sources (such as SQL Server, Oracle, or SQL Server Analysis Services) in a source Excel workbook *if* the data connection is active and has returned data to the workbook. Once a link to Power Query has been established, you can delete the data table itself in the source Excel workbook—and still load the data over the data connection in the source workbook into Power Query.

Power Query will *not* take into account any data filters on an Excel data table, but will load all the data that is in the source table. Consequently, you will have to reapply any filters (of which you'll learn more in Chapter 6) in Power Query if you want to subset the source data.

There are a couple of important points that you need to be aware of at this juncture:

1. Multiple worksheets, tables, or named ranges can all be imported from the same workbook (i.e., Excel file) in a single load operation. However, you need to define a separate load operation for each individual Excel file.

2. It is also possible to load multiple identically structured Excel files simultaneously using Power Query. This is explained in Chapter 10.

Why Use Power Query to Connect to Excel

At this juncture, you might be wondering why you could possibly want to use Power Query to load data from Excel when you can copy and paste from other Excel worksheets or simply link cells across workbooks.

This is a perfectly good question. However, there are several perfectly valid reasons for taking a "detour" via Power Query, even when loading Excel data:

1. The data cleansing and modification options that are available in Power Query are considerably easier than comparable operations in Excel.

2. Filtering source data (and only loading a subset of the data) is unbelievably easy in Power Query.

3. Power Query adapts to fewer—or more—records in the source data automatically.

4. Refreshing the source data is a simple on-click operation.

5. Any changes to the source data can be made available only when you want the data refreshed.

From Table/Range

Sometimes you may inherit an Excel workbook that already contains the data that you need (possibly the result of a connection to external data created using an older technology). It may be that you need to modify and cleanse this data using Power Query—even if the source is already in the same file as you want to place the restructured output. This, too, is perfectly possible.

1. Open the Excel file Chapter02Sample1.xlsx. This is in the folder C:\DataMashupWithExcelSamples.

2. Select a cell inside the table that you want to be the source of the data for modification in Power Query. In this example, you need to make sure that you are in the SourceData tab.

3. In the Excel Data ribbon, click From Table/Range. The Power Query Editor will open.

4. Click inside the Query Settings pane on the query name and enter a new name for this data source.

5. Carry out any modifications that you require to the data in the Power Query Editor (you will learn these techniques in Chapters 6 through 12).

6. Click Close & Load. The transformed data will be loaded into a new worksheet—with a new name.

Note   If you did not click inside an existing table before clicking the From Table/ Range button, you will receive a prompt asking you to select the source data.

Microsoft Access Databases

Another widely used data repository that proliferates in many corporations today is Microsoft Access. It is a powerful desktop relational database and can contain hundreds of tables, each containing millions of records. So we need to see how to load data from this particular source. Moreover, Power Query can be particularly useful when handling Access data because it allows you to see the contents of Access databases without even having to install Access itself.

1. In the Data ribbon, click Get Data ➤ From Database ➤ From Microsoft Access Database.

2. Navigate to the MS Access database containing the data that you want to load (C:\DataMashupWithExcelSamples\ ClientsDatabase.accdb, in this example).

3. Select the Access file and click Import. The Navigator dialog appears; it lists all the tables and queries in the Access database.

4. Select the ClientList dataset. This displays the contents of the table, as you can see in Figure 2-11.

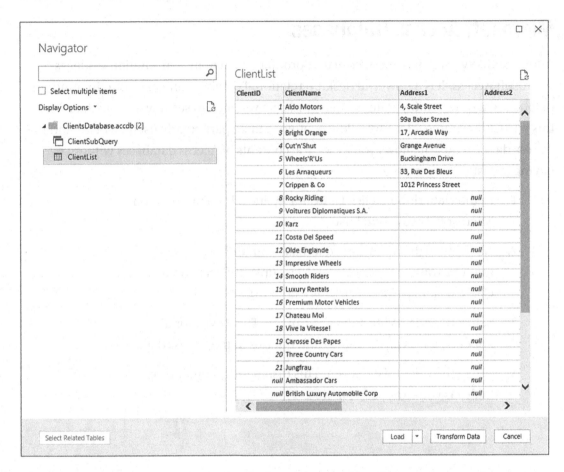

Figure 2-11. *The Navigator dialog before loading data from an Access database*

5. Click Load. The source data from Access is loaded into a new
    worksheet.

Note   If you wish to import several Access tables or queries simultaneously, then
simply ensure that the Select multiple items check box is selected. This will enable
you to select multiple source data tables or views from the Access database.

If you look closely at the left of the Navigator dialog in Figure 2-11, you can see that it
displays two different icons for Access objects:

- A table icon for Access data tables

- An icon representing two small windows for Access queries

This can help you to understand the type of data that you are looking at inside the Access database.

Note   Power Query *cannot* see linked tables in Access, only imported tables or tables that are actually in the Access database. It can, however, read queries overlaid upon native, linked, or imported data.

JSON Files

JSON files are, like XML, a file format that allows users (and computers) to send complex data structures between systems. Generally, JSON files require a little tweaking for them to be loaded in a state that is usable by Power Query. So we will be looking at how to load and prepare JSON files in Chapter 9, once you have assimilated the necessary data transformation techniques in Chapters 6 through 8.

Conclusion

In this chapter, you have seen how this powerful addition to Excel, Power Query, can help you find and load data from a variety of file-based data sources. These sources can be Access, Excel, CSV, XML, or text/CSV files.

You have seen that Power Query will let you see a sample of the contents of the data sources that it can read without needing any other application. This makes it a superb tool for peeking into data sources and deciding if a file actually contains the data that you need. Indeed, Power Query's Navigator can help you filter multiple datasets in Excel or XML files or Access databases, preview each dataset, and only select the ones that you want to load. Of course, it can also load dozens of datasets at once if they all are stored in the same source.

This chapter is not a complete overview of how to load file-based sources. So if you need to load complex XML files or JSON files or need to understand how to load the contents of entire folders—or all the worksheets in an Excel file, for instance—then you can skip straight to Chapter 9 to learn these techniques.

However, file-based data sources are only a small part of the picture. Power Query can also load data from a wide range of relational databases and data warehouses. We will take a look at some of these in the next chapter.

CHAPTER 3

Loading Data from Databases and Data Warehouses

Much of the world's corporate data currently resides in relational databases, data warehouses, and data warehouse appliances either on-premises or in the cloud. Excel—via Power Query—can connect to many of the world's leading commercial and open source databases and data warehouses. This chapter will show you how to extract data from several of these data sources to drive your Excel-based analytics using Power Query. Indeed, you will discover that once you have learned how to connect to one or two databases, you have learned how to use nearly all of them, thanks to the standardized interface and approach that Power Query brings to data extraction.

You need to be aware, however, that the examples in this chapter use sample data that is *not* available on the Apress website. In this chapter, I will let you use your own data or use the sample data that can often be installed with the source databases themselves.

Note   It may be stating the obvious, but connecting to a database means that the database must be installed and running correctly and you already have access to it. Indeed, you may also need specific client software installed on the PC that is running Power Query. This chapter will not explain how to install or use any of the databases (or the client software) that are referenced. For this, you will have to consult the relevant database documentation. Not only that, but many of the data sources outlined in this chapter are only available if you have a Pro version or Enterprise Excel subscription.

© Adam Aspin 2020
A. Aspin, *Data Mashup with Microsoft Excel Using Power Query and M*,
https://doi.org/10.1007/978-1-4842-6018-0_3

Relational Databases

Being able to access the data stored in relational databases is essential for much of today's business intelligence. As enterprise-grade relational databases still hold much of the world's data, you really need to know how to tap into the vast mines of information that they contain. The bad news is that there are many, many databases out there, each with its own intricacies and quirks. The good news is that once you have learned to load data from *one* of them, you can reasonably expect to be able to use *any* of them.

In the real world, connecting to corporate data could require you to have a logon name and usually a password that will let you connect (unless the database can recognize your Windows login or a single sign-on solution has been implemented). I imagine that you will also require permissions to read the tables and views that contain the data. So the techniques described in this chapter are probably the easy bit. The hard part is convincing the guardians of corporate data that you actually *need* the data and you should be allowed to see it.

The databases that Power Query can currently connect to, and can preview and load data from, are given in Table 3-1.

Table 3-1. *Database Sources*

Database	Comments
SQL Server database	Lets you connect to a Microsoft SQL Server on-premises database (on-premises, in a hosted environment, or in a virtual machine in the cloud) and import records from all the data tables and views that you are authorized to access
Access database	Lets you connect to a Microsoft Access file on your network and load queries and tables (which we explored in the previous chapter)
SQL Server Analysis Services database	Lets you connect to a SQL Server Analysis Services (SSAS) data warehouse. This can be either an online analytical processing (OLAP) cube or an in-memory tabular data warehouse
Oracle database	Lets you connect to an Oracle database and import records from all the data tables and views that you are authorized to access. This will likely require client software to be installed

(continued)

Table 3-1. (*continued*)

Database	Comments
IBM DB2 database	Lets you connect to an IBM DB2 database and import records from all the data tables and views that you are authorized to access. This will likely require additional software to be installed
MySQL database	Lets you connect to a MySQL database and import records from all the data tables and views that you are authorized to access
PostgreSQL database	Lets you connect to a PostgreSQL database and import records from all the data tables and views that you are authorized to access. This will likely require additional software to be installed
Sybase database	Lets you connect to a Sybase database and import records from all the data tables and views that you are authorized to access
Teradata database	Lets you connect to a Teradata database and import records from all the data tables and views that you are authorized to access. This will likely require additional software to be installed
SAP HANA database	Lets you connect to a SAP HANA in-memory database and import records from all the objects that you have permission to access. This will likely require additional software to be installed

These are the database connectors that are currently available for Power Query to connect to. As the list of database and data warehouse sources that you can connect to from Power Query continues to evolve, this list could likely be extended to include new items by the time that you read this book.

Note   Although Power Query classifies Microsoft Access as a relational database, I prefer to handle it as a file-based source. For this reason, MS Access data was discussed in the previous chapter.

As well as connections for specific databases, Power Query contains generic connectors that can help you to read data from databases that are not specifically in the list of available databases. These generic connectors are explained in Table 3-2.

Table 3-2. *Generic Database Access*

Source	Comments
ODBC data source	Lets you connect over Open Database Connectivity to a database or data source
OLE DB data source	Lets you connect over Object Linking and Embedding, Database to a database or data source

Be warned that these generic connectors will not work with any database. However, they should work with a database for which you have procured, installed, and configured a valid ODBC or OLE DB driver. These connection types are explained in Chapter 5.

SQL Server

Here I will use the Microsoft enterprise-level relational database—SQL Server—as an example to show you how to load data from a database into Excel using Power Query. The first advantage of this setup is that you probably do not need to install any software to enable access to SQL Server. A second advantage is that the techniques are pretty similar to those used and applied by Oracle, DB2, and the other databases to which Power Query can connect. Furthermore, you can load multiple tables or views from a database at once. To see this in action (on your SQL Server database), take the following steps:

1. Open a new Excel Workbook.

2. In the Data ribbon, click Get Data ➤ From Database ➤ From SQL Server Database. The SQL Server database dialog will appear.

3. Enter the server name in the Server text box. This will be the name of your SQL Server or one of the SQL Server resources used by your organization. It may even be a local version of SQL Server that you have installed on your PC.

4. Enter the database name. The dialog will look like Figure 3-1 (but with your server and database names, of course).

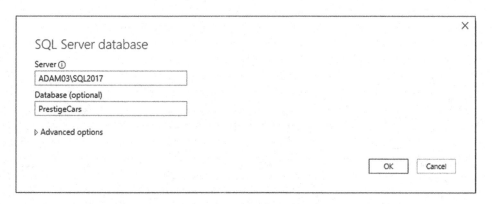

Figure 3-1. *The Microsoft SQL Server database dialog*

5. Click OK. Power Query will connect to the server and display the Navigator dialog containing all the tables and views in the database that you have permission to see on the server you selected.

6. Ensure the Select multiple items check box is checked.

7. Click the check boxes for the tables that you want to load. The data for the most recently selected table appears on the right of the Navigator dialog, as shown in Figure 3-2, where the Stock table is selected.

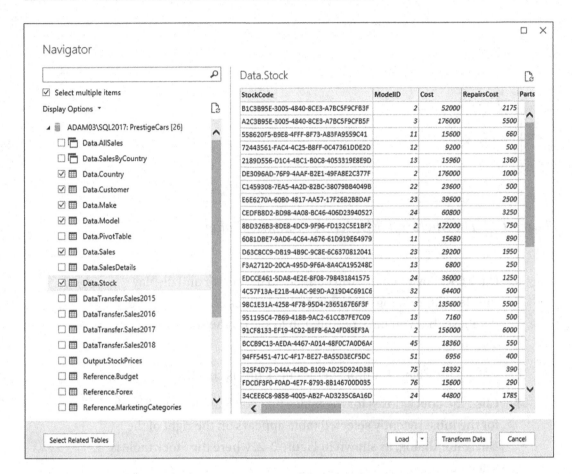

Figure 3-2. *The Navigator dialog when selecting multiple items*

8. Click Load.

9. While the data is being loaded, Power Query will display the Queries & Connections pane and show the load progress for each selected table. You can see this in Figure 3-3.

Figure 3-3. *The Load dialog displaying data load progress*

10. Once the load is complete, the Queries & Connections pane will
     display the final row counts for each source table that has been
     loaded into the data model.

Tip When selecting multiple tables or views, you will only ever see the contents
of a single data source in the Navigator dialog. However, you can preview the
contents of any of the selected data sources (or even any that are not selected)
simply by clicking the table or view name. This will not affect the choice of selected
tables and views that you want to load using Power Query.

Since this is very similar to the way in which you loaded data from Access in the
previous chapter, I imagine that you are getting the hang of how to use database sources
by now. Once again the Navigator dialog is a simple and efficient way to select the
datasets that you want to load into Excel.

Note   You can enter the server IP address instead of the server name if you prefer. If there are several SQL Server instances on the same server, you will need to add a backslash and the instance name. This kind of detailed information can be obtained from corporate database administrators.

Automatically Loading Related Tables

Relational databases are nearly always intricate structures composed of many interdependent tables. Indeed, you will frequently need to load several tables to obtain all the data that you need.

Knowing which tables to select is not always easy. Power Query tries to help you by automatically detecting the links that exist in the source database between tables; this way, you can rapidly isolate the collections of tables that have been designed to work together.

Do the following to see a related group of tables:

1. Connect to the source database as described in the previous section.

2. In the Navigator dialog, click a table that contains data that you need.

3. Click the "Select related tables" button.

Any tables in the database that are linked to the tables that you selected in the Navigator dialog are selected. You can deselect any tables that you do not want, of course. More importantly, you can click the names of the selected tables to see their contents.

Note   Sometimes you have to select several tables in turn and click "Select related tables" to ensure that Power Query will select all the tables that are necessary to underpin your analysis.

Database Options

The world of relational databases is—fortunately or unfortunately—a little more complex than the world of files or MS Access. Consequently, there are a few comments to make about using databases as a data source—specifically, how to connect to them.

First, let's cover the initial connection to the server. The options are explained in Table 3-3.

Table 3-3. *Database Connection Options*

Option	Comments
Server	You cannot browse to find the server, and consequently you need to *type* or *paste* the server name. If the server has an instance name (a concept that I explain later), you need to enter the server and the instance. Your IT department will be able to supply this if you are working in a corporate environment
Database	If you know the database, then you can enter (or paste) it here. This restricts the number of available tables in the Navigator dialog and makes finding the correct table or view easier
SQL statement	You can enter a valid snippet of T-SQL (or a stored procedure or a table-valued function) that returns data from the database

These options probably require a little more explanation. So let's look at each one in turn.

Server Connection

It is fundamental that you know the exact connection string for the database that you want to connect to. This could be the following:

- The database server name.

- The database server name, a backslash, and an instance name (if this physical or virtual server contains several SQL Server instances).

- The database server IP address.

- The database server IP address, a backslash, and an instance name (if there is one).

- If the SQL Server instance is using a custom port, you must end the server name with a comma followed by the port number. This is, inevitably, a question for corporate DBAs.

- If you are running a single SQL Server instance that you have installed on your own PC, then you can use the name *localhost* (or a period) to refer to the local server.

Note   A database instance is a separate SQL Server service running alongside others on the same physical or virtual server. You will always need both the server and this instance name (if there is one) to successfully connect. You can also specify a timeout period if you wish.

Most SQL Server instances host many, many databases. Sometimes these can number in the hundreds. Sometimes, inevitably, you cannot remember which database you want to connect to. Fortunately, the Power Query Navigator can let you browse the databases on a server that you are authorized to access. To do this, do the following:

1. In the Power Query ribbon, click the small triangle at the bottom of the Get Data button and then click SQL Server. The SQL Server database dialog will appear.

2. Enter the server name in the Server text box and click OK. Do *not* enter a database name. The Navigator window opens and displays all the available databases, as shown in Figure 3-4. Of course, the actual contents that are displayed will depend on the server that you are connecting to.

Figure 3-4. *The Navigator dialog when selecting databases*

You can see from Figure 3-4 that if you click the small triangle to the left of a database, then you are able to see all the tables and views that are accessible to you in this database. Although this can mean an overabundance of possible choices when looking for the table(s) or view(s) that you want, it is nonetheless a convenient way of reminding you of the name of the dataset that you require.

Tip   The actual databases that you will be able to see on a corporate server will depend on the permissions that you have been given. If you cannot see a database, then you will have to talk to the database administrators to sort out any permission issues.

Searching for Databases, Tables, and Views in Navigator

If you are overwhelmed by the sheer volume of table(s) and view(s) that appear in the left panel of the Navigator dialog, then you can use Navigator's built-in search facility to help you to narrow down the set of potential data sources.

Searching for Databases

To isolate specific databases, do the following:

1. Carry out steps 1 and 2 in the earlier "SQL Server" section to connect to a SQL Server instance *without* specifying a database.

2. In the Search box of the Navigator dialog, enter a few characters that you know are contained in the name of the table or view that you are looking for. Entering, for example, **US** on my server gives the result that you see in Figure 3-5.

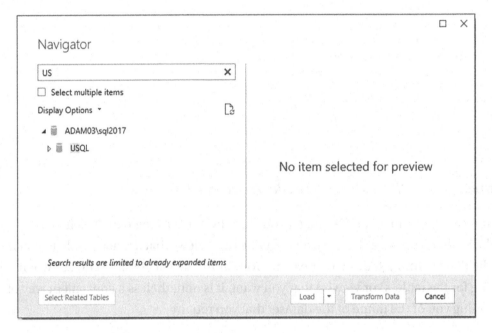

Figure 3-5. Using Search with Navigator to find databases

Searching for Tables

If you are searching for tables, do the following:

1. Expand any databases that you want to search for specific tables.

2. In the Search box of the Navigator dialog, expand the database that interests you and enter a few characters that you know are contained in the name of the table or view that you are looking for. Entering, for example, **cust** on my server gives the result that you see in Figure 3-6.

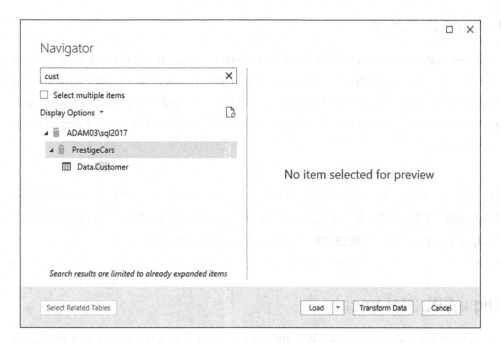

Figure 3-6. *Using Search with Navigator to find tables*

When searching for objects, you can enter the text in uppercase or lowercase (with most SQL Server installations), and the text can appear anywhere in the names of the tables or views—not just at the start of the name. With every character that you type, the list of potential matches gets shorter and shorter. Once you have found the table or view that you are looking for, simply proceed as described earlier to load the data into Excel with Power Query.

If your search does not return the subset of tables in any views that you were expecting, all you have to do is click the cross at the right of the Search box. This cancels the search and displays all the available tables, as well as clears the Search box.

If you are not convinced that you are seeing all the tables and views that are in the database, then click the small icon at the bottom right of the Search box (it looks like a small page with two green circular arrows). This is the Refresh button, which refreshes the connection to the database and displays all the tables and views that you have permission to see. Finally, it is worth noting that filtering tables can also be applied to Excel tables, worksheets, and named ranges as well as Access databases. This is another example of how the unified Navigator interface can help minimize the learning curve when it comes to mastering Power Query.

Database Security

Remember that databases are designed to be extremely secure. Consequently, you only see servers, databases, tables, and views if you are authorized to access them. You might have to talk to your IT department to ensure that you have the required permissions; otherwise, the table that you are looking for could be in the database, but remain invisible to you.

Tip   If you experience a connection error when first attempting to connect to SQL Server, simply click the Edit button to return to the Microsoft SQL Server database dialog and correct any mistakes. This avoids having to start over.

Using a SQL Statement

If there is a downside to using a relational database such as SQL Server as a data source, it is that the sheer amount of data that the database stores—even in a single table—can be dauntingly huge. Fortunately, all the resources of SQL Server can be used to filter the data that is accessed using Power Query before you even load the data. This way, you do not have to load entire tables of data at the risk of drowning in information before you have even started to analyze it.

The following are SQL Server techniques that you can use to extend the partnership between SQL Server and Power Query:

- SQL SELECT statements

- Stored procedures

- Table-valued functions

These are, admittedly, fairly technical solutions. Indeed, if you are not a database specialist, you could well require the services of your IT department to use these options to access data in the server. Nonetheless, it is worth taking a quick look at these techniques in case they are useful now or in the future.

Any of these options can be applied from the SQL Server database dialog. Here is an example of how to filter data from a database table using a SELECT statement:

1. In the Data ribbon, click Get Data ➤ From Database ➤ From SQL Server Database. The SQL Server database dialog will appear.

2. Enter the server name and the database. This will have to be a server and database that you have been granted access to.

3. Click the triangle to the left of Advanced options. This opens a box where you can enter a SQL command.

4. Enter the SQL command that you want to apply. In this example (using a server and database on my PC), it is SELECT CountryName, MakeName, ModelName, Cost FROM Data. AllSales ORDER BY CountryName. The dialog will look like Figure 3-7—only with your SQL in the SQL statement box, of course.

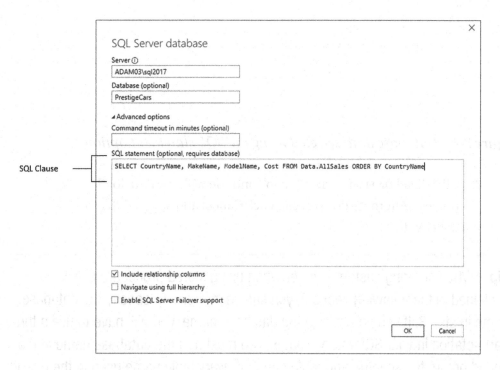

Figure 3-7. *Using SQL to select database data*

5. Click OK. A sample of the corresponding data is eventually displayed in a dialog like the one shown in Figure 3-8. The actual data that is returned will depend on the source system that you are using.

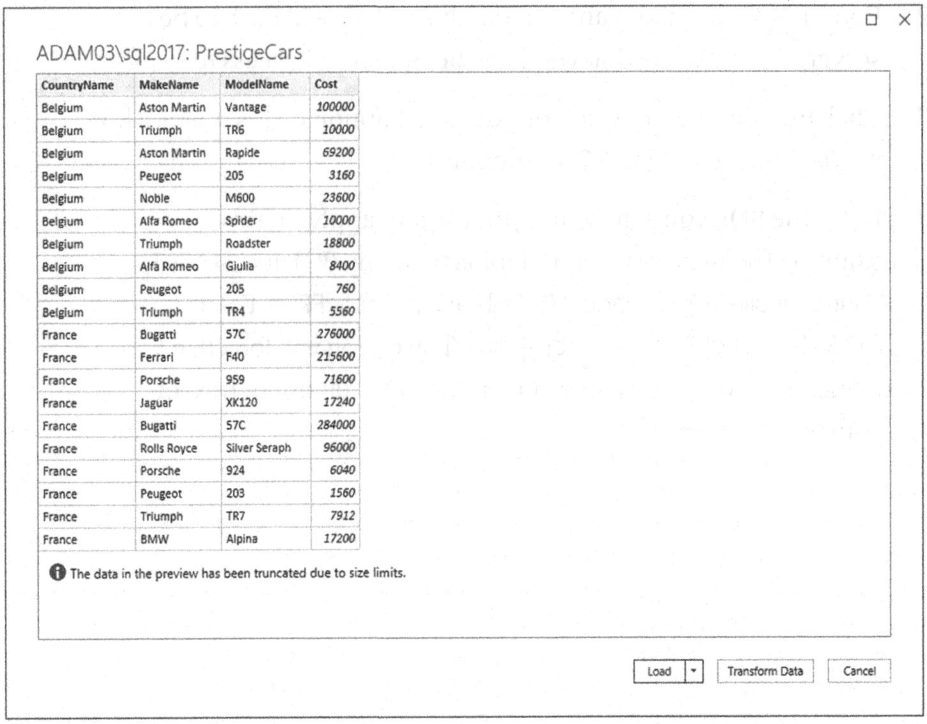

CountryName	MakeName	ModelName	Cost
Belgium	Aston Martin	Vantage	100000
Belgium	Triumph	TR6	10000
Belgium	Aston Martin	Rapide	69200
Belgium	Peugeot	205	3160
Belgium	Noble	M600	23600
Belgium	Alfa Romeo	Spider	10000
Belgium	Triumph	Roadster	18800
Belgium	Alfa Romeo	Giulia	8400
Belgium	Peugeot	205	760
Belgium	Triumph	TR4	5560
France	Bugatti	57C	276000
France	Ferrari	F40	215600
France	Porsche	959	71600
France	Jaguar	XK120	17240
France	Bugatti	57C	284000
France	Rolls Royce	Silver Seraph	96000
France	Porsche	924	6040
France	Peugeot	203	1560
France	Triumph	TR7	7912
France	BMW	Alpina	17200

Figure 3-8. *Database data selected using the SQL statement option*

6. Click Load or Transform Data to continue with the data load process. Alternatively, you can click Cancel and start a different data load.

Tip When entering custom SQL (or when using stored procedures, as is explained in the following section), you should, preferably, specify the database name in step 3. If you do not give the database name, you will have to use a three-part notation in your SQL query. That is, you must add the database name and a period before the schema and table name of *every* table name used in the query.

Stored Procedures in SQL Server

The same principles apply when using stored procedures of functions to return data from SQL Server. You will always use the SQL statement option to enter the command that will return the data. Just remember that to call a SQL Server stored procedure or function, you would enter the following elements into the Microsoft SQL Server database dialog:

- *Server*: <your server name>

- *Database*: <the database name>

- *SQL statement*: EXECUTE (or EXEC) <enter the schema (if there is one, followed by a period) and the stored procedure name, followed by any parameters>

This way, either you or your IT department can create complex and secure ways to allow data from the corporate databases to be read into Power Query from databases.

To see this in practice, here is an example of using a SQL Server stored procedure to return only a subset of the available data. The stored procedure is called *pr_DisplayUKClientData*, and you apply it like this:

- In the Data ribbon, click Get Data ➤ From Database ➤ From SQL Server Database. The SQL Server database dialog will appear.

- Enter the server name and the database.

- Click the triangle to the left of Advanced options. This opens a box where you can enter a SQL command.

- Enter the SQL command that you want to apply. In this case, it is EXECUTE dbo.pr_DisplayUKClientData. The dialog will look like Figure 3-9.

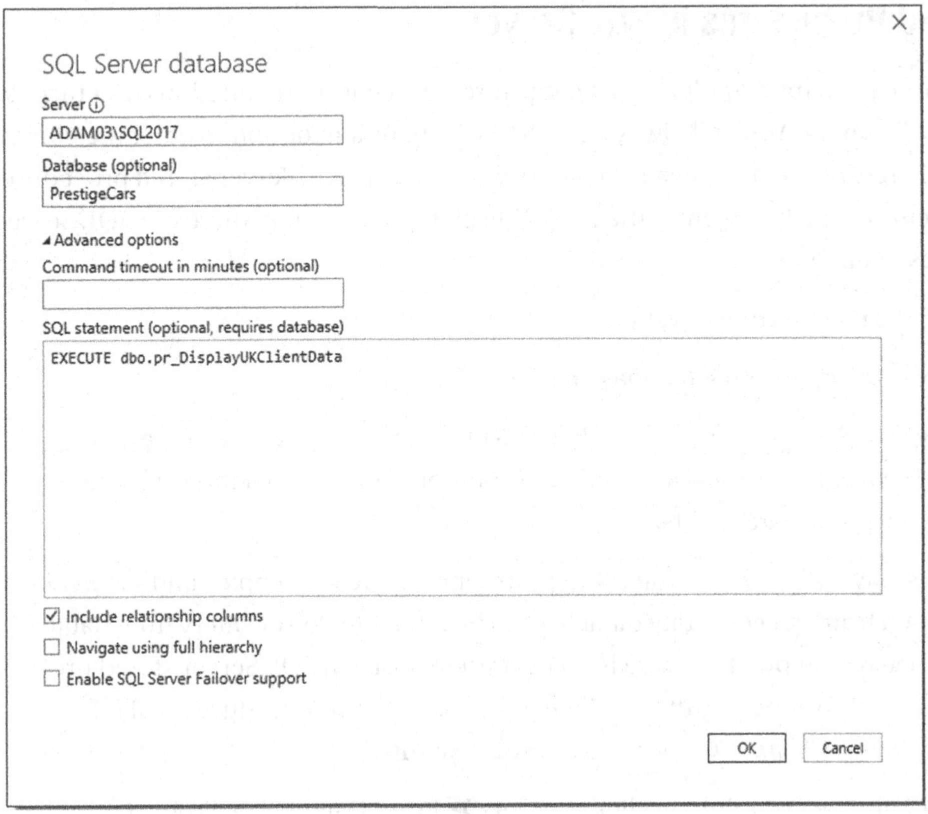

Figure 3-9. *Using SQL to select database data*

- Click OK. A sample of the corresponding data is returned to the Navigator.

- Click Load or Edit to continue with the data load process. Alternatively, you can click Cancel and start a different data load.

The data that is returned in this example is only a subset of the available data that has been selected by the stored procedure. You need to be aware that stored procedures can perform a multitude of tasks on the source data. These can include selecting, sorting, and cleansing the data.

Stored procedures often require *parameters* to be added after the stored procedure name. This is perfectly acceptable when executing a stored procedure in Power Query. An example would be

```
EXECUTE dbo.pr_DisplayUKClientData 2020
```

In this specific example, the parameter is "2020". If you need to enter multiple parameters, they must be comma-separated.

The key thing to remember—and to convey to your IT department—is that the SQL that Power Query expects is the flavor of SQL that the source database uses. So, for SQL Server, that means using T-SQL. In fact, this SQL becomes a "pass-through" query that is interpreted directly by the underlying database.

Note   A SQL statement or stored procedure will only return data as a *single table*. Admittedly, this table could contain data from several underlying tables or views in the source database, but filtering the source data will prevent Power Query from loading data from several tables as separate queries. Consequently, you could have to create multiple queries rather than a single load query to get data from a coherent set of tables in the data source.

Oracle Databases

There are many, many database vendors active in the corporate marketplace today. Arguably the most dominant of them is currently Oracle. While I have used Microsoft data sources to begin the journey into an understanding of how to use databases with Power Query, it would be remiss of me not to explain how to access databases from other suppliers.

So now is the time to show you just how open-minded Power Query really is. It does not limit you to Microsoft data sources—far from it. Indeed, it is every bit as easy to use databases from other vendors as the source of your analytical reports. As an example of this, let's take a look at loading Oracle data into Excel using Power Query.

Installing and configuring an Oracle database is a nontrivial task. Consequently, I am not providing an Oracle sample database, but will leave you either to discover a corporate database that you can connect to or, preferably, consult the many excellent resources available that do an excellent job of explaining how to set up your own Oracle database and install the sample data that is available.

Be aware that connecting to Oracle will require installing Oracle client software on the computer where you are running Power Query. This, too, can be complex to set up. So you might need some help from a corporate resource or a knowledgeable friend if you are planning to test using Oracle data with Power Query.

Should you be feeling brave, you can use the following URLs to find the Oracle client software. For 32-bit versions of Power Query, you could try using the following link to download and install the 32-bit Oracle client:

`www.oracle.com/technetwork/topics/dotnet/utilsoft-086879.html`

For 64-bit versions of Power Query, use the following link to download and install the 64-bit Oracle client:

`www.oracle.com/technetwork/database/windows/downloads/index-090165.html`

Both these links were active as this book went to press.

If you need to check which version of Power Query you are using (32 bit or 64 bit), click File ➤ Help ➤ About. You will see a dialog that tells you which version you are using.

So, assuming that you have an Oracle database available (and that you know the server name or SID as well as a valid user name and password), the following steps show how you can load data from this particular source into Power Query. I will be using standard Oracle sample data that is often installed with sample databases in this example.

1. Open a new Excel workbook.

2. In the Data ribbon, click Get Data ➤ From Database ➤ From Oracle Database.

3. Enter the server name in the Server text box. This will be the name of your Oracle server or one of the Oracle server resources used by your organization.

4. Click the Import button. The dialog will look like Figure 3-10.

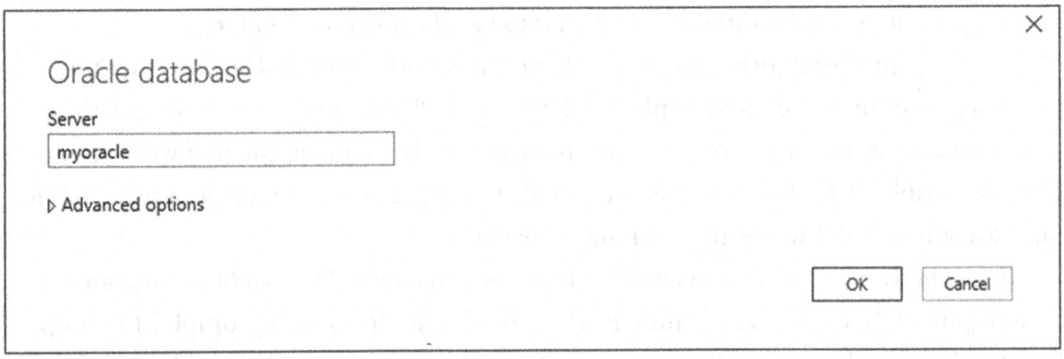

Figure 3-10. *The Oracle database dialog*

5. Click OK. The Oracle database security dialog will appear. Assuming that you are not authorized to use your Windows login to connect to the database, click Database on the left of the dialog.

6. Enter the user name and password that allow you to log in to Oracle. You can see this dialog in Figure 3-11.

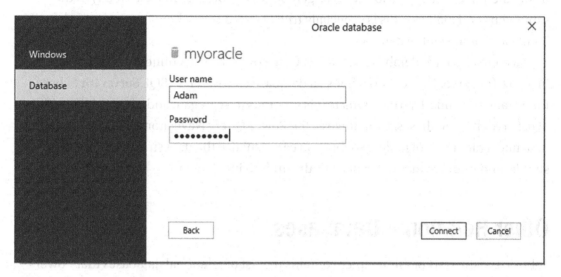

Figure 3-11. *The Oracle database security dialog*

7. Click Connect. Power Query will connect to the server and display the Navigator dialog containing all the tables and views in the database that you have permission to see on the server you selected. In some cases, you could see a dialog saying that the data source does not support encryption. If you feel happy with an unencrypted connection, then click the OK button for this dialog.

8. Expand the HR folder. This is a standard Oracle sample schema that could be installed on your Oracle instance. If not, you will have to choose another schema.

9. Check the Select multiple items check box.

10. Click the check boxes for the tables that interest you. The data for the most recently selected data appears on the right of the Navigator dialog, exactly as was the case with SQL Server.

11. Click Load. The Queries & Connections pane will appear and show the query for each selected table.

If you have already followed the example earlier in this chapter to load data from SQL Server, you will probably appreciate how much the two techniques have in common. Indeed, one of the great advantages of using Power Query is that loading data from different data sources follows a largely similar approach and uses many of the same steps and dialogs. This is especially true of databases, where the steps are virtually identical—whatever the database.

Of course, no two databases are alike. Consequently, you connect to an Oracle instance (or server) but cannot choose a database as you can in SQL Server (or Sybase, for instance). Similarly, where Oracle has schemas to segregate and organize data tables, SQL Server has databases. Nonetheless, the Power Query Navigator will always organize data into a hierarchy of folders so that you can visualize the data structures in a clear, simple, and intuitive manner, whatever the underlying database.

Other Relational Databases

Table 3-1 at the start of this chapter contains the list of relational databases that Power Query could connect to as this book went to press. I imagine that the list has grown since this book was published. However, the good news is that you probably do not need much more information to connect to any of the databases that are available for you to use as data sources. Simply put, if you know how to connect to one of them, you can probably connect to any of them.

So I am not going to fill out reams of pages with virtually identical explanations of how to get data from a dozen or more relational databases. Instead I suggest that you simply try to connect, using the techniques that you have learned in this chapter for Oracle and SQL Server.

Be warned, though, that to connect to a relational database, you will inevitably need to know the following details:

- The server name

- A database name (possibly)

- A valid username (depending on the security that has been implemented)

- A valid password for the user that you are connecting as (this, too, will depend on the security in place)

However, if you have these elements, then nothing should stop you from using a range of corporate data sources as the basis for your analysis with Power Query. You will, of course, need all the necessary permissions to access the database and the data that it contains.

It is also worth knowing that connecting to DB2, MySQL, PostgreSQL, Sybase, IBM Informix, IBM Netezza, SAP HANA, or Teradata can require not only that the database administrator has given you the necessary permissions but also that connection software (known as *drivers* or *providers*) has been installed on your PC. Given the "corporate" nature of the requirements, it may help if you talk directly to your IT department to get this set up in your enterprise IT landscape.

One way to find out if the software that is required to enable a connection to a specific database has been installed is to select the database from the list available in the Get Data dialog. If the drivers have not been installed, you will see a warning similar to the one in Figure 3-12.

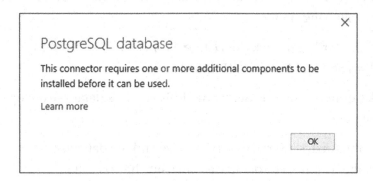

Figure 3-12. *The missing driver alert*

Clicking the "Learn more" link will take you to the download page for the missing drivers. Be warned, however, that configuring data providers can, in some cases, require specialist knowledge as well as local admin rights on the computer where the drivers have to be installed.

Microsoft SQL Server Analysis Services Data Sources

An Analysis Services database is a data warehouse technology that can contain vast amounts of data that has been optimized to enable decision making. *SSAS cubes* (as these databases are also called) are composed of facts (measures or values) and dimensions (descriptive attributes).

In fact—and with apologies to data warehouse purists—an SSAS cube is, essentially, a gigantic pivot table. So, if you have used pivot tables in Excel, you are ready to access data warehouse sources in Power Query and slice and dice the data they contain.

Note   In this section I will be explaining access to *dimensional* (disk-based) SSAS data warehouses. I explain *tabular* SSAS in the next section.

Please note that there is no sample SSAS database supplied with this book. This is because installing and configuring SSAS is a considerable task that requires specialist knowledge. So I will leave you to obtain the login details for your corporate Analysis Services database(s) and use those to experiment with.

If your work environment uses Analysis Services databases, you can access them by carrying out the following steps:

1. In the Data ribbon, click Get Data ➤ From Database ➤ From Analysis Services Database (Import).

2. Click Connect. The SQL Server Analysis Services database dialog will appear.

3. Enter the Analysis Services server name and the database (or "cube") name. The database I am using here is called CarSalesOLAP; you will have to specify your own SSAS database name. In any case, you will need to use the name of your own SSAS server. The dialog will look something like the one shown Figure 3-13—only with your server and database names, of course.

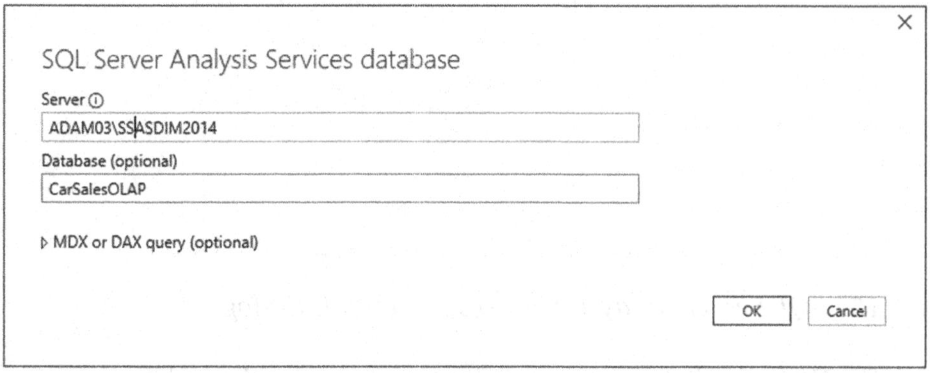

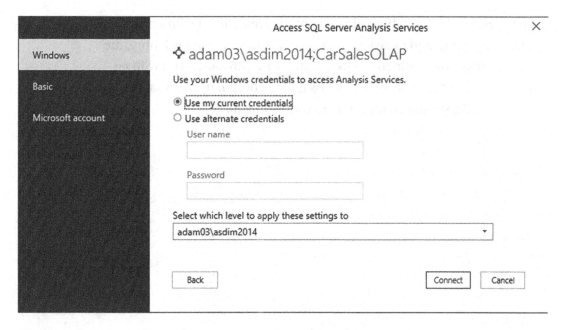

Figure 3-13. *Connecting to an SSAS (multidimensional) database*

Figure 3-14. *Specifying the appropriate security when connecting to an SSAS (multidimensional) database*

4. Click Connect. You will probably see the Connecting dialog, briefly, as shown in Figure 3-15.

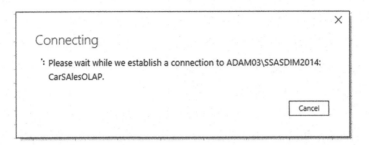

Figure 3-15. *SQL Server Analysis Services credentials dialog*

5.   The Navigator dialog will appear. Expand the folders in the left
     pane of the dialog. This way, you can see all the fact tables and
     dimensions contained in the data warehouse.

6.   Select the fact tables, dimensions, or even only the dimension
     attributes and measures that you want to load. On my laptop, the
     dialog looks something like Figure 3-16. Obviously, you will see
     the fact tables and dimensions that are hosted by the Analysis
     Services instance that you are connecting to.

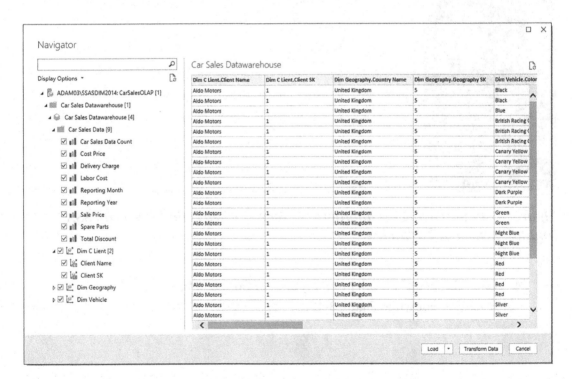

Figure 3-16. *Selecting attributes and measures from an SSAS cube*

7. Click Load. The Queries & Connections pane will display a new query, and the measures and attributes that you selected will appear in a new worksheet. You can see an example of this in Figure 3-17.

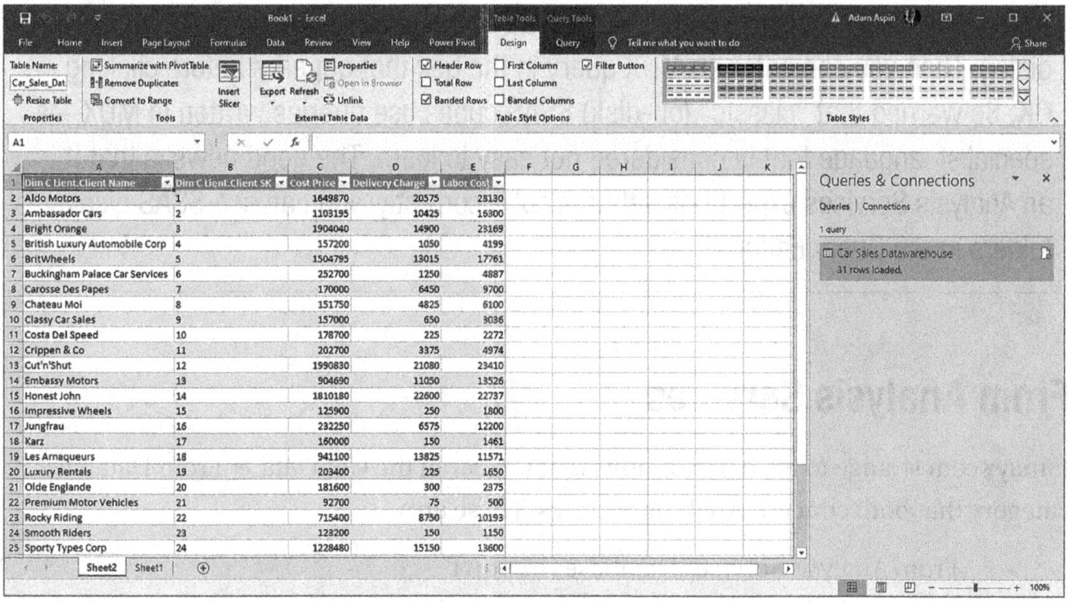

Figure 3-17. *The output from an SSAS cube in an Excel worksheet*

In step 7 you can, of course, click the popup triangle at the right of the Load button and choose from the other possible load options that you saw in Chapter 2.

Note   If you did not enter the cube (database) name in step 3, then the Navigator dialog will display all the available cubes on the SSAS server. From here you can drill down into the cube that interests you to query the data you require.

SSAS cubes are potentially huge. They can contain dozens of dimensions, many fact tables, and literally thousands of measures and attributes. Understanding multidimensional cubes and how they work is beyond the scope of this book. Nonetheless, it is important to understand that for Power Query, a cube is just another data source. This means that you can be extremely selective as to the cube elements that you load into Power Query and only load the elements that you need for your analysis. You can load entire dimensions or just a few attributes, just like you can load whole fact tables or just a selection of measures.

Note   You can filter the data that is loaded from an SSAS cube by expanding the MDX or DAX query (optional) item in the SQL Server Analysis Services database dialog. Then you can enter an MDX query in the box that appears before clicking OK. Be warned that "classic" (on-disk) SSAS cubes use queries written in MDX—a specialist language that is considered not easy to learn. The good news is that if an Analysis Services expert has set up a cube correctly, you can see SSAS display folders in the Query Editor.

From Analysis Services

It may seem strange to have two options that appear in the Get Data ➤ From Database category that both concern Analysis Services. These are

- From Analysis Services Database (Import)

- From Analysis Services

The first is the one you saw in the previous section and is a totally standard Power Query connection process. The second has, surprisingly, nothing to do with Power Query at all. It is, in fact, an older type of connection that has existed in Excel since the 2007 version. It is called an Office Data Connection.

So, even if this type of connection cannot be used in the context of Power Query (and therefore is, technically, outside the scope of this book), I prefer to explain it anyway—even if this is only to clear up the confusion felt by many users when faced with these two different methods of accessing SSAS data.

To connect to an Analysis Services database using Office Data Connection:

1. In the Data ribbon, click Get Data ➤ From Database ➤ From Analysis Services Database. The Connect to Database Server dialog will appear.

2. Enter the Analysis Services server name as shown in Figure 3-18. You will, of course, have to use your Analysis Services instance name.

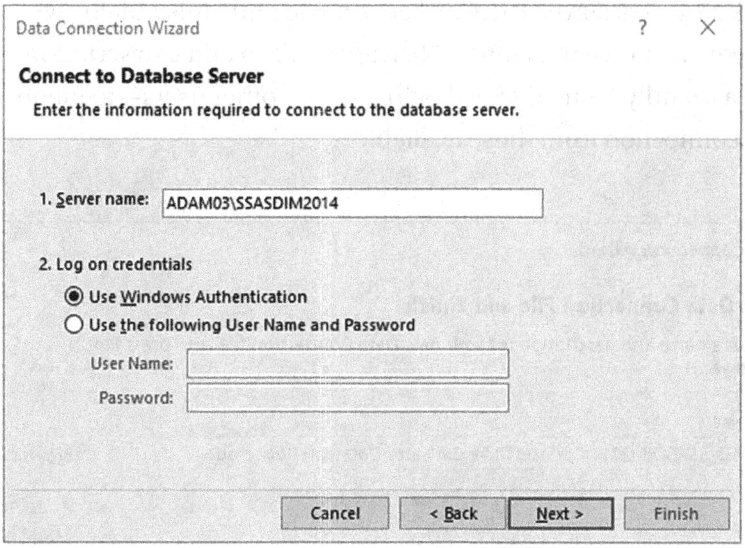

Figure 3-18. *The Connect to Database Server dialog*

3. Click Next. The Select Database and Table dialog will appear, as shown in Figure 3-19. Here you can select from any available databases on the Analysis Services server.

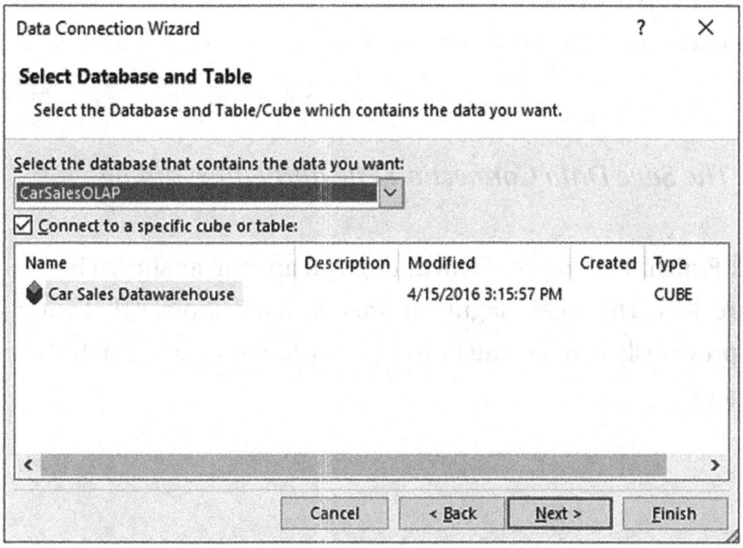

Figure 3-19. *The Select Database and Table dialog*

4.   Click Next. The Save Data Connection File and Finish dialog will
     appear, as shown in Figure 3-20. Here you can add a description
     and a friendly name that will help you—or other users—to identify
     this connection from those available.

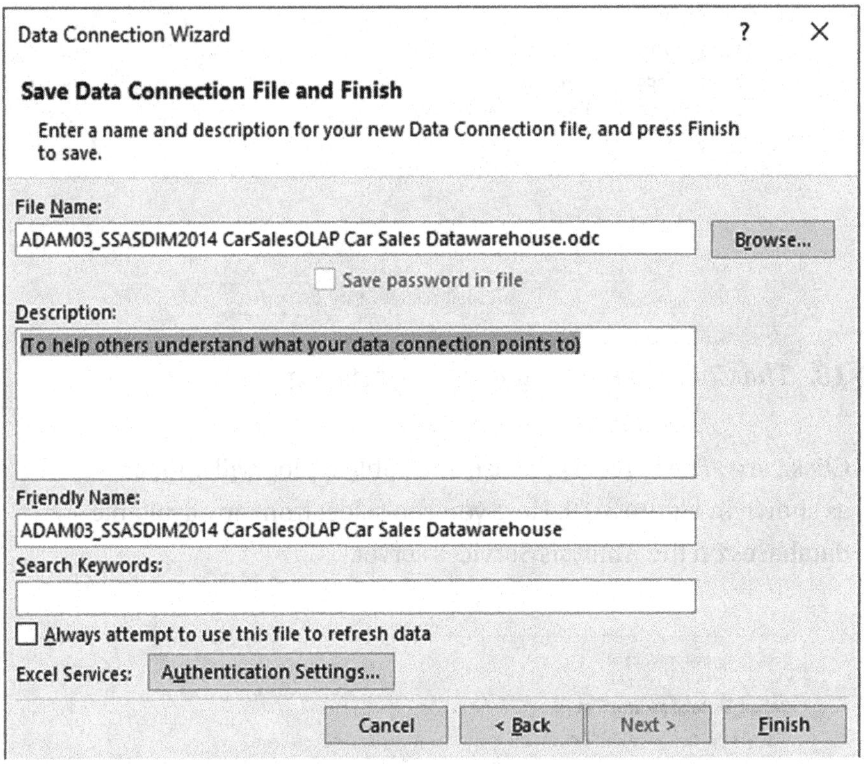

Figure 3-20. *The Save Data Connection File and Finish dialog*

5.   Click Finish. The Import Data dialog will appear, as shown in
     Figure 3-21. This offers slightly more restricted choices that you
     saw previously when using Power Query to connect to Analysis
     Services.

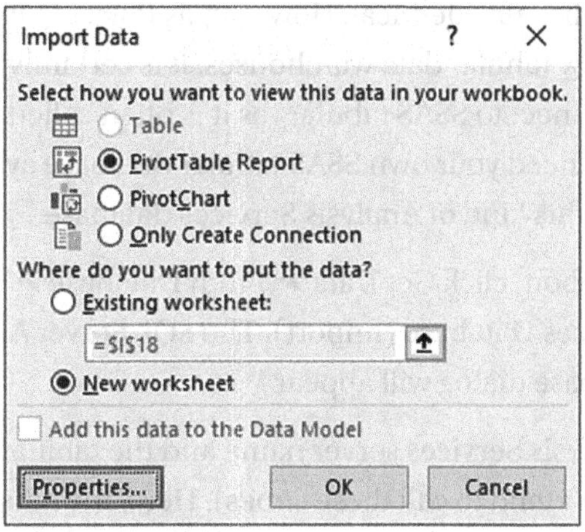

Figure 3-21. *The Import Data dialog*

6.   Click OK. Excel will create a pivot table (or a pivot chart if this is
     what you have selected) based on the Analysis Services data in
     either a new or an existing worksheet.

I must reemphasize that the source data *cannot* be cleansed, modeled, or tweaked in
Power Query when you are using this type of connection and that, consequently, you will
not see a query appear in the Queries & Connections pane.

SSAS Tabular Data Warehouses

The previous section showed you how to connect to a "classic" SQL Server Analysis
Services cube. However, there are now two types of SQL Server Analysis Services data
warehouses:

- The "traditional" dimensional cube

- The "newer" tabular data warehouse

As more and more data warehouses (at least the ones that are based on Microsoft
technologies) are being built using the newer, tabular technology, it is probably worth
your while to see how quickly and easily you can use to connect to these data sources
with Power Query. Indeed, the steps that you follow to connect to either of these data

warehouse sources are virtually identical. However, as Power Query is rapidly becoming the tool of choice to query tabular data warehouses, it is certainly worth a few minutes to learn how to use it to connect to SSAS tabular (as it is often called, for short).

Once again, you will need your own SSAS tabular database available to attempt making a connection to this kind of Analysis Services database.

1. In the Data ribbon, click Get Data ➤ From Database ➤ From
    Analysis Services Database (Import). The SQL Server Analysis
    Services database dialog will appear.

2. Enter the Analysis Services server name and the tabular database
    name (we don't tend to call these cubes). Here, the database is
    CarSalesTabular on my PC; you will have to specify your own
    tabular database name. In any case, you will need to use the name
    of your own SSAS server.

3. Click Import.

4. The dialog will look like Figure 3-22.

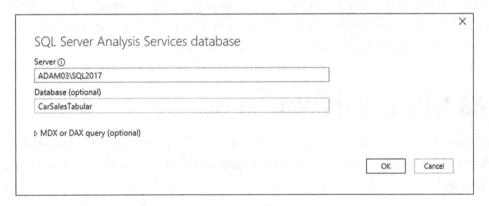

Figure 3-22. *Connecting to an SSAS (multidimensional) database*

5. Click OK. If this is the first time that you are connecting to the
    tabular data warehouse, then the Access SQL Server Analysis
    Services dialog will appear so that you can define the credentials
    that you are using to connect to the Analysis Services database,
    where you will have to accept or alter the credentials. You can see
    this dialog in Figure 3-23.

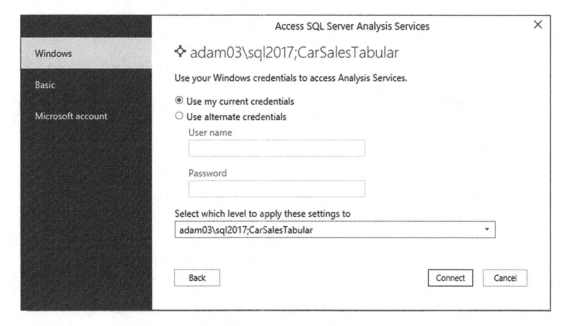

Figure 3-23. *The credentials dialog*

6. Click Connect. The Navigator dialog will appear.

7. Expand the folders in the left pane of the dialog. This way, you can see all the tables contained in the data warehouse. These may—or may not—be structured as facts and dimensions as was the case with a "classic" SSAS data warehouse.

8. Select the tables that you want to load. The dialog will look something like Figure 3-24.

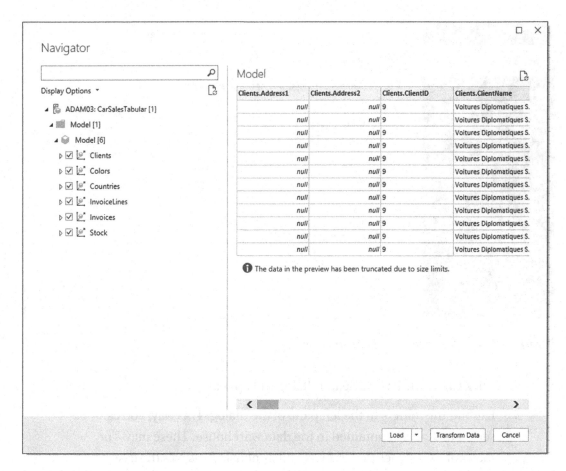

Figure 3-24. *Selecting attributes and measures from an SSAS tabular data source*

9. Click Load. The data will be loaded (most probably into a new
    worksheet—but this will depend on your environment).

Tip   You can filter the data that is loaded from an SSAS tabular database by
expanding the MDX or DAX query (optional) item in the SQL Server Analysis
Services database dialog. Then you can enter a DAX query in the box that appears
before clicking OK. SSAS tabular databases use queries written in a specific
language called DAX.

Types of Credentials When Connecting

When connecting to just about any database—be it a Microsoft database such as SQL Server or Analysis Services or one of the non-Microsoft databases for which there are connectors available in Excel—you will have to choose how to be authenticated by the database. This will involve specifying the type of credentials that you want to pass through to the database from which you want to extract data.

There are essentially three types of connections available (as you saw in Figure 3-14):

- *Windows*: This means using your Windows login to the corporate network or local workgroup to authenticate against the database. This presumes that your Windows login has been given the rights to access the database and the data it contains.

- *Basic*: This means entering a user name and password that will be recognized by the database that has been given the rights to access the database and the data it contains. Clearly you will need to have this information to hand before attempting this kind of connection.

- *Microsoft account*: This means using your Microsoft account to access the database and the data it contains. Once again, this account must have been given the rights to access the database and the data it contains.

Power Query saves a data source credential, or sign-in identity, for each data source connection you have used.

Unable to Connect

There will, inevitably, be times when you cannot connect to an external database from Power Query in Excel. You will discover this pretty quickly when you see the dialog shown in Figure 3-25.

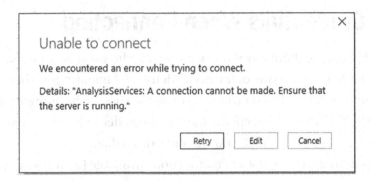

Figure 3-25. *The Unable to connect dialog*

Quite simply, the solution is to click the Edit button, which will redisplay the connection dialog for this specific data source. Then you enter the correct connection information—and try to connect, again.

Other Database Connections

Power Query does not limit you to a predefined set of available data sources. Provided that your source database comes complete with one of the generic data providers—ODBC or OLE DB—then Power Query can, in all probability, access these sources too. You will learn about these in Chapter 5.

Conclusion

In this chapter, you have seen how to connect Power Query to some of the plethora of databases and data warehouses that currently exist. Moreover, you have seen that Power Query comes equipped "out of the box" with connections to some of the most widely used databases that currently exist in a corporate environment.

CHAPTER 4

Loading Data from the Web and the Cloud

In this chapter, we will take a look at a subset of the fast-growing and wide-ranging set of data sources available over the Internet that you can use as a source of analytical data for Excel. While the data sources that you will see in the following pages may be extremely diverse, they all have one thing in common: they are stored outside the enterprise and are available using an Internet connection.

Looking at all the available sources in detail would take up an entire book, so I will only show you how to access *some* of the mainstream services that are currently on offer. Once you have learned how to access a few of them, you should be able to extend the basic techniques to access just about any of the web and cloud services that can currently be used by Power Query to import data into Excel.

The ever-increasing range of data sources that are accessible using Power Query are provided by several different suppliers. So nearly all of the data connections outlined in this chapter require access to a specific online source. Most of these sources are industrial strength—and not free. However, if your enterprise is not a subscriber to these services, and you wish, nevertheless, to experiment with them, it could be worth taking a look at the free trial offers available from many (if not all) of the service providers whose offerings are outlined in this chapter. Consequently, many of these data sources are only available with an Excel Pro or Enterprise licence.

Web and Cloud Services

Before delving into the details of some of the web and cloud services that are available, let's take an initial high-level look at what these really are. These data sources include (among others)

© Adam Aspin 2020
A. Aspin, *Data Mashup with Microsoft Excel Using Power Query and M*,
https://doi.org/10.1007/978-1-4842-6018-0_4

- Web pages

- Online services, such as Salesforce or MS Dynamics 365

- Microsoft Azure, which covers hosting files in Azure Blob services, storing data in an Azure SQL Database, or storing data in an Azure Synapse Analytics (or even reading big data in Azure HDInsight)

Web Pages

If you need to collect some data that you can see as a table in a web browser, you can use Power Query to connect to the URL for the page in question and then load all the data from any table on the page.

Online Services

Online services is a catch-all phrase used to describe data that you can access using the Internet. Most of the online services available to Power Query are what are called "platforms." These are (often huge) software and data resources that either are only available online or were once housed in corporate systems but are now available as services on the Internet. There are currently several online services that are available to connect to using Power Query. They are listed in Table 4-1.

Table 4-1. *Online Services Currently Available to Power Query*

Source	Comments
Salesforce Objects	Lets you access data in Salesforce
Salesforce Reports	Lets you access the prestructured data objects (both native and custom) that underlie built-in Salesforce reports
Facebook	Accesses Facebook data
SharePoint Online	Connects to the cloud-hosted version of Microsoft SharePoint
Microsoft Exchange Online	Connects to the cloud-hosted version of Microsoft Exchange
Dynamics 365 Online	Connects to the cloud-hosted version of Microsoft Dynamics 365—the MS CRM and ERP solution

Microsoft Azure

Azure is the Microsoft Cloud. The Azure data sources that Power Query can currently connect to, and can preview and load data from, are given in Table 4-2.

Table 4-2. *Azure Sources*

Source	Comments
Microsoft Azure SQL Database	Lets you connect to a Microsoft SQL Server cloud-based database and import records from all the data tables and views that you are authorized to access
Microsoft Azure SQL data warehouse (now rebranded as Azure Synapse Analytics)	Lets you connect to Microsoft's cloud-based, elastic, enterprise data warehouse
Microsoft Azure Blob Storage	Reads from a cloud-based unstructured data store
Microsoft Azure Table Storage	Reads from Microsoft Azure tables
Microsoft Azure Data Lake Storage (Gen1 and Gen2)	Lets you connect to Microsoft's raw data cloud storage
Microsoft Azure HDInsight	Reads cloud-based Hadoop files in the Microsoft Azure environment

Obviously, more Azure connection options may be added to Power Query in Excel by Microsoft as the Azure offering is extended.

Note   Power Query can also access SharePoint on-premises and MS Exchange data. However, I shall not be examining these connections in this book.

Web Pages

As a first and extremely simple example, let's grab some data from a web page. This is made extremely easy by Power Query, as it can read the tables of data present in any web page. Since I want to concentrate on the method rather than the data, I will use a web page that has nothing to do with the sample data used elsewhere in this book. I will not be using this other than as a simple introduction to the process of loading data from web pages using Power Query.

Assuming that you have launched Excel

1. In the Data ribbon, click From Web.

2. Enter the following URL (it is a Microsoft help page for Power Query that contains a few tables of data): `http://office.microsoft.com/en-gb/excel-help/guide-to-the-power-query-ribbon-HA103993930.aspx`. I am, of course, hoping that it is still available when you read this book. Of course, if you have a URL that you want to try out, then feel free! The dialog will look something like Figure 4-1.

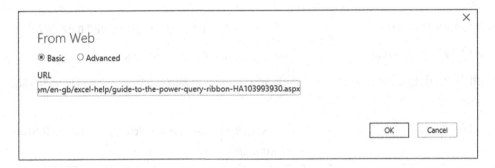

Figure 4-1. *The From Web dialog*

3. Click OK. The Navigator dialog will appear. After a few seconds, during which Power Query is connecting to the web page, the list of available tables of data in the web page will be displayed.

4. Click one of the table names on the left of the Navigator dialog. The contents of the table will appear on the right of the Navigator dialog to show you what the data in the chosen table looks like, as shown in Figure 4-2.

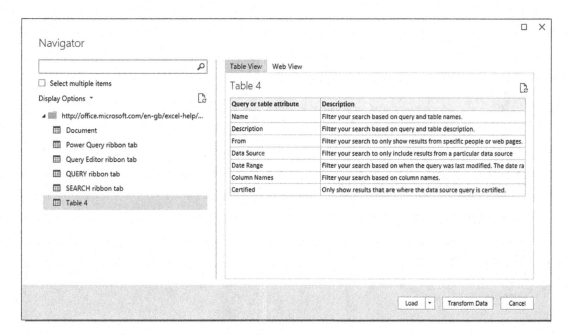

Figure 4-2. The Navigator dialog previewing the contents of a table on a web page

5. Select the check box in the Navigator dialog (shown to the left of Table 4 in Figure 4-2).

6. Click Load at the bottom of the window. The data will be loaded into a new worksheet.

Tip   Another way of accessing web pages is to click the small triangle at the bottom of the Get Data button in the Data ribbon and select From Other Sources ➤ From Web from the menu that appears.

This simple example showed how you can select tables of data from a web page and load them into Excel.

Advanced Web Options

In step 3 of the previous example, you could have selected the Advanced button. Had you done this, the From Web dialog would have expanded to allow you to build complex URLs by adding URL parts. You can see an example of this in Figure 4-3.

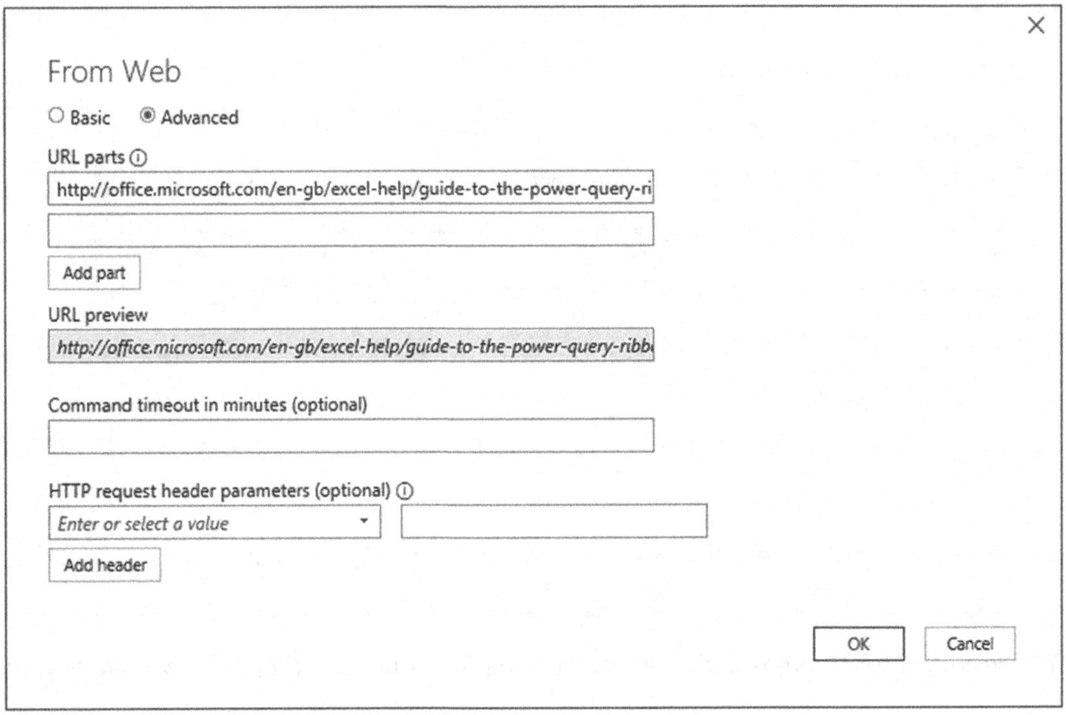

Figure 4-3. *The Advanced options in the From Web dialog*

Clicking the Add part button allows you to define multiple URL parts.

If necessary, you can also specify HTTP request header parameters that will be used when submitting the URL. These could be required by certain web pages. A discussion of these is outside the scope of this book.

Viewing the Source Web Page

It can be more than a little disconcerting to see only the tables from a web page—and not the actual page itself—in the Navigator. After all, the Web is a quintessentially visual medium.

So Power Query has a useful addition to the Navigator that applies only to web pages. This is the possibility to see the actual page itself in the Navigator—just as it appears in a web browser. To try this out:

1.   Follow steps 1 through 3 as described earlier.

2.   Click Web View on the right of the Navigator. You should see something like the page shown in Figure 4-4.

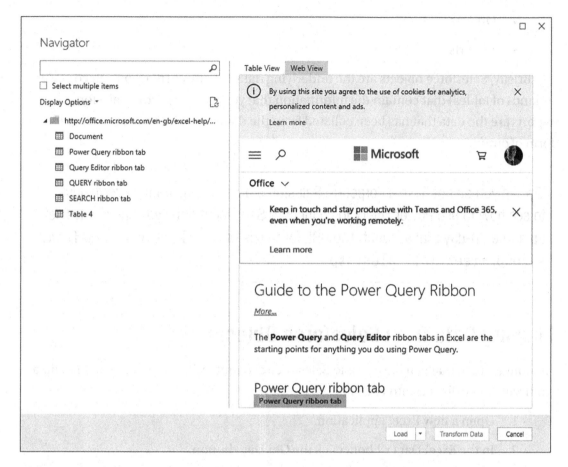

Figure 4-4. *Viewing the source web page in the From Web dialog*

You can now scroll down the page—and flip back to viewing only the data in the tables in the page by clicking Table View on the right-hand side of the dialog.

Salesforce

One of the pioneers in the software as a service (SaaS) space—and now, indisputably, one of the leaders—is Salesforce. So it is perhaps inevitable that Power Query will allow you to connect to Salesforce and load into Excel any data that you have permission to view using your Salesforce account.

Indeed, Salesforce is such a wide-ranging and complete service that you have two possible methods of accessing your data:

- Objects

- Reports

Briefly, Salesforce objects are the underlying data structures (that you can consider as kinds of tables) that contain the information that you want to access. Salesforce reports are the data that has been collated from the data tables into a more accessible form of output.

Tip   If you do not have a corporate Salesforce account but want, nevertheless, to see how to use Power Query to connect to Salesforce data, you can always set up a free 30-day trial account. The URL for this is `www.salesforce.com/form/signup/freetrial-sales.jsp`.

Loading Data from Salesforce Objects

Assuming, then, that you have a valid Salesforce account, here is how you can load data from Salesforce objects into Excel:

1. Open a new Excel application.

2. In the Excel Data ribbon, click the Get Data button.

3. Click From Online Services ➤ From Salesforce Objects. The Salesforce Objects dialog will appear. It should look like the one shown in Figure 4-5.

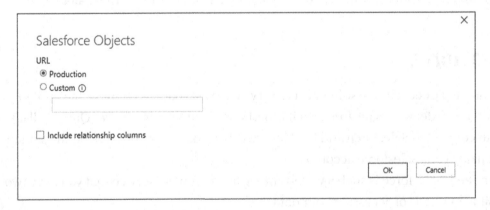

Figure 4-5. *The Salesforce Objects dialog*

4. Select the Production button and click OK. The Access Salesforce
    login dialog will appear. It should look like the one shown in
    Figure 4-6.

Figure 4-6. *The Access Salesforce login dialog*

5. Unless you are already signed in, click Sign in. The Salesforce sign-
    in dialog will appear.

6. Enter your Salesforce user name and password. The dialog should
    look something like the one shown in Figure 4-7.

Figure 4-7. *The Salesforce sign-in dialog*

7. If this is the first time that you are connecting to Salesforce from
    Power Query (or if you have requested that Salesforce request
    confirmation each time that you log in), you will be asked to
    verify your identity. The Salesforce Verify Your Identity dialog will
    appear, as shown in Figure 4-8.

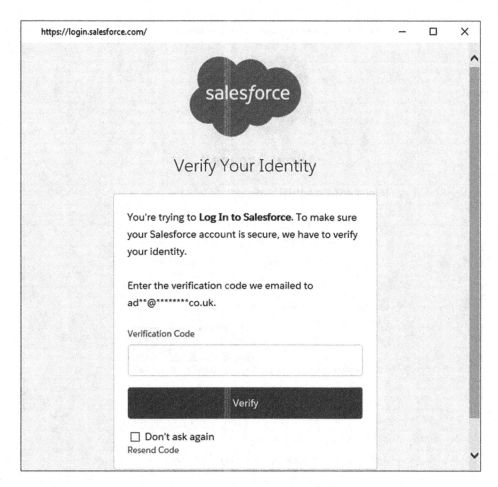

Figure 4-8. *The Salesforce Verify Your Identity dialog*

8. Click Verify. Salesforce will send a verification code to the email account that you are using to log in to Salesforce.

9. Enter the code in the Verification Code field and click OK. You will see the Allow Access dialog, as in Figure 4-9.

Figure 4-9. *The Salesforce Allow Access dialog*

10.   Click Allow. You will return to the Access Salesforce dialog, only now you are logged in.

11.   Click Connect. The Navigator will appear, showing the Salesforce objects that you have permissions to access. You can see an example of this in Figure 4-10.

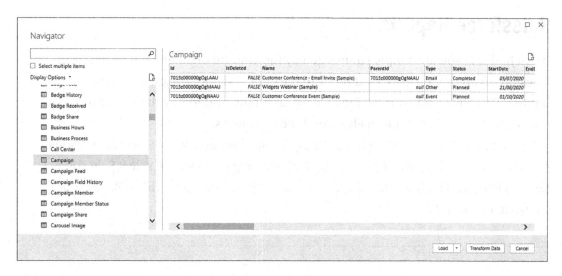

Figure 4-10. *Salesforce objects viewed in the Navigator*

12. Select the objects whose data you wish to load into Excel and click Load. The data will be loaded into Excel ready for you to create reports based on your Salesforce data.

Tip To avoid having to confirm your identity to Salesforce every time that you create a new suite of Excel reports using Salesforce data, you can check "Remember me" in the Salesforce sign-in dialog and "Don't ask again" in the Salesforce Verify Your Identity dialog.

Salesforce objects contain a vast amount of data. However, from the point of view of Power Query, this is similar to accessing a database structure. This means that you have to have some understanding of how the underlying data is stored. Should you wish to learn about the way that Salesforce data is structured, then I suggest that you start with the Salesforce documentation currently available at https://trailhead.salesforce.com/en/modules/data_modeling/units/objects_intro.

Salesforce Reports

If you find that you are simply submerged by the amount of data that is available in Salesforce, you can, instead, go directly to the data that underlies standard Salesforce reports. This will avoid your having to learn about the underlying data structures. The downside is that you cannot easily extend these datasets.

To access Salesforce report data, simply follow the steps outlined in the previous section. However, instead of choosing Salesforce Objects in step 3, select Salesforce Reports instead. The Navigator dialog will, in this case, look something like the one shown in Figure 4-11.

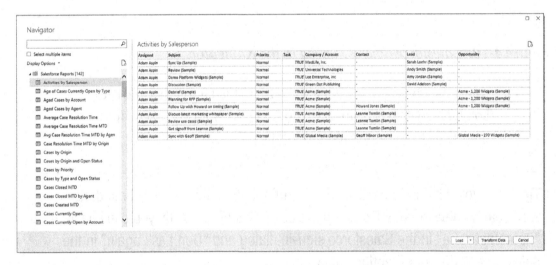

Figure 4-11. *The Navigator dialog showing the data for Salesforce Reports*

From here you can select and load the reports data from Salesforce that you want to use for further analysis.

Microsoft Dynamics 365

Another online service that contains much valuable enterprise data is Microsoft Dynamics 365. As you would probably expect, Power Query in Excel can connect easily to Microsoft online sources such as Dynamics. Here is how to do this if your organization uses this specific platform:

1. Open a new Excel application.

2. In the Excel Data ribbon, click the Get Data button.

3. Click From Online Services ➤ From Dynamics 365 (online)

4. Click Connect. The Dynamics 365 (online) dialog will appear.

5. Enter the URL that you use to connect to Dynamics 365 and add /api/data/v8.1 (at least, this was the case as this book went to press). It could look like the one shown in Figure 4-12. Note, however, that this URL will vary depending on where you are in the world.

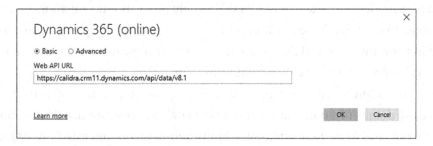

Figure 4-12. *The Dynamics 365 (online) dialog*

6. Click OK. The OData feed dialog will appear. This is because Power Query uses OData to connect to Dynamics 365 Online.

7. Select Organizational Account as the security access method.

8. Click Sign In to sign in to your Dynamics 365 account and follow the Microsoft sign-in process.

9. Click Connect. The Navigator dialog will appear showing all the Dynamics objects that you have permissions to connect to.

Note   In step 6 you saw that an MS Dynamics 365 connection is really an OData connection. OData is explained in more detail in the following chapter.

There are a huge number of Dynamics 365 tables—and this number will vary depending on the subscription that your organization has taken out. However, you are, in reality, accessing a database structure. This means that you have to have some understanding of how the underlying data is stored. Should you wish to learn about Dynamics 365 tables, then I suggest that you start with the Microsoft online help at `https://docs.microsoft.com/en-us/dynamics365/unified-operations/dev-itpro/data-entities/data-entities`.

Azure SQL Database

SQL Server does not only exist as an on-premises database. It is also available as a "platform as a service" (also known as PaaS). Simply put, this lets you apply a pay-as-you-go model to your database requirements where you can fire up a database server in the cloud in a few minutes and then scale it to suit your requirements, rather than buying hardware and software and having to maintain them.

Connecting to Microsoft's PaaS offering, called Azure SQL Database, is truly simple. If you have the details of a corporate Azure SQL Database, you can use this to connect to. If you do not, and nonetheless want to experiment with connecting Power Query to Azure SQL Database, you can always request a free trial account from Microsoft and set up an Azure SQL Database database in a few minutes. If this is the path that you are taking, then you can find instructions on how to do this (including loading the sample data that you will connect to later in this section) at the following URL: `https://docs.microsoft.com/en-gb/azure/sql-database/sql-database-get-started-portal`.

Tip   When you are creating your own Azure SQL Database to test connectivity from Power Query, be sure to define the source to be *Sample*. This will ensure that the MS sample data is loaded into your test database.

To connect from Excel to an Azure SQL Database using Power Query:

1. Open a new Excel application.

2. In the Excel Data ribbon, click Get Data ➤ From Azure ➤ From Azure SQL Database. The SQL Server database dialog will appear (after all, an Azure SQL Database is a SQL Server database—but in the cloud).

3. Enter the Azure SQL Database server name that you obtained
    from the Microsoft Azure Management Portal (or that was given to
    you by a corporate DBA). The SQL Server database dialog will look
    like the one shown in Figure 4-13.

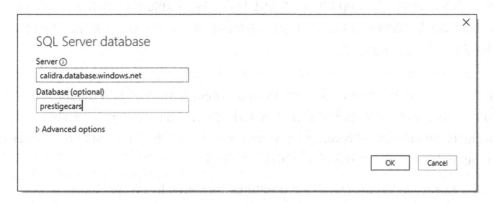

Figure 4-13. *The SQL Server database dialog for an Azure SQL Database connection*

4. Click OK. The credentials dialog will appear.

5. Click Database on the left and enter a valid user name and
    password. The credentials dialog will look like the one shown in
    Figure 4-14.

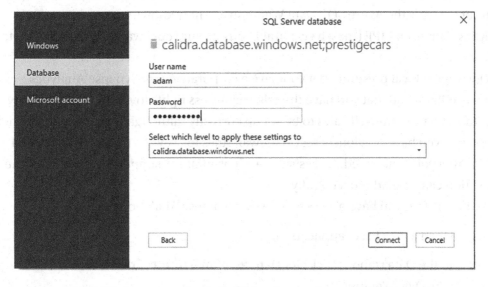

Figure 4-14. *The SQL Server credentials dialog for an Azure SQL Database connection*

6. Click Connect. The Navigator dialog will appear showing the database(s) that you have permission to access in the Azure SQL Server Database.

Note   If you are setting up an Azure SQL Database, make sure that you include firewall rules to allow connection from the computer where you are running Excel to the Azure SQL Database.

If you followed the steps to connect to an on-premises SQL Server database in Chapter 3, then you are probably feeling that the approach used here is virtually identical. Fortunately, the Power Query development team has worked hard to make the two processes as similar as possible. This extends to

- Ensuring that the DataSource settings are stored by Power Query and can be updated just as you can for an on-premises database connection

Azure SQL Data Warehouse (Azure Synapse Analytics)

Azure has many available platforms to store data. One that is particularly well adapted to Power Query is the Azure SQL Data Warehouse—now known as Azure Synapse Analytics. This is an MPP (massively parallel processing) data warehouse that is hosted in Azure.

Once again I will presume that you have a corporate Azure Synapse Analytics instance at hand and that you have the relevant access rights to Azure Synapse Analytics. Here, too, you need firewall rules to be set up correctly (although this may not be strictly necessary if you have previously set up firewall rules for, say, Azure SQL Database). I imagine that you could need the assistance of corporate IT support to ensure that the connection can be made successfully.

Assuming that you have access to an Azure Synapse Analytics instance:

1. Open a new Excel application.

2. In the Data ribbon, click Get Data ➤ From Azure ➤ From Azure SQL Data Warehouse.

3. Enter the Azure SQL Data Warehouse server name that you obtained from the Microsoft Azure Management Portal (or that was given to you by a corporate IT). The SQL Server database dialog will look like the one shown in Figure 4-15. This is because Azure Synapse Analytics is, essentially, a SQL Server database.

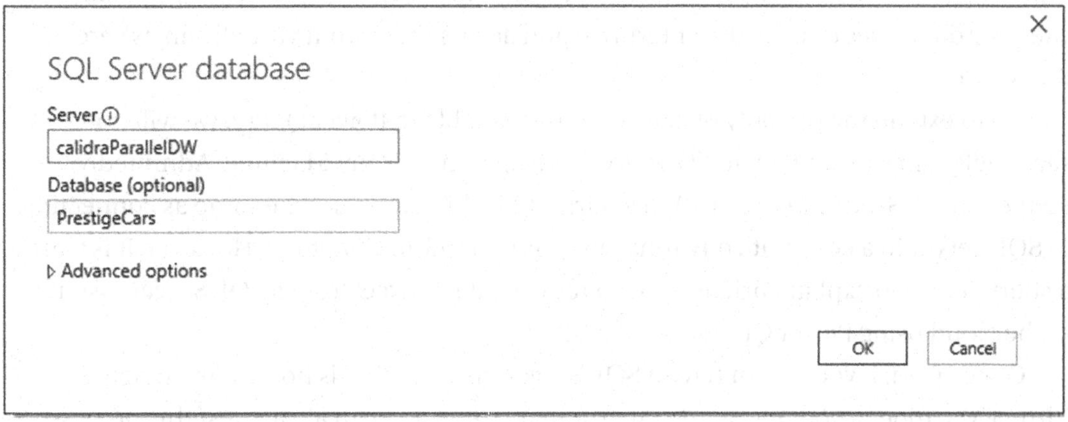

Figure 4-15. *The SQL Server database dialog for an Azure Synapse Analytics connection*

4. Select the Import button and then click OK. The credentials dialog will appear.

5. Click Database on the left and enter a valid user name and password.

6. Click Connect. The Navigator dialog will appear showing the database(s) that you have permission to access in the Azure SQL Server database.

7. Select the tables that you need and click Load or Edit to return to Excel. Remember to click Select multiple items if you want to import several tables simultaneously.

Note   Do not be phased by the fact that the title for the dialog where you specify the server and database says "SQL Server database." This will connect you to the Azure SQL Data Warehouse correctly.

Connecting to SQL Server on an Azure Virtual Machine

More and more databases are now hosted outside a corporate environment by cloud service providers. With a provider such as Amazon (with RDS for SQL Server) or Microsoft (that offers virtual machines—or VMs—for SQL Server in Azure), you can now site your databases outside the enterprise and access them from virtually anywhere in the world.

So, to extend the panoply of data sources available to Power Query, we will now see, briefly, how to connect to SQL Server on an Azure Virtual Machine. Admittedly, connecting to SQL Server on an Azure Virtual Machine is nearly the same as connecting to SQL Server in a corporate environment—as you saw in Chapter 3. However, it is worth a short detour to explain, briefly, how to return data to Excel from a SQL Server instance in the cloud using Power Query.

Once again, if you do not have a SQL Server instance that is hosted on an Azure Virtual Machine in your corporate environment, then you can always test this process using an Azure trial account. I cannot, however, explain here how to set up a SQL Server instance on a VM, as this is a large and separate subject that is outside the scope of this book. There are, however, many resources available that can explain how to do this should you need them.

To connect to SQL Server on a Virtual Machine in Azure:

1. Open a new Excel application.

2. In the Excel ribbon, click the small triangle at the bottom of the Get Data button and then click SQL Server. The SQL Server database dialog will appear.

3. Enter the full string that describes the server in the Server text box. Either this will be given to you by a corporate DBA or, if you are using your own Azure account, you can find it in the Azure Management Portal.

4. Enter the database name corresponding to the database that you have the right to access. The dialog will look like Figure 4-16.

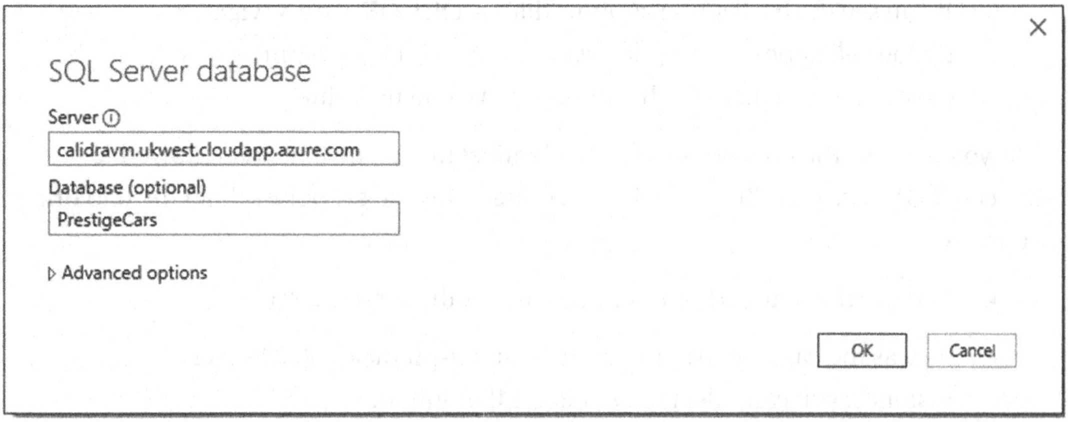

Figure 4-16. *The Microsoft SQL Server database dialog for an Azure VM*

5.   Click OK. The Access a SQL Server Database dialog will appear.
     Select Database as the security mode and enter the user name
     and password, as shown in Figure 4-17. If you are using your own
     Azure account, these can be the user name and password that you
     specified when setting up the virtual machine.

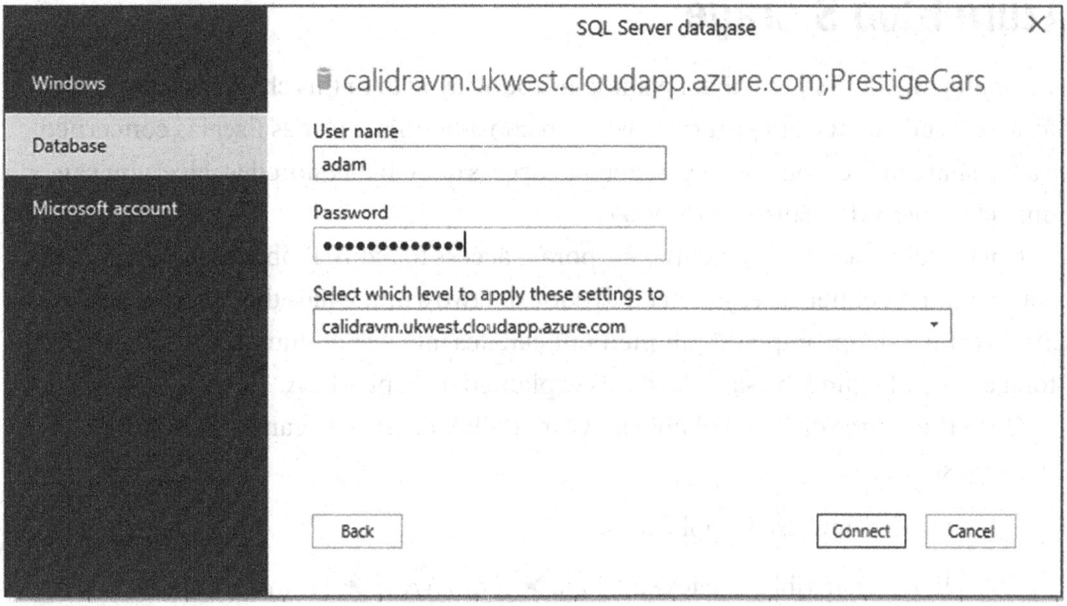

Figure 4-17. *The SQL Server database dialog when connecting to a virtual machine*

6. If you see the encryption support dialog, click OK. The Navigator
    dialog will appear listing all the tables that you have permissions
    to see on the SQL Server hosted by the virtual machine.

As you can see, the process is virtually identical to the one that you followed to
connect to SQL Server in Chapter 3. I have, nonetheless, a few points that I need to bring
to your attention:

- You use the Azure VM multipart name as the server name.

- As was the case when connecting to an on-premises SQL Server
  instance, you can select the database if required.

- You can use the server's IP address as the database name if the VM
  has specified a public IP address.

- Security is a big and separate question. In a corporate environment,
  you *might* be able to use Windows security to connect. You will
  almost certainly have to use database security for a test VM.

- As is always the case in Azure, firewalls must be set up correctly.

Azure Blob Storage

The final Azure data source that I want to introduce you to in this chapter is Azure Blob
Storage. To all intents and purposes, you can consider this, as far as Excel is concerned,
as a file share in the cloud. So if you need to access data that is stored as files, you can
connect to them via Azure Blob Storage.

Once again, you will need either corporate access to Azure Blob Storage or an Azure
trial account. In either case, you need to copy the two sample files that are in the folder
C:\PowerBiDesktopSamples\MultipleIdenticalFiles into a container in your Azure Blob
Storage. Downloading the sample files is explained in Appendix A.

Once the source data is available in Azure Blob Storage, you can carry out the
following steps:

1. Open a new Excel application.

2. In the Data ribbon, click Get Data ➤ From Azure ➤ From Azure
    Blob Storage.

3. Enter the account name that you are using to connect to Azure Blob Storage. The Azure Blob Storage dialog will look like the one shown in Figure 4-18. If you are using a corporate Azure Blob Storage account, then your system administrator will provide this. In a test scenario, you can find this in the Azure Management Portal by opening the Storage Account blade and copying the Blob Service Endpoint.

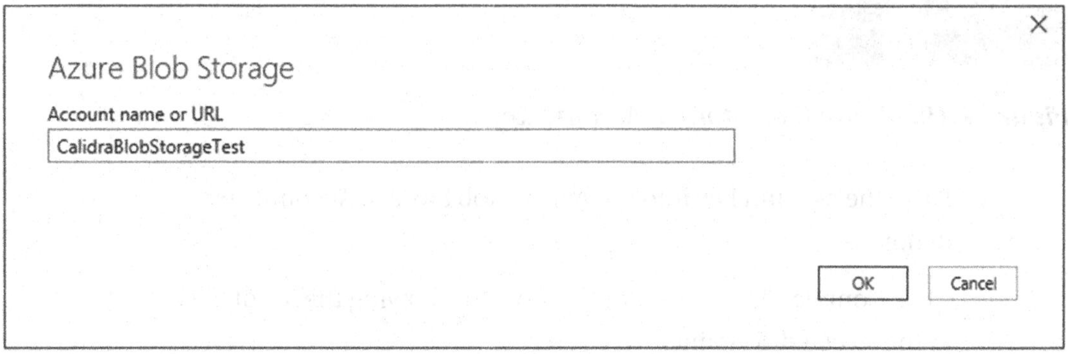

Figure 4-18. *Connecting to an Azure Blob Storage*

4. Click OK. The Azure Blob Storage Account Key dialog will appear.

5. In the Azure Management Portal, copy an account key. These can be found in the Azure Management Portal by clicking the Storage Account blade and then clicking Access Keys. If you have been sent an account key by a system administrator, then use that instead. You can see this dialog in Figure 4-19.

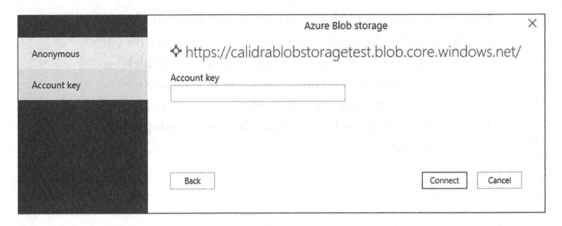

Figure 4-19. *Azure Blob Storage Account key*

6.   Paste the account key into the Azure Blob Storage Account key
dialog.

7.   Click Connect. The Navigator will appear, showing the list of files
in the selected container.

8.   Click Load. The list of files stored in Azure will appear in Power
Query.

Note   It is important to note that, for the moment at least, what you have returned
from Azure is a list of available files. Chapter 9 explains how to select and load
data from some or all of the available files into Excel, where they can be used as a
basis for analytics.

Azure Security

All cloud service providers take security extremely seriously. As you have seen in this
chapter, you will always be obliged to enter some form of security token and/or specify a
valid user name and password to connect to cloud-based data.

Other Source Types

Clearly it would be impossible to explain how to use all of the potential data sources without devoting a considerable number of pages to the subject. Moreover, not everybody will need to access every place where external data is stored. Indeed, most users only ever need to ingest data from two or three external data sources at most.

Inevitably, this means that there are several data sources available in Power Query in Excel that you will not be seeing in this book. However, as I have mentioned, one of the fundamental advantages of Power Query is that once you have learned how to connect to a couple of data sources, you have learned how to use pretty nearly all of them.

So, there are a handful of data sources that I am not covering in this book. They include

- Azure Data Lake

- SharePoint (on-premises and online)

- Microsoft Exchange (on-premises and online)

- Microsoft Dynamics online

- Active Directory

- Hadoop

- Azure HDInsight

- Facebook

Connecting to SharePoint, Exchange, Microsoft Dynamics, Azure HDInsight, or Hadoop will mean, inevitably, that these are used by your organization—and that you have the necessary access rights.

I prefer to add a word of warning if you are using Power Query in Excel to connect to Azure HDInsight or Hadoop. These are "big data" sources and, as the moniker implies, they can contain vast amounts of data. The sheer size of the data that they contain can easily swamp Excel. Consequently, I advise you to read the next few chapters that explain how to select and filter data before loading it *before* you attempt to connect to big data sources.

Conclusion

In this chapter, you saw, briefly, how to retrieve data that you access using the Internet. This can range from a table of data on a web page to a massive Azure Synapse Analytics Data Warehouse. You may even need to access data held in Azure Blob Storage or in an Azure Data Lake. Alternatively, perhaps you need to create reports based on your Salesforce or MS Dynamics 365 data. In any case, Power Query can connect and access the data available in these services and repositories.

Given the number of online sources, this chapter could only scratch the surface of this range of potential data repositories. However, as Power Query is rigorous about standardizing access to data, you should be able to apply the approaches you have learned in this chapter to many other data services, both current and future.

CHAPTER 5

Generic Data Sources

If you take a good look at the Get Data options, you will find that there are currently 40 data sources for which Power Query connectors are available. However, even this range of connectors pales into insignificance when faced with the vast array of potential source data repositories. So what can you do when faced with a source of external data that is not among those currently available?

One solution is to use a generic data connector to access data stores that are not directly accessible. To conclude our whistle-stop tour of some of the available source data, then, this chapter will introduce you to

- ODBC data

- OLE DB data

- OData feeds

The only difficulty when using generic data connectors is that they are, well, generic. This means that they take a "lowest common denominator" approach. This can mean that

- You depend on external providers of third-party software.

- Documentation is sparse or incomprehensible to the nontechnical user.

- You are on your own if you encounter any technical challenges.

Despite these caveats, the main generic connectors do, nonetheless, open up the possibility of connecting to and ingesting data from an immense range of potential sources of external data. So I always advise attempting to make these connections work if you possibly can, as the results are often much simpler and better than attempting to export source data as text or CSV files and then loading them.

© Adam Aspin 2020
A. Aspin, *Data Mashup with Microsoft Excel Using Power Query and M,*
https://doi.org/10.1007/978-1-4842-6018-0_5

If you wish to practice the ODBC and OLE DB connections described in this chapter, you will need to have access to source data that has these connection types enabled. In other words, you will need to have ODBC or OLE DB drivers already installed and functioning.

ODBC Sources

As you have seen in this book so far, Excel can connect to a wide range of data sources. However, there will always be external applications for which there is no specific connector built in to Excel.

This is where a generic solution called Open Database Connectivity (or ODBC) comes into play. ODBC is a standard way to connect to data sources, most of which are databases or structured like databases. Simply put, if an ODBC driver exists for the application that you want to connect to, then you can load data from it into Excel.

Hundreds of ODBC drivers have been written. Some are freely available; others require you to purchase a license. They exist for a wide spectrum of applications ranging from those found on most PCs to niche products. Some products have an ODBC driver that is installed with the application itself; others require you to download an ODBC driver separately. Some ODBC drivers are freely distributed, whereas others require you to purchase a license.

Although ODBC is designed as a standard way of accessing data in applications, each ODBC driver is slightly different from every other ODBC driver. Consequently, you might have to spend a little time learning the quirks of the interface for the driver that you want to use with the application that you want to connect to.

In this section, we will use FileMaker Pro as a data source. This product is a desktop and server database system that has been around for quite some time. However, there is currently no specific Power Query connector for it. The good news is that FileMaker Pro *does* have an ODBC driver. So we will use FileMaker Pro as an example of how to use ODBC to connect to Excel using Power Query.

I have to add that I am not expecting you to install a copy (even if it is only a trial copy) of FileMaker Pro and its companion ODBC driver to carry out this exercise. What I do want to explain, however, is how you can use ODBC to connect to a data source where an ODBC driver is available. So feel free to download and install FileMaker Pro and its ODBC driver if you wish, but you will have to refer to the FileMaker Pro documentation for an explanation of how to do this.

Assuming that you have an ODBC-compliant data source and a working ODBC driver for this data source, here is one example of how to load data into Excel using ODBC and Power Query:

1. Run the ODBC Data Source Administrator app. This is normally in the folder C:\ProgramData\Microsoft\Windows\Start Menu\ Programs\Administrative Tools. Be sure to use the 64-bit version if you are using 64-bit Excel or the 32-bit version if you are using 32-bit Excel.

2. Click the System DSN tab. You should see the dialog shown in Figure 5-1.

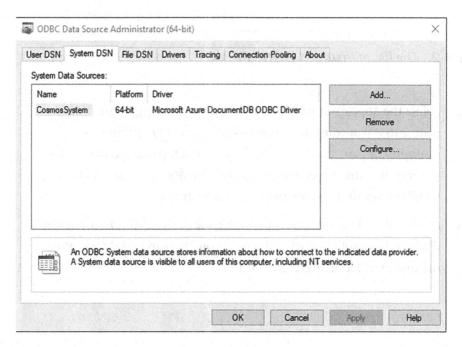

Figure 5-1. *The ODBC Data Source Administrator*

3. Click Add. You will see the list of all currently installed ODBC drivers on your computer. This should look something like the dialog shown in Figure 5-2.

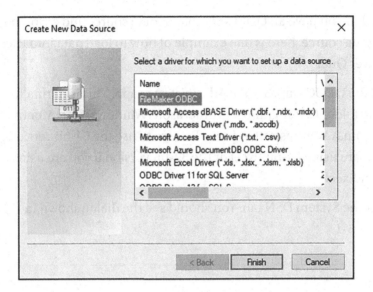

Figure 5-2. *The list of installed ODBC drivers*

4. Select the appropriate ODBC driver corresponding to the data
    source that you want to connect to (FileMaker ODBC in this
    example). If you cannot see the ODBC driver, you need to install—
    or reinstall—the driver. Please consult the documentation for the
    ODBC driver that you are using for these details.

5. Click Finish. The configuration dialog for the specific ODBC driver
    that you have selected will appear. If you are using FileMaker Pro,
    the dialog will look like Figure 5-3.

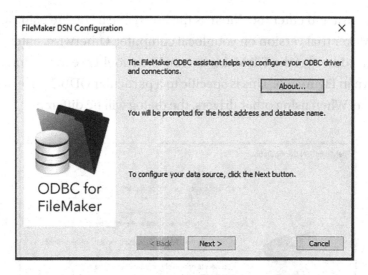

Figure 5-3. *The FileMaker Pro ODBC configuration assistant*

6. Click Next, and enter a name and a description for this particular
    ODBC connection. This could look something like the dialog
    shown in Figure 5-4.

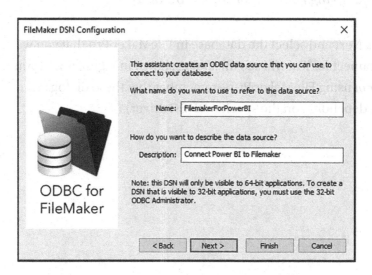

Figure 5-4. *Naming the ODBC connection for FileMaker Pro*

119

7. Click Next and enter **localhost** as the hostname if you are using a FileMaker trial version on your local computer. Otherwise, enter the IP address of the FileMaker server. You should see the dialog shown in Figure 5-5. This is specific to a particular ODBC driver, of course. When using other drivers, the dialog will be different.

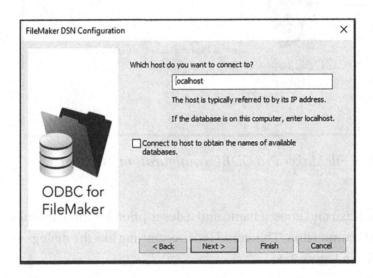

Figure 5-5. *Specifying the host for the ODBC data*

8. Click Next and select the database in FileMaker Pro that you want to connect to. You will see the dialog shown in Figure 5-6 (if you are *not* using FileMaker Pro—remember that these dialogs can vary depending on the specific ODBC driver).

Figure 5-6. *Specifying the database for the ODBC data*

9. Click Next. The ODBC configuration dialog will resume the specifications for the connection. This could look something like the one shown in Figure 5-7.

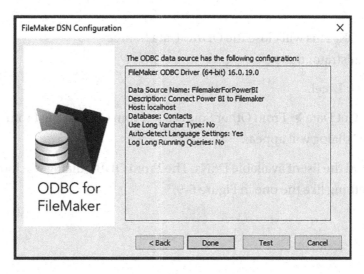

Figure 5-7. *The ODBC connection confirmation dialog*

10. Click Done. You will return to the ODBC Data Source Administrator, where you will see the System DSN that you just created. The ODBC Data Source Administrator dialog should look something like the one shown in Figure 5-8.

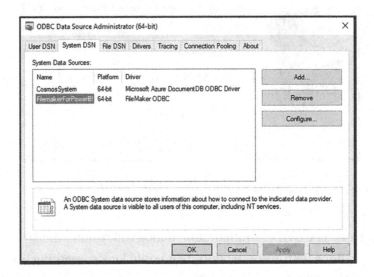

Figure 5-8. *The ODBC Data Source Administrator dialog with an ODBC driver configured*

11. Click OK. This will close the ODBC Data Source Administrator dialog.

12. Launch Excel.

13. Click Get Data ➤ From Other Sources ➤ From ODBC. The From ODBC dialog will appear.

14. Expand the list of available DSNs. The From ODBC dialog will look something like the one in Figure 5-9.

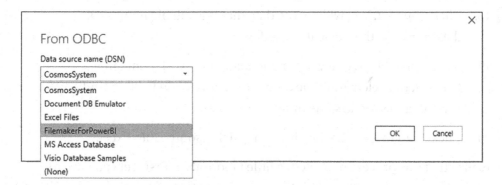

Figure 5-9. *The Excel From ODBC dialog to select an ODBC data source*

15. Select the DSN that you created previously (FilemakerForPowerBI in this example).

16. Click OK. The credentials dialog will appear.

17. Choose Windows integrated security or click Database on the left and enter the user name that has permissions to connect using the ODBC driver. The credentials dialog will look something like the one in Figure 5-10.

	ODBC driver	×
Default or Custom	✧ dsn=FilemakerForPowerBI	
Windows	Use a username and password to access a data source with an ODBC driver.	
Database	User name	
	admin	
	Password	
	••••••••••	
	Credential connection string properties (optional) ⓘ	
	Back	Connect Cancel

Figure 5-10. *The ODBC driver security dialog*

18. Click Connect. You will see the data that is available in the ODBC data source in the Navigator window.

19. Select the table(s) that you want to load into Excel. Remember to check the Select multiple items check box if you want to load several tables at the same time.

20. Click Load to load the data from the ODBC source into Excel.

I realize that this process may seem a little laborious at first. Yet you have to remember that you will, in all probability, only set up the ODBC connection *once*. After that you can use it to connect to the source data as often as you want.

Tip   Once you have created an ODBC DSN, you can use it in multiple scenarios— and with many different products—that require data from the source that you are using ODBC to connect to. This means that the ODBC source I created here can be used for Power Query in Excel, Power BI, and many other applications where you need to access FileMaker Pro data.

You need to be aware that each and every ODBC driver is different. So the appearance of the dialogs in steps 5 to 10 will vary slightly with each different ODBC driver that you configure. The key elements will, nonetheless, always be the same. They are

- Name the DSN

- Specify the host computer for the data

- Define the data repository (or database)

- Specify any credentials needed to access the data source

There is much more that could be written about creating and using ODBC connections to load data into Excel—or indeed into any number of destination applications. However, I will have to refer you to the wealth of available resources both in print and online if you need to learn more about this particular technology. A good starting point is the Microsoft documentation that explains the difference between System, User, and File DSNs and describes many of the key elements that you might need to know.

Note   The data source application (FileMaker Pro in this example) must be open and/or running for an ODBC connection to work. Other ODBC sources could have their own specific quirks.

As a final comment, I can only urge you to procure all the relevant documentation for the ODBC driver that you intend to use with Power Query in Excel. Indeed, if you are using an enterprise data source that uses ODBC drivers, you may have corporate resources who can either assist or even configure ODBC for you.

OLE DB Data Sources

OLE DB (short for Object Linking and Embedding, Database) is technically what is known as an application programming interface (API). Less technically, it is a technique for connecting to database sources in a generic manner.

So, in a somewhat similar fashion to ODBC, you can use OLE DB to connect to data sources (which are often databases, although they can be other sources of data). Indeed, you may find that OLE DB is a useful way to connect to a database even if another method exists.

So, whatever the use that you find for OLE DB, it is well worth getting to know how it works. In this example, I will use OLE DB to connect to SQL Server and a sample database.

1. Open a new Excel application.

2. In the Data ribbon, click Get Data ➤ From Other Sources ➤ From OLE DB. The From OLE DB dialog will appear.

3. Click Connect. The From OLE DB dialog will appear. It should look like Figure 5-11.

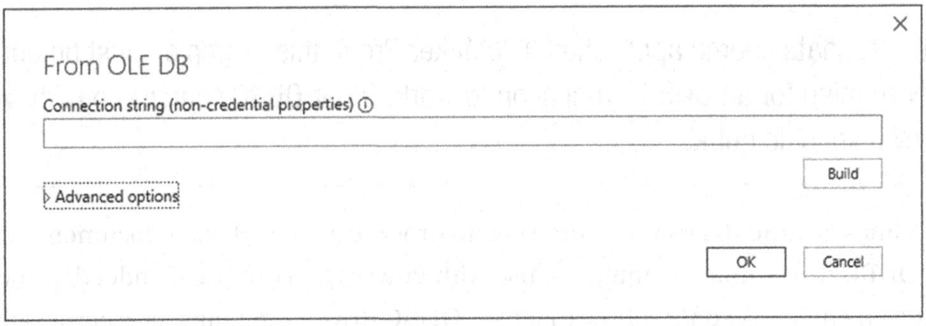

×

From OLE DB

Connection string (non-credential properties) ⓘ

[   ]

Build

▷ Advanced options

OK   Cancel

Figure 5-11. *The From OLE DB dialog*

4. If you have a fully working connection string, enter it in the
    Connection string text box.

5. If you do not have a connection string, click the Build button. The
    OLE DB Data Link Properties dialog will be displayed, as shown in
    Figure 5-12.

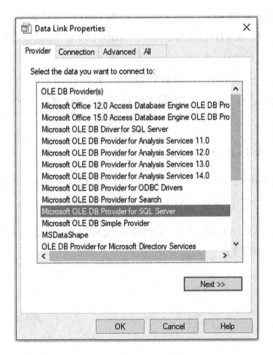

Figure 5-12. *The OLE DB Data Link Properties dialog*

6. Select the OLE DB data provider that you want to use. In this
    example, it will be Microsoft OLE DB Provider for SQL Server.
    Of course, you must select the OLE DB provider that you have
    installed for the data source that you want to access.

7. Click Next. The Connection properties pane of the OLE DB Data
    Link Properties dialog will appear.

8. Select an available SQL Server (or enter its name) from the "Select
    or enter a server name" popup.

9. Select the type of security, and enter a user name and password
    if you have selected to use a specific user name instead of using
    Windows NT Integrated security.

10. Select the source database from the "Select the database on the
    server" popup. The dialog will look something like the one shown
    in Figure 5-13.

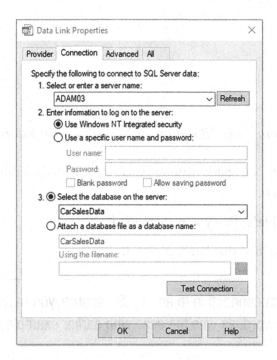

Figure 5-13. *The Connection properties of the OLE DB Data Link Properties*
dialog

11. Click the Test Connection button to ensure that the connection is valid. You should see the message in Figure 5-14.

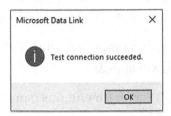

Figure 5-14. *The test connection alert*

12. Click OK. Excel will build the connection string and insert it into the From OLE DB dialog, as shown in Figure 5-15.

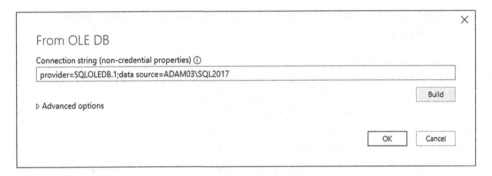

Figure 5-15. *The From OLE DB dialog with a valid connection string*

13. Click OK. The Navigator window will appear with the appropriate data displayed.

14. Select the table(s) that you want to load.

15. Click Load to load the data into Excel.

Note   If this is a first connection to an OLE DB source, you may be asked for a user name and password, as was the case with earlier examples in this chapter.

Steps 8 through 10 are specific to the SQL Server OLE DB driver. For other drivers, these steps could be different.

You need to be aware that an OLE DB connection requires that the OLE DB driver (or "provider") is installed on the computer where you are running Excel. However, what is really interesting is that an OLE DB connection can be reduced to a simple connection string. So if you need to share the connection with other users, you can simply email the connection string to them in many cases. Your colleagues can then simply paste the connection string into the From OLE DB dialog in Excel. In other words (and using this example as a model), you can simply send the following text to a coworker:

```
provider=SQLOLEDB.1;initial catalog=CarSalesData;data source=ADAM03\
SQLSERVER2016
```

They can use this string to connect to a specified database by pasting it into the From OLE DB dialog. Equally, your IT department might be able to provide you with the appropriate connection string that you can use directly.

There are other advantages to using OLE DB connections too. Specifically, you (or your IT department) can provide an advanced level of configuration in the connection string to speed up or otherwise improve the access to the data. This could be by specifying a mirrored server that is to be used for reporting to relieve the pressure on a main server, for instance. At this level the technical ramifications will depend on the OLE DB data source as well as the driver used and are so manifestly wide-ranging that they are outside the scope of this book.

OData Feeds

OData is a short way of referring to the Open Data Protocol. This protocol allows web clients to publish and edit resources, identified as URLs. The data that you connect to using OData can be in a tabular format or indeed in different structures.

OData is something of a generic method of connecting to web-based data. Consequently, each OData source could differ from others that you may have used previously.

There are a multitude of OData sources that are available. Some are public, some are only accessible if you have appropriate permissions. However, the access method will always be broadly similar. Here, then, is an example of how to connect to an OData sample source that Odata.org has made freely available (at least when this book went to press):

1. In the Excel Data ribbon, click Get Data ➤ From Other Sources ➤ From OData Feed. The OData feed dialog will appear.

2. Enter the URL that you are using to connect to the OData source. In this example, I will use a publicly available OData feed that you can find at `https://services.odata.org/TripPinRESTierService/People`. The dialog should look like Figure 5-16.

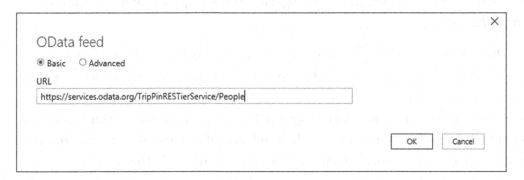

Figure 5-16. *The OData feed dialog*

3. Click OK. The OData feed credentials dialog will appear. You can see this in Figure 5-17.

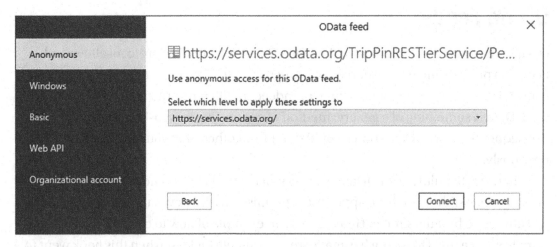

Figure 5-17. *The OData feed credentials dialog*

4. Select the type of credential from the available list on the left of the dialog. In this example, anonymous credentials are accepted, so you do not have to enter a user name or password. For other services, you may well need to select the appropriate security method on the left and then enter the required credentials.

5. Click Connect. The Navigator dialog will be displayed and will show the data available using the specified URL. You can see the data returned from this sample URL in Figure 5-18.

https://services.odata.org/TripPinRESTierService/People

UserName	FirstName	LastName	MiddleName	Gender	Age	Emails	AddressInfo	HomeAddress	FavoriteFeature	Features	Friends
russellwhyte	Russell	Whyte	null	Male	null	List	Table	null	Feature1	List	Table
scottketchum	Scott	Ketchum	null	Male	null	List	Table	null	Feature1	List	Table
ronaldmundy	Ronald	Mundy	null	Male	null	List	Table	null	Feature1	List	Table
javieralfred	Javier	Alfred	null	Male	null	List	Table	null	Feature1	List	Table
willieashmore	Willie	Ashmore	null	Male	null	List	Table	null	Feature1	List	Table
vincentcalabrese	Vincent	Calabrese	null	Male	null	List	Table	null	Feature1	List	Table
clydeguess	Clyde	Guess	null	Male	null	List	Table	Record	Feature1	List	Table
keithpinckney	Keith	Pinckney	null	Male	null	List	Table	null	Feature1	List	Table
marshallgaray	Marshall	Garay	null	Male	null	List	Table	null	Feature1	List	Table
ryantheriault	Ryan	Theriault	null	Male	null	List	Table	null	Feature1	List	Table
elainestewart	Elaine	Stewart	null	Female	null	List	Table	null	Feature1	List	Table
salliesampson	Sallie	Sampson	null	Female	null	List	Table	null	Feature1	List	Table
jonirosales	Joni	Rosales	null	Female	null	List	Table	null	Feature1	List	Table
georginabarlow	Georgina	Barlow	null	Female	null	List	Table	null	Feature1	List	Table
angelhuffman	Angel	Huffman	null	Female	null	List	Table	null	Feature1	List	Table
laurelosborn	Laurel	Osborn	null	Female	null	List	Table	null	Feature1	List	Table
sandyosborn	Sandy	Osborn	null	Female	null	List	Table	null	Feature1	List	Table
ursulabright	Ursula	Bright	null	Female	null	List	Table	null	Feature1	List	Table
genevievereeves	Genevieve	Reeves	null	Female	null	List	Table	null	Feature1	List	Table
kristakemp	Krista	Kemp	null	Female	null	List	Table	null	Feature1	List	Table

Load ▾   Transform Data   Cancel

Figure 5-18. Data returned from an OData feed in the Power Query Navigator

6. Click Load. The data will be loaded into a new Excel worksheet and/or the data model, depending on the load configuration options that you choose.

Note Interestingly, Dynamics 365 Online uses OData as the connection method.

OData Options

The OData feed dialog (rather like the From Web dialog that you saw earlier in this chapter) also contains an Advanced button. Selecting this will expand the dialog to allow you to add one or more URL parts to the URL. You can see this in Figure 5-19.

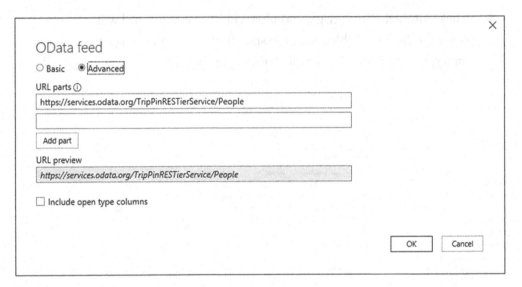

Figure 5-19.   *The OData feed dialog Advanced options*

Note   URL parts can be parameterized in the Power Query Editor. I will explain parameterization in Chapter 11.

Refreshing Data

Loading data from databases and data warehouses only means that a snapshot of the source data is copied into Excel. If the source data is updated, extended, or deleted, then you will need to get the latest version of the data if you want your analyses to reflect the current state of the data.

Essentially you have two options to do this:

- Refresh all the source data from all the data sources that you have defined.

- Refresh one or more tables individually.

Refreshing the Entire Data in the Excel In-Memory Model

There is only one way to be certain that all your data is up to date. Refreshing the entire data may take longer, but you will be sure that your Excel file contains the latest available data from all the sources that you have connected to.

To carry out a complete refresh:

1. In the Home ribbon, click the Refresh button. The Queries & Connections pane will show all the data sources that are currently being refreshed. The Queries & Connections pane will look like the one in Figure 5-20.

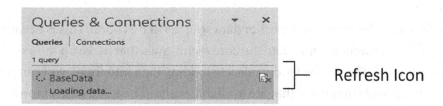

Figure 5-20. *The Refresh dialog*

The data currently in any worksheets or the Power Pivot data model will be updated to display the latest data available in the source.

Note   A full data refresh can take quite a while if the source data is voluminous or if the network connection is slow.

Refreshing an Individual Query

If you are certain that only one or more tables need to be refreshed in your Excel data model, then you can choose to refresh tables individually. To do this:

1. In the Queries & Connections pane, click the refresh icon for the table that you want to refresh. This is illustrated in Figure 5-20.

The existing data for this table will be replaced with the latest data.

Conclusion

In this chapter, you have learned that you can use generic data access connectors—ODBC, OLE DB, and OData—to connect to sources of data for which there is not (yet) a built-in Power Query connector. You also saw how to refresh the data in Excel.

This chapter concludes the set of five chapters that introduced you to some of the many and varied data sources that you can use with Power Query in Excel. In the course of these pages, you have seen how to load data from a selection of the available sources. The good news is that Excel can read data from many more sources than those we covered here. The even better news is that you can use the knowledge that you have acquired to connect to any other available data source using the standardized Power Query interface.

So I will not be describing any further data sources in this book. This is because now that you have come to appreciate the core techniques that make up the extremely accessible approach that Power Query takes to loading data into Excel, you can probably load any of the connection types that are available without needing much more information from me.

Now that you can find, access, and load the data you need into Excel, it is time to move on to the next step. This means cleansing and restructuring the datasets so that they suit your analytical requirements. Handling these challenges is the subject of the next seven chapters.

CHAPTER 6

Structuring Imported Data

In the previous five chapters, you saw some of the ways in which you can find and load (or connect to) data into either Excel worksheets or the Excel data model. Inevitably, this is the first part of any process that you follow to extract, transform, and load data. Yet it is quite definitely only a first step. Once the data is accessed using Power Query, you need to know how to adapt it to suit your requirements in a multitude of ways. This is because not all data is ready to be used immediately. Quite often, you have to do some initial work on the data to make it more easily usable. Tweaking source data in Power Query is generally referred to as *data transformation*, which is the subject of this chapter as well as the next three.

The range of transformations that Power Query offers is extensive and varied. Learning to apply the techniques that Power Query makes available enables you to take data as you find it, then cleanse it and push it back into either Excel worksheets or the Excel data model as a series of coherent and structured data tables. Only then is it ready to be used to create compelling analysis.

As it is all too easy to be overwhelmed (at least initially) by the extent of the data transformation options that Power Query has to offer, I have grouped the possible modifications into four categories. These categories are my own and are merely a suggestion to facilitate understanding:

- *Data transformation*: This includes adding and removing columns and rows, renaming columns, as well as filtering data.

- *Data modification*: This covers altering the actual data in the rows and columns of a dataset.

- *Extending datasets*: This encompasses adding further columns, possibly expanding existing columns into more columns or rows, and adding calculations.

- *Joining datasets*: This involves combining multiple separate datasets—possibly from different data sources—into a single dataset.

135

© Adam Aspin 2020
A. Aspin, *Data Mashup with Microsoft Excel Using Power Query and M*,
https://doi.org/10.1007/978-1-4842-6018-0_6

This chapter introduces you to the core data transformation techniques that you can apply to shape each individual dataset that you have loaded. These transformations include

- Renaming, removing, and reordering columns

- Removing groups or sets of rows

- Deduplicating datasets

- Sorting the data

- Excluding records by filtering the data

- Grouping records

In Chapter 7, you learn how to cleanse and modify data. In Chapter 8, you see how to subset columns to extract part of the available data in a column, calculate columns, merge data from separate queries, and add further columns containing different types of calculations, and you learn about pivoting and unpivoting data. So, if you cannot find what you are looking for in this chapter, there is a good chance that the answer is in the following two chapters.

In this chapter, I will also use a set of example files that you can find on the Apress website. If you have followed the instructions in Appendix A, then these files are in the C:\DataMashupWithExcelSamples folder.

Extending Queries in Power Query

In Chapter 1, you saw how to load external source data directly into Excel for reporting and analysis. Clearly, this approach presumes that the data that you are using is perfectly structured, clean, and error-free. Source data is nearly always correct and ready to use in analytics when it comes from "corporate" data sources such as data warehouses (held in relational, dimensional, or tabular databases). This is not always the case when you are faced with multiple disparate sources of data that have not been precleansed and prepared for you. The everyday reality is that you could have to cleanse and transform much of the source data that you will use in Excel.

The really good news is that the kind of data transformation that used to require expensive servers and industrial-strength software is now available for free. Yes, Power Query is an awesome ETL (**E**xtract, **T**ransform, and **L**oad) tool that can rival many applications that cost hundreds of thousands of dollars.

Power Query data transformation is carried out using *queries*. As you saw in previous chapters, you do not have to modify source data. You can load it directly if it is ready for use. Yet if you need to cleanse the data, you add an intermediate step between connecting the data and loading it into the Excel data model. This intermediate step uses the Power Query Editor to tweak the source data.

So how do you apply queries to transform your data? You have two choices:

- Load the data first from one or more sources, and then transform it later.

- Edit each source data element in a query before loading it.

Power Query is extremely forgiving. It does not force you to select one or the other method and then lock you into the consequences of your decision. You can load data first and then realize that it needs some adjustment, switch to the Query Editor and make changes, and then return to extending a spreadsheet based on this data. Or you can first focus on the data and try to get it as polished and perfect as possible before you start building reports. The choice is entirely up to you.

To make this point, let's take a look at both of these ways of working.

Note   At risk of being pedantic and old-fashioned, I would advise you to make notes when creating really complex transformations, because going back to a solution and trying to make adjustments later can be painful when they are not documented at all.

Editing Data After a Data Load

In Chapter 1, you saw how to load the Excel workbook CarSales.xlsx directly into Excel for use in further analysis. Now let's presume that you want to make some changes to the data structure of the data that you have already loaded. Specifically, you want to rename the CostPrice column. The file that you want to modify is Chapter06Sample1.xlsx file in the C:\DataMashupWithExcelSamples directory.

1. Launch Excel.

2. Open the Excel file C:\DataMashupWithExcelSamples\
   Chapter06Sample1.xlsx. You can see the sample data already
   loaded into a worksheet.

3.   Click Data ➤ Queries & Connections. You will now also see the
     query that carried out this load process (BaseData) in the Queries
     & Connections pane in Figure 6-1.

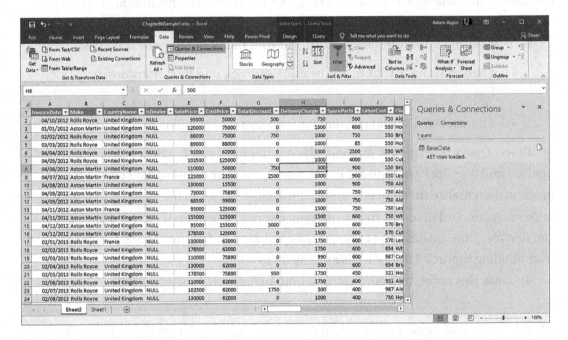

Figure 6-1. *An initial data load*

4.   In the Queries & Connections pane on the right, double-click the
     connection BaseData. This will connect to—and open—Power
     Query. The Power Query window will look like the one in
     Figure 6-2. You may see an alert dialog telling you that you are
     connecting to an as yet unknown external data source. In this
     case, click OK.

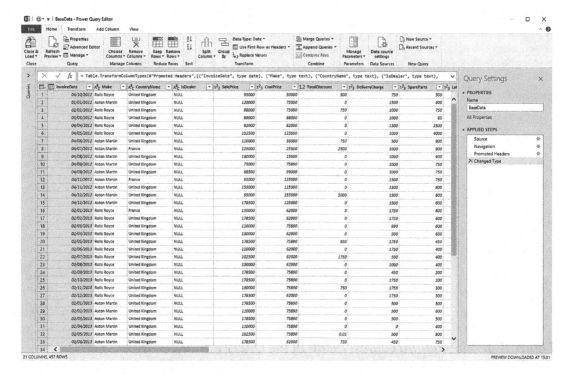

Figure 6-2.   *The Power Query Editor*

5.   Right-click the title of the CostPrice column (do not click the
     arrow to the right of the column). The column will be selected.

6.   Select Rename from the context menu. You can see the context
     menu in Figure 6-3.

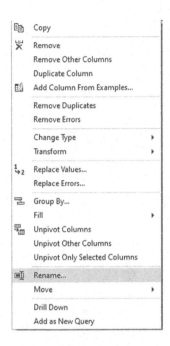

Figure 6-3. *The column context menu in the Query Editor*

7. Type **VehicleCost** and press Enter. The column title will change to VehicleCost.

8. In the Power Query Editor Home ribbon, click the Close & Load button. The Power Query Editor will close and return you to Excel where the source data has been loaded into a new worksheet.

I hope that this simple example makes it clear that transforming the source data is a quick and painless process. The technique that you applied—renaming a column—is only one of many dozens of possible techniques that you can apply to transform your data. However, it is not the specific transformation that is the core idea to take away here. What you need to remember is that the data that underpins your analytics is always present and it is only a click away. At any time, you can "flip" to the data and make changes, simply by double-clicking the relevant query in the Queries & Connections pane. Any changes that you make and confirm will update your data in Excel almost instantaneously.

Transforming Data Before Loading

On some occasions, you might prefer to juggle with your data before you load it. This is a variation on the approach that you have used in Chapter 2 when loading data using the Query Editor. Do the following to transform your data *before* it appears in the Excel window:

1. Open a new Excel workbook.

2. In the Data ribbon, click the tiny triangle in the Get Data button.

3. Select From File ➤ From Workbook and click Import for the Excel file C:\DataMashupWithExcelSamples\CarSales.xlsx.

4. In the Navigator window, select the CarData worksheet.

5. Click the Transform data button (*not* the Load button).

6. The Power Query Editor will open and display the source data as a table.

7. Carry out steps 4 through 6 from the previous example to rename the CostPrice column.

8. In the Power Query Editor Home ribbon, click the Close & Load button. The Power Query Editor will close and return you to the Excel window.

This time, you have made a simple modification to the data *before* loading the dataset into Excel. The data modification technique was exactly the same. The only difference between loading the data directly and taking a detour via Power Query was clicking Edit Data instead of Load in the Navigator dialog. This means that the data was only loaded once you had finished making any modifications to the source data in the Power Query Editor.

Query or Load?

Excel always gives you the choice of loading data directly or taking a constructive detour via Power Query. The path that you follow is entirely up to you and clearly depends on each set of circumstances. Nonetheless, you might want to consider the following basic principles when faced with a new challenge using unfamiliar data:

- Are you convinced that the data is ready to use? That is, is it clean and well structured? If so, then you can try loading it directly into Excel.

- Are you faced with multiple data sources that need to be combined and molded into a coherent structure? If this is the case, then you really need to transform the data using the Power Query Editor.

- Does the data come from an enterprise data warehouse or a coherently structured external source? This could be held in a relational database, a SQL Server Analysis Services cube, an in-memory tabular data warehouse, or a cloud-based service. As these data sources are nearly always the result of many hundreds—or even thousands—of hours of work cleansing, preparing, and structuring the data, you can probably load these straight into the data model or an Excel worksheet.

- Does the data need to be preaggregated and filtered? Think Power Query.

- Are you likely to need to change the field names to make the data more manageable? It could be simpler to change the field names in the Query Editor.

- Are you faced with lots of lookup tables that need to be added to a "core" data table? Then Power Query is your friend.

- Does the data contain many superfluous or erroneous elements? Then use Power Query to remove these as a first step.

- Does the data need to be rationalized and standardized to make it easier to handle? In this case, the path to success is via the Power Query Editor.

- Is the data source enormous? If this is the case, you could save time by editing and subsetting and filtering the data first in the Power Query Editor. This is because the Power Query Editor only loads a *sample* of the data for you to tweak. The entire dataset will only be loaded when you confirm all your modifications and close the Query Editor.

These kinds of questions are only rough guidelines. Yet they can help to point you in the right direction when you are working with Power Query. Inevitably, the more that you work with this application, the more you will develop the reflexes and intuition that will help you make the correct decisions. Remember, however, that Power Query is there to help and that even a directly loaded dataset is based on a query. So you can always load data and then decide to tweak the query structure later if you need to. Alternatively, editing data in a Query window can be a great opportunity to take a closer look at your data before loading it into Excel—and it only adds a couple of clicks.

This all means that you are free to adopt a way of working that you feel happy with. Power Query will adapt to your style easily and almost invisibly, letting you switch from data to Excel so fluidly that it will likely become second nature.

The remainder of this chapter will take you through some of the core techniques that you need to know to cleanse and shape your data. However, before getting into all the detail, let's take a quick, high-level look at the Power Query Editor and the way that it is laid out.

The Power Query Editor

All of your data transformation will take place in the Power Query Editor. It is a separate window from the Excel interface that you are used to, and it has a slightly different layout.

The Power Query Editor consists of six main elements:

- The four principal ribbons: Home, Transform, Add Column, and View. Other ribbons are available when carrying out specific types of data transformations.

- The Query list pane containing all the queries that have been added to an Excel file.

- The Data window, where you can see a sample of the data for a selected query.

- The Query Settings pane that contains the list of steps used to transform data.

- The formula bar above the data that shows the code (written in the "M" language that you will discover in Chapter 12) that performs the selected transformation step.

- The status bar (at the bottom of the window) that indicates useful information, such as the number of rows and columns in a query table and the date when the dataset was downloaded

The callouts for these elements are shown in Figure 6-4.

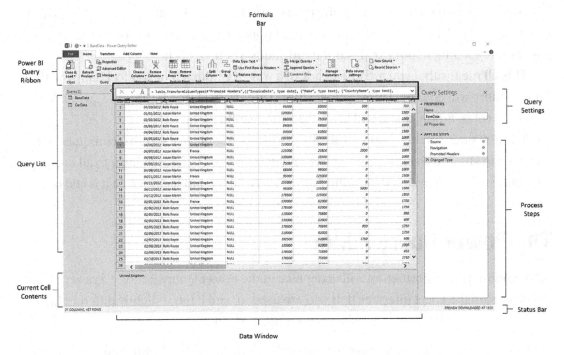

Figure 6-4. *The Power Query Editor, explained*

Note   If you do not see the formula bar, just click View ➤ Formula Bar in the Power Query Editor menu.

The Applied Steps List

Data transformation is by its very nature a sequential process. So the Query window stores each modification that you make when you are cleansing and shaping source data. The various elements that make up a data transformation process are listed in the Applied Steps list of the Query Settings pane in the Power Query Editor.

The Power Query Editor does not number the steps in a data transformation process, but it certainly remembers each one. They start at the top of the Applied Steps list (nearly always with the Source step) and can extend to dozens of individual steps that trace the evolution of your data until you load it into the data model. You can, if you want, consider the Query Editor as a kind of "macro recorder."

Moreover, as you click each step in the Applied Steps list, the data in the Data window changes to reflect the results of each transformation, giving you a complete and visible trail of all the modifications that you have applied to the dataset.

The Applied Steps list gives a distinct name to the step for each and every data modification option that you cover in this chapter and the next. As it can be important to understand exactly what each function actually achieves, I will always draw to your attention the standard name that Power Query applies.

The Power Query Editor Ribbons

Power Query Editor uses four core ribbons. They are fundamental to what you learn in the course of this chapter. They are as follows:

- The Home ribbon

- The Transform ribbon

- The Add Column ribbon

- The View ribbon

I am not suggesting for a second that you need to memorize what all the buttons in these ribbons do. What I hope is that you are able to use the following brief descriptions of the Query Editor ribbon buttons to get an idea of the amazing power of Power Query in the field of data transformation. So if you have an initial dataset that is not quite as you need it, you can take a look at the resources that Power Query has to offer and how they can help. Once you find the function that does what you are looking for, you can jump to the relevant section for the full details on how to apply it.

The Home Ribbon

Since we will be making intense use of the Power Query Editor Home ribbon to transform data, it is important to have an idea of what it can do. I explain the various options in Figure 6-5 and in Table 6-1.

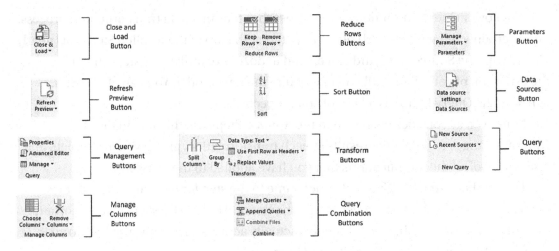

Figure 6-5. *The Query Editor Home ribbon*

Table 6-1. *Query Editor Home Ribbon Options*

Option	Description
Close & Load	Finishes the processing steps; saves and closes the query
Refresh Preview	Refreshes the preview data
Query Management	Lets you delete, duplicate, or reference a query
Manage Columns	Lets you select the columns to retain from all the columns available in the source data or remove one or more columns
Reduce Rows	Keeps or removes the specified number of rows at the top or bottom of the table
Sort	Sorts the table using the selected column as the sort key
Split Column	Separates the column into two or more separate columns
Group By	Groups and potentially aggregates the data
Data Type	Sets the column data type
Use First Row as Headers	Promotes the first record as the header definitions
Replace Values	Replaces values in a column with other values
Merge Queries	Joins data from two separate queries

(continued)

Table 6-1. (*continued*)

Option	Description
Append Queries	Adds data from one or more queries into another identically structured query
Combine Files	Merges all files in a given column into a single table
Manage Parameters	Lets you view and modify any parameters defined for this ETL process in Power Query
Data Source Settings	Allows you to manage and edit settings for data sources that you have already connected to
New Query	Allows you to connect to additional external data or reuse existing connections

The Transform Ribbon

The Transform ribbon, as its name implies, contains a wealth of functions that can help you to transform your data. The various options it contains are explained in Figure 6-6 and Table 6-2.

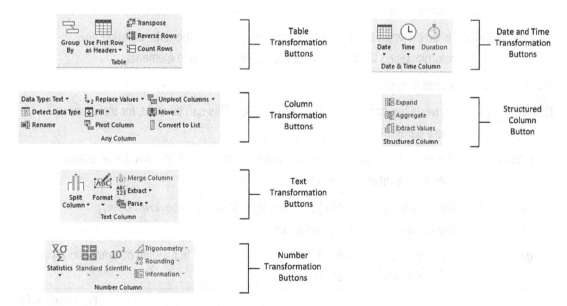

Figure 6-6. *The Query Editor Transform ribbon*

Table 6-2. *Query Editor Transform Ribbon Options*

Option	Description
Group By	Groups the table using a specified set of columns; aggregates any numeric columns for this grouping
Use First Row As Headers	Uses the first row as the column titles
Transpose	Transforms the columns into rows and the rows into columns
Reverse Rows	Displays the source data in reverse order, showing the final rows at the top of the window
Count Rows	Counts the rows in the table and replaces the data with the row count
Data Type	Applies the chosen data type to the column
Detect Data Type	Detects the correct data type to apply to multiple columns
Rename	Renames a column
Replace Values	Carries out a search-and-replace operation inside a column, replacing a specified value with another value
Fill	Copies the data from cells above or below into empty cells in the column
Pivot Column	Creates a new set of columns using the data in the selected column as the column titles
Unpivot Columns	Takes the values in a set of columns and unpivots the data, creating new columns using the column headers as the descriptive elements
Move	Moves a column
Convert to List	Converts the contents of a column to a list. This can be used, for instance, as query parameters
Split Column	Splits a column into one or many columns at a specified delimiter or after a specified number of characters
Format	Modifies the text format of data in a column (uppercase, lowercase, capitalization) or removes trailing spaces
Merge Columns	Takes the data from several columns and places it in a single column, adding an optional separator character

(continued)

Table 6-2. (*continued*)

Option	Description
Extract	Replaces the data in a column using a defined subset of the current data. You can specify a number of characters to keep from the start or end of the column, set a range of characters beginning at a specified character, or even list the number of characters in the column
Parse	Creates an XML or JSON document from the contents of an element in a column
Statistics	Returns the Sum, Average, Maximum, Minimum, Median, Standard Deviation, Count, or Distinct Value Count for all the values in the column
Standard	Carries out a basic mathematical calculation (add, subtract, divide, multiply, integer-divide, or return the remainder) using a value that you specify applied to each cell in the column
Scientific	Carries out a basic scientific calculation (square, cube, power of n, square root, exponent, logarithm, or factorial) for each cell in the column
Trigonometry	Carries out a basic trigonometric calculation (Sine, Cosine, Tangent, ArcSine, ArcCosine, or ArcTangent) using a value that you specify applied to each cell in the column
Rounding	Rounds the values in the column either to the next integer (up or down) or to a specified factor
Information	Replaces the value in the column with simple information: Is Odd, Is Even, or Positive/Negative
Date	Isolates an element (day, month, year, etc.) from a date value in a column
Time	Isolates an element (hour, minute, second, etc.) from a date/time or time value in a column
Duration	Calculates the duration from a value that can be interpreted as a duration in days, hours, minutes, etc.
Expand	Adds the (identically structured) data from another query to the current query
Aggregate	Calculates the sum or product of numeric columns from another query and adds the result to the current query
Extract Values	Extracts the values of the contents of a column as a single text value

The Add Column Ribbon

The Add Column ribbon does a lot more than just add columns. It also contains functions to break columns down into multiple columns and to add columns containing dates and calculations based on existing columns. The various options it contains are explained in Figure 6-7 and Table 6-3.

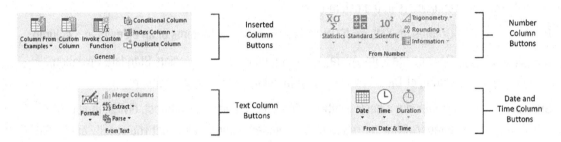

Figure 6-7. *The Query Editor Add Column ribbon*

Table 6-3. *Query Editor Add Column Ribbon Options*

Option	Description
Column From Examples	Lets you use one or more columns as examples to create a new column
Custom Column	Adds a new column using a formula to create the column's contents
Invoke Custom Function	Applies an "M" language function to every row
Conditional Column	Adds a new column that conditionally adds the values from the selected column
Index Column	Adds a sequential number in a new column to uniquely identify each row
Duplicate Column	Creates a copy of the current column
Format	Modifies the text format of data in a new column (uppercase, lowercase, capitalization) or removes trailing spaces
Merge Columns	Takes the data from several columns and places it in a single column, adding an optional separator character

(continued)

Table 6-3. (*continued*)

Option	Description
Extract	Creates a new column using a defined subset of the current data. You can specify a number of characters to keep from the start or end of the column, set a range of characters beginning at a specified character, or even list the number of characters in the column
Parse	Creates a new column based on the XML or JSON in a column
Statistics	Creates a new column that returns the Sum, Average, Maximum, Minimum, Median, Standard Deviation, Count, or Distinct Value Count for all the values in the column
Standard	Creates a new column that returns a basic mathematical calculation (add, subtract, divide, multiply, integer-divide, or return the remainder) using a value that you specify applied to each cell in the column
Scientific	Creates a new column that returns a basic scientific calculation (square, cube, power of n, square root, exponent, logarithm, or factorial) for each cell in the column
Trigonometry	Creates a new column that returns a basic trigonometric calculation (Sine, Cosine, Tangent, ArcSine, ArcCosine, or ArcTangent) using a value that you specify applied to each cell in the column
Rounding	Rounds the values in a new column either to the next integer (up or down) or to a specified factor
Information	Replaces the value in the column with simple information: Is Odd, Is Even, or Positive/Negative
Date	Isolates an element (day, month, year, etc.) from a date value in a new column
Time	Isolates an element (hour, minute, second, etc.) from a date/time or time value in a new column
Duration	Calculates the duration from a value that can be interpreted as a duration in days, hours, minutes, and seconds in a new column

The View Ribbon

The View ribbon lets you alter some of the Query Editor settings and see the underlying data transformation code. The various options that it contains are explained in the next chapter.

Dataset Shaping

So you are now looking at a data table that you have loaded into Excel. For argument's sake, let's assume that it is the C:\DataMashupWithExcelSamples\Chapter06Sample1. xlsx file from the sample data directory and that you have double-clicked the BaseData query in the Queries & Connections pane to display the Power Query Editor. What can you do to the BaseData dataset that is now visible? It is time to take a look at some of the core techniques that you can apply to shape the initial dataset. These include the following:

- Renaming columns

- Reordering columns

- Removing columns

- Merging columns

- Removing records

- Removing duplicate records

- Filtering the dataset

I have grouped these techniques together as they affect the initial size and shape of the data. Also, it is generally not only good practice but also easier for you, the data modeler, if you begin by excluding any rows and columns that you do not need. I also find it easier to understand datasets if the columns are logically laid out and given comprehensible names from the start. All in all, this makes working with the data easier in the long run.

Renaming Columns

Although we took a quick look at renaming columns in the first pages of this chapter, let's look at this technique again in more detail. I admit that renaming columns is not actually modifying the form of the data table. However, when dealing with data, I consider it vital to have all data clearly identifiable. This implies meaningful column names being applied to each column. Consequently, I consider this modification to be fundamental to the shape of the data and also as an essential best practice when importing source data.

To rename a column:

1. Click inside (or on the column header for) the column that you want to rename.

2. Click Transform to activate the Transform ribbon.

3. Click the Rename button. The column name will be highlighted.

4. Enter the new name or edit the existing name.

5. Press Enter or click outside the column title.

The column will now have a new title. The Applied Steps list on the right will now contain another element, Renamed Columns. This step will be highlighted.

Note   As an alternative to using the Transform ribbon, you can right-click the column title and select Rename.

Reordering Columns

Power Query will load data as it is defined in the data source. Consequently, the column sequence will be entirely dependent on the source data (or by a SQL query if you used a source database, as described in Chapter 3). This column order need not be definitive, however, and you can reorder the columns if that helps you understand and deal with the data. Do the following to change column order:

1. Click the header of the column you want to move.

2. Drag the column left or right to its new position. You will see the column title slide laterally through the column titles as you do this, and a thicker gray line will indicate where the column will be placed once you release the mouse button. Reordered Columns will appear in the Applied Steps list.

Figure 6-8 shows this operation.

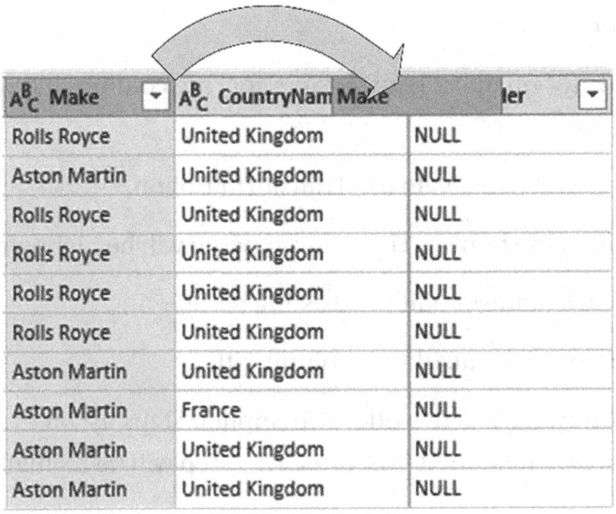

A^B_C Make	A^B_C CountryNam	Make	ler
Rolls Royce	United Kingdom	NULL	
Aston Martin	United Kingdom	NULL	
Rolls Royce	United Kingdom	NULL	
Rolls Royce	United Kingdom	NULL	
Rolls Royce	United Kingdom	NULL	
Rolls Royce	United Kingdom	NULL	
Aston Martin	United Kingdom	NULL	
Aston Martin	France	NULL	
Aston Martin	United Kingdom	NULL	
Aston Martin	United Kingdom	NULL	

Figure 6-8. *Reordering columns*

If your query contains dozens—or even hundreds—of columns, you may find that dragging a column around can be slow and laborious. Equally, if columns are extremely wide, it can be difficult to "nudge" a column left or right. Power Query can come to your aid in these circumstances with the Move button in the Transform ribbon. Clicking this button gives you the menu options that are outlined in Table 6-4.

Table 6-4. *Move Button Options*

Option	Description
Left	Moves the currently selected column to the left of the column on its immediate left
Right	Moves the currently selected column to the right of the column on its immediate right
To Beginning	Moves the currently selected column to the left of all the columns in the query
To End	Moves the currently selected column to the right of all the columns in the query

The Move command also works on a set of columns that you have selected by Ctrl-clicking and/or Shift-clicking. Indeed, you can move a selection of columns that is not contiguous if you need to.

Note   You need to select a column (or a set of columns) before clicking the Move button. If you do not, then the first time that you use Move, Power Query selects the column(s) but does not move it.

Removing Columns

So how do you delete a column or series of columns? Like this:

1. Click inside the column you want to delete, or if you want to delete several columns at once, Ctrl-click the titles of the columns that you want to delete.

2. Click the Remove Columns button in the Home ribbon. The column(s) will be deleted and Removed Columns will be the latest element in the Applied Steps list.

Tip   Another way to remove selected columns is to press the delete key. This will also add a "Removed Columns" step to the Applied Steps list.

When working with imported datasets over which you have had no control, you may frequently find that you only need a few columns of a large data table. If this is the case, you will soon get tired of Ctrl-clicking numerous columns to select those you want to remove. Power Query has an alternative method. Just select the columns you want to keep and delete the others. To do this:

1. Ctrl-click the titles of the columns that you want to keep.

2. Click the small triangle in the Remove Columns button in the Home ribbon. Select Remove Other Columns from the menu. All unselected columns will be deleted and Removed Other Columns will be added to the Applied Steps list.

When selecting a contiguous range of columns to remove or keep, you can use the standard Windows Shift-click technique to select from the first to the last column in the block of columns that you want to select.

Note   Both of these options for removing columns are also available from the context menu, if you prefer. It shows Remove (or Remove Columns, if there are several columns selected) when deleting columns, as well as Remove Other Columns if you right-click a column title.

Choosing Columns

If you prefer not to scroll through a wide dataset, yet still need to select a subset of columns as the basis for your reports, then there is another way to define the collection of fields that you want to use. You can choose the columns that you want to keep (and, by definition, those that you want to exclude) like this:

1. Open the sample file Chapter06Sample1.xlsx in the folder C:\DataMashupWithExcelSamples unless it is already open.

2. In the Queries & Connections pane on the right (that you can toggle on and off from the Data ribbon Queries & Connections option), double-click the connection BaseData. The Query Editor will open.

3. In the Home ribbon of the Query Editor, click the Choose Columns button.

4. Click (Select All Columns) to deselect the entire collection of columns in the dataset.

5. Select the columns Make, Model, Color, and SalePrice. The Choose Columns dialog will look like the one in Figure 6-9.

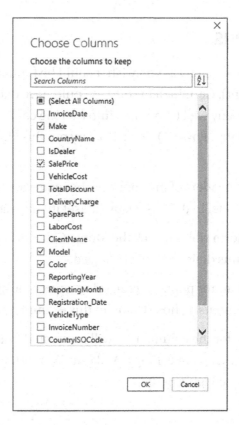

Figure 6-9. The Choose Columns dialog

6. Click OK. The Query Editor will only display the columns that you selected.

The Choose Columns dialog comes with a couple of extra functions that you might find useful when choosing the set of columns that you want to work with:

- You can sort the column list in alphabetical order (or, indeed, revert to the original order) by clicking the Sort icon (the small A-Z) at the top right of the Choose Columns dialog and selecting the required option.

- You can filter the list of columns that is displayed simply by entering a few characters in the Search Columns field at the top of the dialog.

- The (Select All Columns) option switches between selecting and deselecting all the columns in the list.

Merging Columns

Source data is not always exactly as you wish it could be (and that is sometimes a massive understatement). Certain data sources could have data spread over many columns that could equally well be merged into a single column. So it probably comes as no surprise to discover that Power Query can carry out this kind of operation too. Here is how to do it:

1. Ctrl-click the headers of the columns that you want to merge (Make and Model in the BaseData dataset in this example).

2. In the Transform ribbon, click the Merge Columns button. The Merge Columns dialog will be displayed.

3. From the Separator popup menu, select one of the available separator elements. I chose Colon in this example.

4. Enter a name for the column that will be created from the two original columns (I am calling it MakeAndModel). The dialog should look like Figure 6-10.

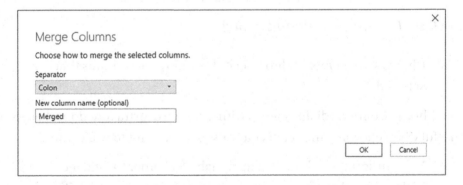

Figure 6-10. *The Merge Columns dialog*

5. Click OK. The columns that you selected will be replaced by the data from all the columns that you selected in step 1, as shown in Figure 6-11.

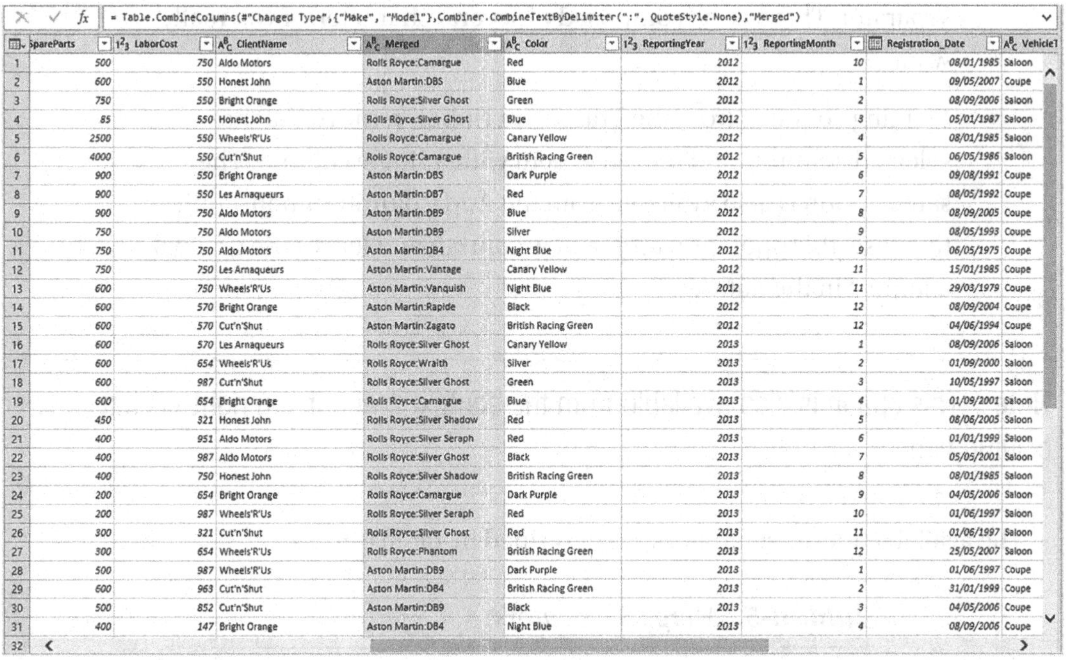

Figure 6-11. *The result of merging columns*

6. Rename the resulting column (named Merged by Power Query).

I need to make a few comments about this process:

- You can select as many columns as you want when merging columns.

- If you do not give the resulting column a name in the Merge Columns dialog, it will simply be renamed Merged. You can always rename it later if you want.

- The order in which you select the columns affects the way that the data is merged. So, always begin by selecting the column whose data must appear at the left of the merged column, then the column whose data should be next, and so forth. You do not have to select columns in the order that they initially appeared in the dataset.

- If you do not want to use any of the standard separators that Power Query suggests, you can always define your own. Just select --Custom-- in the popup menu in the Merge Columns dialog. A new box will appear in the dialog, in which you can enter your choice of separator. This can be composed of several characters if you really want.

- Merging columns from the Transform ribbon removes all the selected columns and replaces them with a single column. The same option is also available from the Add Column ribbon—only in this case, this operation *adds* a new column and leaves the original columns in the dataset.

Note   This option is also available from the context menu if you right-click a column title.

The available merge separators are described in Table 6-5.

Table 6-5. *Merge Separators*

Option	Description
Colon	Uses the colon (:) as the separator
Comma	Uses the comma (,) as the separator
Equals Sign	Uses the equals sign (=) as the separator
Semi-Colon	Uses the semicolon (;) as the separator
Space	Uses the space ( ) as the separator
Tab	Uses the tab character as the separator
Custom	Lets you enter a custom separator

Tip   You can split, remove, and duplicate columns using the context menu if you prefer. Just remember to right-click the column title to display the correct context menu.

Moving to a Specific Column

Power Query can load datasets that contain hundreds of columns. As scrolling left and right across dozens of columns can be more than a little frustrating, you can always jump to a specific column at any time.

1. In the Home ribbon of the Query Editor, click the small triangle at the bottom of the Choose Columns button. Select Go to Column. The Go to Column dialog will appear.

2. Select the column you want to move to. The dialog will look like Figure 6-12.

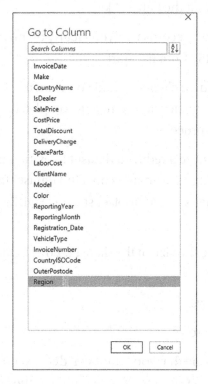

Figure 6-12. *The Go to Column dialog*

3. Click OK. Power Query will select the chosen column.

Tip   If you prefer, you can double-click a column name in the Go to Column dialog to move to the chosen column.

Removing Records

You may not always need *all* the data that you have loaded into a Power Query. There could be several possible reasons for this:

- You are taking a first look at the data, and you only need a sample to get an idea of what the data is like.

- The data contains records that you clearly do not need and that you can easily identify from the start.

- You are testing data cleansing and you want a smaller dataset to really speed up the development of a complex data extraction and transformation process.

- You want to analyze a reduced dataset to extrapolate theses and inferences, and to save analysis on a full dataset for later, or even use a more industrial-strength toolset such as SQL Server Integration Services.

To allow you to reduce the size of the dataset, Power Query proposes two basic approaches out of the box:

- Keep certain rows

- Remove certain rows

Inevitably, the technique that you adopt will depend on the circumstances. If it is easier to specify the rows to sample by inclusion, then the keep-certain-rows approach is the best option to take. Inversely, if you want to proceed by exclusion, then the remove-certain-rows technique is best. Let's look at each of these in turn.

Keeping Rows

This approach lets you specify the rows that you want to continue using. It is based on the application of one of the following three choices:

- Keep the top n records.

- Keep the bottom n records.

- Keep a specified range of records—that is, keep n records every y records.

Most of these techniques are very similar, so let's start by imagining that you want to keep the top 50 records in the sample C:\DataMashupWithExcelSamples\ Chapter06Sample1.xlsx file.

1. Open the source file and then open the Power Query Editor by double-clicking the BaseData query in the Queries & Connections pane.

2. In the Home ribbon of the Query Editor, click the Keep Rows button. The menu will appear.

3. Select Keep Top Rows. The Keep Top Rows dialog will appear.

4. Enter **50** in the "Number of rows" box, as shown in Figure 6-13.

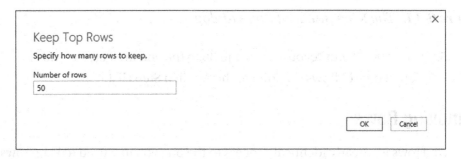

Figure 6-13. The Keep Top Rows dialog

5. Click OK. All but the first 50 records are deleted and Kept First Rows is added to the Applied Steps list.

To keep the bottom *n* rows, the technique is virtually identical. Follow the steps in the previous example, but select *Keep Bottom Rows* in step 2. In this case, the Applied Steps list displays Kept Last Rows.

To keep a range of records, you need to specify a starting record and the number of records to keep from then on. For instance, suppose that you wish to lose the first 10 records but keep the following 25. This is how to go about it:

1. In the Home ribbon, click the Keep Rows button.

2. Select Keep Range of Rows. The Keep Range of Rows dialog will appear.

3. Enter **11** in the "First row" box.

4. Enter **25** in the "Number of rows" box, as shown in Figure 6-14.

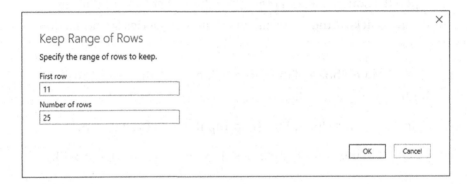

Figure 6-14. *The Keep Range of Rows dialog*

5. Click OK. All but records 1–10 and 36 to the end are deleted and Kept Range of Rows is added to the Applied Steps list.

Removing Rows

Removing rows is a nearly identical process to the one you just used to keep rows. As removing the top or bottom *n* rows is highly similar, I will not go through it in detail. All you have to do is click the Remove Rows button in the Home ribbon and follow the process as if you were keeping rows. The Applied Steps list will read Removed Top Rows or Removed Bottom Rows in this case, and rows will be removed instead of being kept in the dataset, of course.

The remove rows approach does have one very useful option that can be applied as a sampling technique. It allows you to remove one or more records every few records to produce a subset of the source data. To do this, you need to do the following:

1. Click the Remove Rows button in the Query window Home ribbon. The menu will appear.

2. Select Remove Alternate Rows. The Remove Alternate Rows dialog will appear.

3. Enter **10** as the First row to remove.

4. Enter **2** as the Number of rows to remove.

5. Enter **10** as the Number of rows to keep.

The dialog will look like Figure 6-15.

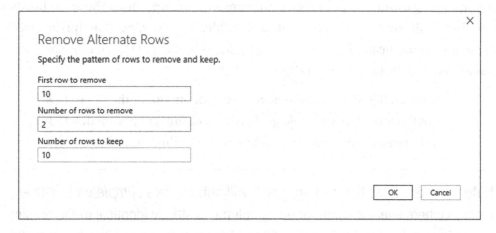

Figure 6-15. *The Remove Alternate Rows dialog*

6. Click OK. All but the records matching the pattern you entered in the dialog are removed. Removed Alternate Rows is then added to the Applied Steps list.

Note   If you are really determined to extract a sample that you consider to be representative of the key data, then you can always filter the data before subsetting it to exclude any outliers. Filtering data is explained later in this chapter.

Removing Blank Rows

If your source data contains completely blank (empty) rows, you can delete these as follows:

1. Click the Remove Rows button in the Query window Home ribbon. The menu will appear.

2. Select Remove Blank Rows.

This results in empty rows being deleted. Removed Blank Rows is then added to the Applied Steps list.

Removing Duplicate Records

An external source of data might not be quite as perfect as you might hope. One of the most annoying features of poor data is the presence of duplicates. These are insidious since they falsify results and are not always visible. If you suspect that the data table contains *strict* duplicates (i.e., where *every* field is identical in two or more records), then you can remove the duplicates like this:

1. Click the Remove Duplicates in the popup menu for the table (this is at the top left of the table grid). All duplicate records are deleted and Removed Duplicates is added to the Applied Steps list.

Note   I must stress that this approach will only remove *completely* identical records where every element of every column is strictly identical in the duplicate rows. If two records have just one different character or a number but everything else is identical, then they are *not* considered duplicates by Power Query. Alternatively, if you want to isolate and examine the duplicate records, then you can display only completely identical records by selecting Keep Duplicates from the popup menu for the table.

So if you suspect or are sure that the data table you are dealing with contains duplicates, what are the practical solutions? This can be a real conundrum, but there are some basic techniques that you can apply:

- Remove all columns that you are sure you will not be using later in the data-handling process. This way, Power Query will only be asked to compare essential data across potentially duplicate records.

- Group the data on the core columns (this is explained later in this chapter).

Note   As you have seen, Power Query can help you to home in on the essential elements in a dataset in just a few clicks. If anything, you need to be careful that you are *not removing* valuable data—and consequently skewing your analysis— when excluding data from the query.

Sorting Data

Although not strictly a data modification step, sorting an imported table will probably be something that you want to do at some stage, if only to get a clearer idea of the data that you are dealing with. Do the following to sort the data:

1. Open the sample file Chapter06Sample1.xlsx in the folder C:\DataMashupWithExcelSamples unless it is already open.

2. In the Queries & Connections pane on the right, double-click the connection BaseData. The Query Editor will open.

3. Click inside the column you wish to sort by.

4. Click Sort Ascending (the A/Z icon) or Sort Descending (the Z/A icon) in the Home ribbon.

The data is sorted in either alphabetical (smallest to largest) or reverse alphabetical (largest to smallest) order. If you want to carry out a complex sort operation (i.e., first by one column and then by another if the first column contains the same element over several rows), you do this simply by sorting the columns one after another. Power Query Editor adds a tiny 1, 2, 3, and so on to the right of the column title to indicate the sort sequence. You can see this in Figure 6-16, where I sorted *first* on the column Make and *finally* on the column Model.

Figure 6-16. *Sorting multiple columns*

If you look closely at the column headings, you will see a small "1" and "2" that indicate the sort priority as well as the arrows that indicate that the columns are sorted in ascending order.

Note   An alternative technique for sorting data is to click the popup menu for a column (the downward-facing triangle at the right of a column title) and select Sort Ascending or Sort Descending from the popup menu.

Reversing the Row Order

If you find that the data that you are looking at seems upside down (i.e., with the bottom rows at the top and vice versa), you can reverse the row order in a single click, if you want. To do this, do the following:

In the Transform ribbon, click the Reverse Rows button.

The entire dataset will be reversed and the bottom row will now be the top row.

Undoing a Sort Operation

If you subsequently decide that you do not want to keep your data sorted, you can undo the sort operation at any time, as follows:

1. Click the sort icon at the right of the name of the column that you used as the basis for the sort operation. The context menu will appear, as you can see in Figure 6-17.

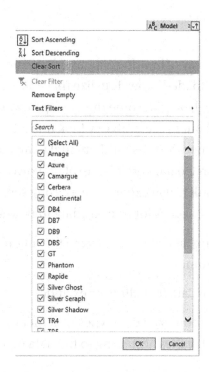

Figure 6-17. *Removing a sort operation*

 2. Click Clear Sort.

The sort order that you applied will be removed, and the data will revert to its original row order.

As sorting data is considered part of the data modification process, it also appears in the Applied Steps list as Sorted Rows. This means that you can also remove a sort operation by deleting the relevant step in the Applied Steps list.

Note   If you sorted the dataset on several columns, you can choose to remove all the sort order that you applied by clicking the *first* column that you used to sort the data. This will remove the sort order that you applied to *all* the columns that you used to define the sort criteria. If all you want to do is undo the sort on the final column in a set of columns used to sort the recordset, then you can clear only the sort operation on this column.

Filtering Data

The most frequently used way of limiting a dataset is, in my experience, the use of filters on the table that you have loaded. Now, I realize that you may be coming to Power Query after years with Excel, or after some time using Power Pivot, and that the filtering techniques that you are about to see probably look much like the ones you have used in those two tools. However, because it is fundamental to include and exclude appropriate records when loading source data, I prefer to explain Power Query filters in detail, even if this means that certain readers will experience a strong sense of déjà vu.

Here are two basic approaches for filtering data in Power Query:

- Select one or more specific values from the unique list of elements in the chosen column.

- Define a range of data to include or exclude.

The first option is common to all data types, whether they are text, number, or date/time. The second approach varies according to the data type of the column that you are using to filter data.

Selecting Specific Text Values

Selecting one or more values present in a column of data is as easy as this (assuming that you are still using the Excel file Chapter06Sample1.xlsx and are in the Query Editor):

1. Click a column's popup menu. (I used Make in the sample dataset Chapter06Sample1.xlsx here.) The filter menu appears.

2. Check all elements that you want to retain and uncheck all elements that you wish to exclude. In this example, I kept Bentley and Rolls Royce, as shown in Figure 6-18.

Figure 6-18. *A filter menu*

3.   Click OK. Filtered Rows is added to the Applied Steps list.

Note   You can deselect all items by clicking the (Select All) check box; reselect all the items by selecting this box again. It follows that if you want to keep only a few elements, it may be faster to unselect all of them first and then only select the ones that you want to keep. If you want to exclude any records without a value in the column that you are filtering on, then select Remove Empty from the filter menu.

Finding Elements in the Filter List

Scrolling up and down in a filter list can get extremely laborious. A fast way of limiting the list to a subset of available elements is to do the following (assuming that you are still in the Query Editor for the Excel file C:\DataMashupWithExcelSamples\ Chapter06Sample1.xlsx):

1.   Click the popup menu for a column. (I use Model in the sample dataset in this example.) The filter menu appears.

2. Enter a letter or a few letters in the Search box. The list shortens with every letter or number that you enter. If you enter **ar**, then the filter popup will look like Figure 6-19.

Figure 6-19. *Searching the filter menu*

3. Select the elements that you want to filter on and click OK.

To remove a filter, all that you have to do is click the cross that appears at the right of the Search box.

Filtering Text Ranges

If a column contains text, then you can apply specific options to filter the data. These elements are found in the filter popup of any text-based column in the Text Filters submenu. The choices are given in Table 6-6.

Table 6-6. *Text Filter Options*

Filter Option	Description
Equals	Sets the text that must match the cell contents
Does Not Equal	Sets the text that must *not* match the cell contents
Begins With	Sets the text at the left of the cell contents
Does Not Begin With	Sets the text that must *not* appear at the left of the cell contents
Ends With	Sets the text at the right of the cell contents
Does Not End With	Sets the text that must *not* appear at the right of the cell contents
Contains	Lets you enter a text that will be part of the cell contents
Does Not Contain	Lets you enter a text that will *not* be part of the cell contents

Filtering Numeric Ranges

If a column contains numbers, then there are also specific options that you can apply to filter the data. You'll find these elements in the filter popup of any text-based column in the Number Filters submenu. The choices are given in Table 6-7.

Table 6-7. *Numeric Filter Options*

Filter Option	Description
Equals	Sets the number that must match the cell contents
Does Not Equal	Sets the number that must not match the cell contents
Greater Than	Cell contents must be greater than this number
Greater Than Or Equal To	Cell contents must be greater than or equal to this number
Lesser Than	Cell contents must be less than this number
Lesser Than Or Equal To	Cell contents must be less than or equal to this number
Between	Cell contents must be between the two numbers that you specify

Filtering Date and Time Ranges

If a column contains dates or times (or both), then specific options can also be applied to filter the data. These elements are found in the filter popup of any text-based column in the Date/Time Filters submenu. The choices are given in Table 6-8.

Table 6-8. *Date and Time Filter Options*

Filter Element	Description
Equals	Filters data to include only records for the selected date
Before	Filters data to include only records up to the selected date
After	Filters data to include only records after the selected date
Between	Lets you set an upper and a lower date limit to exclude records outside that range
In the Next	Lets you specify a number of days, weeks, months, quarters, or years to come
In the Previous	Lets you specify a number of days, weeks, months, quarters, or years up to the date
Is Earliest	Filters data to include only records for the earliest date
Is Latest	Filters data to include only records for the latest date
Is Not Earliest	Filters data to include only records for dates not including the earliest date
Is Not Latest	Filters data to include only records for dates not including the latest date
Day ➤ Tomorrow	Filters data to include only records for the day after the current system date
Day ➤ Today	Filters data to include only records for the current system date
Day ➤ Yesterday	Filters data to include only records for the day before the current system date
Week ➤ Next Week	Filters data to include only records for the next calendar week
Week ➤ This Week	Filters data to include only records for the current calendar week
Week ➤ Last Week	Filters data to include only records for the previous calendar week
Month ➤ Next Month	Filters data to include only records for the next calendar month

(continued)

Table 6-8. (*continued*)

Filter Element	Description
Month ➤ This Month	Filters data to include only records for the current calendar month
Month ➤ Last Month	Filters data to include only records for the previous calendar month
Month ➤ Month Name	Filters data to include only records for the specified calendar month
Quarter ➤ Next Quarter	Filters data to include only records for the next quarter
Quarter ➤ This Quarter	Filters data to include only records for the current quarter
Quarter ➤ Last Quarter	Filters data to include only records for the previous quarter
Quarter ➤ Quarter Name	Filters data to include only records for the specified quarter
Year ➤ Next Year	Filters data to include only records for the next year
Year ➤ This Year	Filters data to include only records for the current year
Year ➤ Last Year	Filters data to include only records for the previous year
Year ➤ Year To Date	Filters data to include only records for the calendar year to date
Custom Filter	Lets you set up a specific filter for a chosen date range.

Filtering Numeric Data

Filtering data uses a globally similar approach, whatever the type of data that is being filtered—text, numeric, logical, or date/time. As a simple example, here is how to apply a number filter to the sale price to find vehicles that sold for less than £5,000.00 (once again in the Query Editor for the file Chapter06Sample1.xlsx):

1. Click the popup menu for the SalePrice column.

2. Click Number Filters. The submenu will appear.

3. Select Less Than. The Filter Rows dialog will be displayed.

4. Enter **5000** in the box next to the "is less than" box, as shown in Figure 6-20.

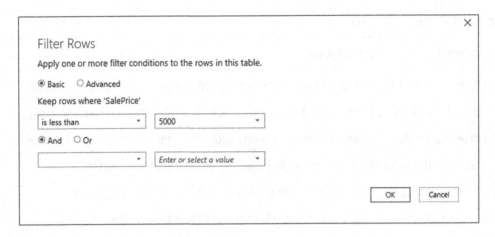

Figure 6-20. *The Filter Rows dialog*

  5. Click OK. The dataset only displays rows that conform to the filter
      that you have defined.

Although extremely simple to apply, filters do require a few comments:

- You can combine up to two elements in a basic filter. These can be
  mutually inclusive (an AND filter) or they can be an alternative (an
  OR filter).

- You can combine several elements in an advanced filter—as you will
  learn in the next section.

- You should not apply any formatting when entering numbers.

- Any text that you filter on is not case-sensitive.

- If you choose the wrong type of filter (for instance, greater than rather
  than less than), you do not have to cancel and start over. Simply
  select the correct filter type from the popup in the left-hand boxes in
  the Filter Rows dialog.

Tip   If you set a filter value that excludes all the records in the table, Power Query
displays an empty table except for the words "This table is empty." You can always
remove the filter by clicking the cross to the left of Filtered Rows in the Applied
Steps list. This will remove the step and revert the data to its previous state.

Applying Advanced Filters

Should you ever need to be extremely specific when filtering data, you can always use Power Query's advanced filters. These let you extend the filter elements so that you can include or exclude records to a fine-grained level of detail. Here is the procedure in the Query Editor for the file Chapter06Sample1.xlsx:

1. Click the popup menu for the SalePrice column.

2. Click Number Filters. The submenu will appear.

3. Select Equals. The Filter Rows dialog will be displayed.

4. Click Advanced.

5. Enter **5000** as the value for the first filter element in the dialog.

6. Select Or from the popup as the filter type for the second filter element.

7. Select equals as the operator.

8. Enter **89000** as the value for the second filter in the dialog.

9. Click Add Clause. A new filter element will be added to the dialog under the existing elements.

10. Select Or as the filter type and equals as the operator.

11. Enter **178500** as the value for the third filter element in the dialog. The Filter Rows dialog will look like the one shown in Figure 6-21.

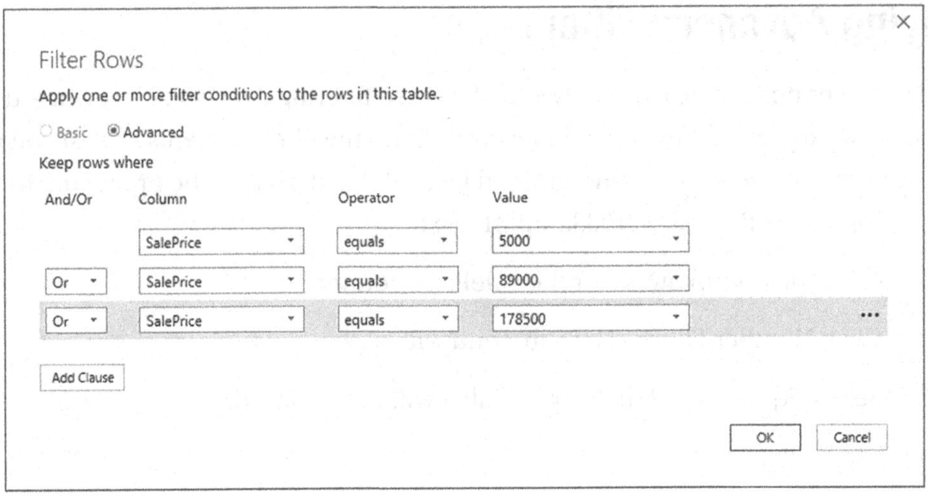

Filter Rows

Apply one or more filter conditions to the rows in this table.

○ Basic ◉ Advanced

Keep rows where

And/Or	Column	Operator	Value
	SalePrice ▾	equals ▾	5000 ▾
Or ▾	SalePrice ▾	equals ▾	89000 ▾
Or ▾	SalePrice ▾	equals ▾	178500 ▾	⋯

Add Clause

OK   Cancel

Figure 6-21. Advanced filters

12. Click OK. Only records containing the figures that you entered in the Filter Rows dialog will be displayed in the Power Query Editor.

I would like to finish on the subject of filters with a few comments:

- In the Advanced filter dialog, you can "mix and match" columns and operators to achieve the filter result that you are looking for.

- You can also order the sequence of filters if you ever need to. To do this, simply click inside a filter row and it will appear with a gray background (like the third filter in Figure 6-21). Then click the ellipses at the right of the filter row and select Move Up or Move Down from the popup menu. You can see this in Figure 6-22.

Figure 6-22. Ordering filters

- To delete a filter, click the ellipses at the right of the filter row and select Delete.

Note   When you are dealing with really large datasets, you may find that a filter does not always show all the available values from the source data. This is because the Query Editor has loaded only a sample subset of the data. In cases like these, you will see an alert in the filter popup menu and a "Load more" link. Clicking this link will force Power Query to reload a larger sample set of data. However, memory restrictions may prevent it from loading all the data that you need. In cases like this, you should consider modifying the source query (if this is possible, of course, such as when connecting to a database) so that it brings back a representative dataset that can fit into memory.

Grouping Records

At times, you will need to transform your original data in an extreme way—by grouping the data. This is very different from filtering data, removing duplicates, or cleansing the contents of columns. When you group data, you are altering the structure of the dataset to "roll up" records where you do the following:

- Define the attribute columns that will become the unique elements in the grouped data table

- Specify which aggregations are applied to any numeric columns included in the grouped table

Grouping is frequently an extremely selective operation. This is inevitable, since the fewer attribute (i.e., nonnumeric) columns you choose to group on, the fewer records you are likely to include in the grouped table. However, this will always depend on the particular dataset you are dealing with, and grouping data efficiently is always a matter of flair, practice, and good, old-fashioned trial and error.

Simple Groups

To understand how grouping works—and how it can radically alter the structure of your dataset—let's see a simple example of row grouping in action:

1. In Power Query for the sample file Chapter06Sample1.xlsx, click inside the Make column.

2. In either the Home ribbon or Transform ribbon, click the Group By button. The Group By dialog will appear, looking like the one in Figure 6-23.

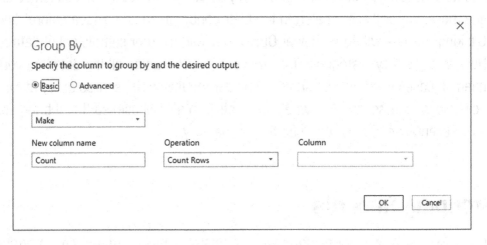

Figure 6-23. *Simple grouping*

3. Click OK. The dataset will now only contain the list of makes of vehicle and the number of records for each make. You can see this in Figure 6-24.

	Make	Count
1	Rolls Royce	63
2	Aston Martin	110
3	Jaguar	129
4	Bentley	71
5	TVR	14
6	MGB	36
7	Triumph	34

Figure 6-24. *Simple grouping output*

Power Query will add a step named Grouped Rows to the Applied Steps list when you apply grouping to a dataset.

Note   The best way to cancel a grouping operation is to delete the Grouped Rows step in the Applied Steps list.

Although Power Query defaults to counting rows, there are several other operations that you can apply when grouping data. These are outlined in Table 6-9.

Table 6-9. *Aggregation Operations When Grouping*

Aggregation Operation	Description
Count Rows	Counts the number of records
Count Distinct Rows	Counts the number of unique records
Sum	Returns the total for a numeric column
Average	Returns the average for a numeric column
Median	Returns the median value of a numeric column
Min	Returns the minimum value of a numeric column
Max	Returns the maximum value of a numeric column
All Rows	Creates a table of records for each grouped element

Complex Groups

Power Query can help you shape your datasets in more advanced ways by creating more complex data groupings. As an example, you could try out the following to group by make and model and add columns showing the total sales value and the average cost:

1. Open the sample file C:\DataMashupWithExcelSamples\ Chapter06Sample1.xlsx.

2. Double-click the BaseData Connection to open the Query Editor.

3. Select the following columns (by Ctrl-clicking the column headers):

    a.   Make

    b.   Model

4. In either the Home ribbon or Transform ribbon, click Group By.

5. In the New Column Name box, enter **TotalSales**.

6. Select Sum as the operation.

7. Choose SalePrice as the source column in the Column popup list.

8. Click the Add Aggregation button and repeat the operation, only this time, use the following:

   a. *New Column Name*: **AverageCost**

   b. *Operation*: Average

   c. *Column*: CostPrice

The Group By dialog should look like the one in Figure 6-25.

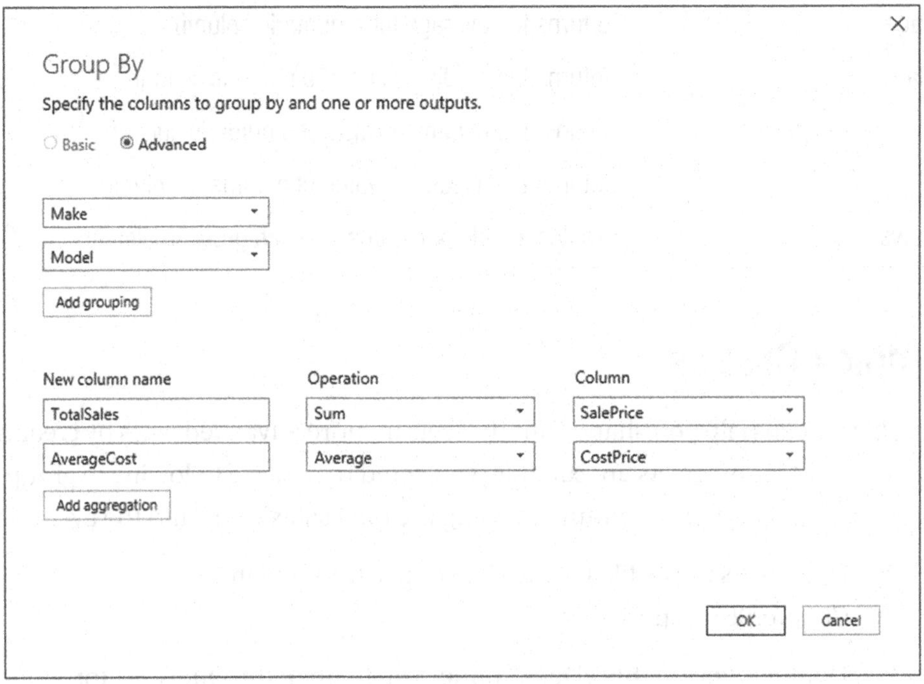

Figure 6-25. The Group By dialog

9. Click OK. All columns, other than those that you specified in the Group By dialog, are removed, and the table is grouped and aggregated, as shown in Figure 6-26. Grouped Rows will be added to the Applied Steps list. I have also sorted the table by the Make and Model columns to make the grouping easier to comprehend.

	Make	Model	TotalSales	AverageCost
1	Rolls Royce	Camargue	4116900	61002.69231
2	Aston Martin	DBS	465500	68000
3	Rolls Royce	Silver Ghost	1315500	75630
4	Aston Martin	DB7	1023480	23703.125
5	Aston Martin	DB9	5423860	59132.96296
6	Aston Martin	DB4	793000	84167.5
7	Aston Martin	Vantage	658200	38750
8	Aston Martin	Vanquish	1506750	89700
9	Aston Martin	Rapide	455500	142500
10	Aston Martin	Zagato	359750	127500
11	Rolls Royce	Wraith	359750	64500
12	Rolls Royce	Silver Shadow	622500	71445
13	Rolls Royce	Silver Seraph	582500	71445
14	Rolls Royce	Phantom	359750	64500
15	Jaguar	XK	4461250	39803.15789
16	Jaguar	XJ6	1239750	32630.76923
17	Jaguar	XJ12	618000	33750
18	Bentley	Continental	3662250	49256.86275
19	Bentley	Arnage	90750	28200
20	Bentley	Azure	489500	28200
21	Bentley	Turbo R	708750	35460
22	TVR	Tuscan	374250	41000
23	TVR	Cerbera	124500	40000
24	MGB	GT	1011000	9500
25	Triumph	TR4	566500	18704.54545
26	Triumph	TR5	207500	19500
27	Triumph	TR7	101000	15250

Figure 6-26. *Grouping a dataset*

If you have created a really complex group and then realized that you need to change the order of the columns, all is not lost. You can alter the order of the columns in the output by clicking the ellipses to the right of each column definition in the Group By dialog and selecting Move Up or Move Down. The order of the columns in the Group By dialog will be the order of the columns (left to right) in the resulting dataset.

Note   You do not have to Ctrl-click to select the grouping columns. You can add them one by one to the Group By dialog by clicking the Add Aggregation button. Equally, you can remove grouping columns (or added and aggregated columns) by clicking the ellipses to the right of a column name and selecting Delete from the popup menu.

Count Rows

One simple option that you may find useful in certain circumstances is the Count rows function. This—as its name implies—displays the full number of rows available in the source dataset.

1.   In the Power Query Transform menu, click Count rows. The number of records will appear in the place of the existing dataset as shown in Figure 6-27.

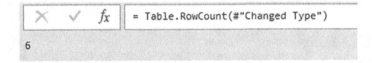

Figure 6-27.   *Returning the row count of a source dataset*

Saving Changes in the Query Editor

Contrary to what you might expect, you *cannot* save any changes that you have made when using the Power Query Editor at any time. Instead you must first exit the Query Editor and then save the underlying Excel file as you would normally.

Exiting the Query Editor

In a similar vein to the Save options just described, you can choose how to exit the Query Editor and return to your reports in Excel. The default option (when you click the Close & Load button) is to apply all the changes that you have made to the data, update the data model with the new data (if this option has been selected), and return to Excel.

However, you have another option that may prove useful. This appears in the File menu for the Query Editor.

1.   In the Query Editor, click File.

2.   Select Discard & Close. You can see this option in Figure 6-28.

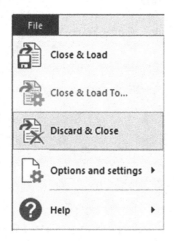

Figure 6-28. *Discard modifications in Power Query*

If you choose not to apply the changes that you have made, then you will return to the Excel workbook and lose any modifications you have made—*without any confirmation.*

Conclusion

This chapter started you on the road to transforming datasets with Power Query. You saw how to trim datasets by removing rows and columns. You also learned how to subset a sample of data from a data source by selecting alternating groups of rows.
You also saw how to choose the columns that you want to use in Excel, how to move columns around in the dataset, and how to rename columns so that your data is easily comprehensible when you use it later as the basis for your analysis. Then, you saw how to filter and sort data, as well as how to remove duplicates to ensure that your dataset only contains the precise rows that you need for your upcoming visualizations. Finally, you learned how to group and aggregate data.

It has to be admitted, nonetheless, that preparing raw data for use in analytics is not always easy and can take a while to get right. However, Power Query can make this task really easy with a little practice. So now that you have grasped the basics, it is time to move on and discover some further data transformation techniques. Specifically, you will see how to transform and potentially cleanse the data that you have imported. This is the subject of the next chapter.

CHAPTER 7

Data Transformation

Once a dataset has been filtered and shaped (as covered in the previous chapter), it probably still needs a good few modifications to make it ready for consumption. Many of these modifications are, at their heart, a series of fairly simple yet necessary techniques that you apply to make the data cleaner and more standardized. I have chosen to group these approaches under the heading *data transformation*.

The sort of things that you may be looking to do before finally loading source data into the data model normally cover a range of processes that *cleanse* the data. They can include the following:

- Change the data type for a column—by telling Power Query that the column contains numbers, for example

- Ensure that the first row is used as headers (if this is required)

- Remove part of a column's contents

- Replace the values in a cell with other values

- Transform the column contents—by making the text uppercase, for instance, or by removing decimals from numbers

- Fill data down or up over empty cells to ensure that records are complete

- Apply math or statistical (or even trigonometric) functions to columns of numbers

- Convert date or time data into date elements such as days, months, quarters, years, hours, or minutes

© Adam Aspin 2020

A. Aspin, *Data Mashup with Microsoft Excel Using Power Query and M*, https://doi.org/10.1007/978-1-4842-6018-0_7

Transforming data does not only consist of reducing it. Sometimes you may have to *extend* the data to make it usable. This normally means adding further columns to a data table. The techniques to do this include

- Duplicating a column and possibly altering the format of the data in the copied column

- Extracting part of the data in a column into a new column

- Separating all the multiple data elements in a column so that each data element appears in a separate column

- Merging columns into a new column

- Adding custom columns that possibly contain calculations or extract part of a column's data into a new column or even concatenate columns

- Adding "index" columns that number the rows to ensure uniqueness or memorize a sort order

This chapter will take you on a tour of these kinds of essential data transformations. Once you have finished reading it, you should be confident that you can take a rough and ready data source as a starting point and convert it into a polished and coherent data table that is ready to become a pivotal part of your Excel analytics. Not only that, but you will have carried out really heavy lifting much faster and more easily than you could have done using enterprise-level tools or most of the Excel techniques that you know already.

The sample data that you will need to follow the exercises in this chapter is in the folder C:\DataMashupWithExcelSamples.

Viewing a Full Record

Before even starting to cleanse data, you probably need to take a good look at it. While the Power Query Editor is great for scrolling up and down columns to see how data compares for a single field, it is often less easy to appreciate the entire contents of a single record.

So to avoid having to scroll frenetically left and right across rows of data, the Power Query Editor has another brilliantly simple solution. If you click a row (or more specifically, on the number of a row in the grid on the left), the Power Query Editor will display the contents of an entire record in a single window under the dataset. You can see an example of this in Figure 7-1.

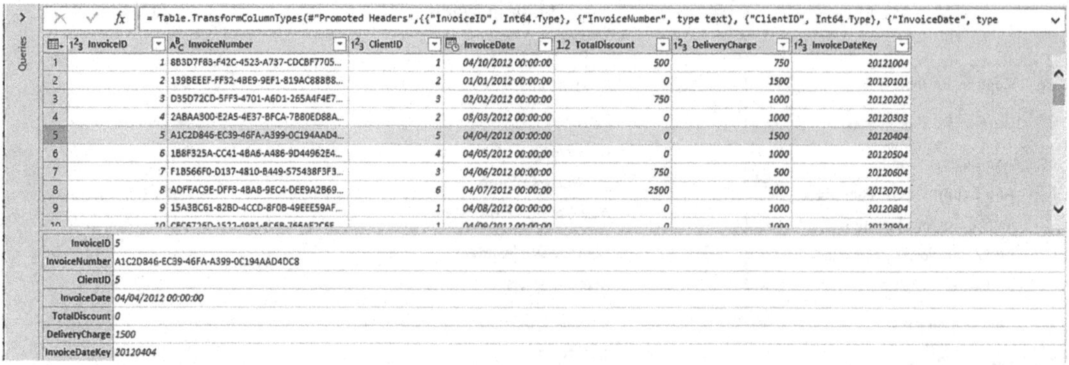

Figure 7-1. *Viewing a full record*

Note   You can alter the relative height of the recordset and dataset windows simply by dragging the gray separator line between the upper and lower windows up or down.

Power Query Editor Context Menus

As is normal for Windows programs, Power Query Editor makes full use of context (or "right-click") menus as an alternative to using the ribbons. When transforming datasets, there are three main context menus that you will probably find yourself using:

- *Table menu*: This menu appears when you right-click the top corner of the grid containing the data (or click the small triangle at the top left of the data grid).

- *Column menu*: This menu appears when you right-click a column title.

- *Cell menu*: This menu appears when you right-click a data cell.

While I have referred copiously to the context menus when explaining how to transform data, it is probably easier to take a quick look at them now so that you can see the various options. Figure 7-2 gives you a quick overview of these three context menus.

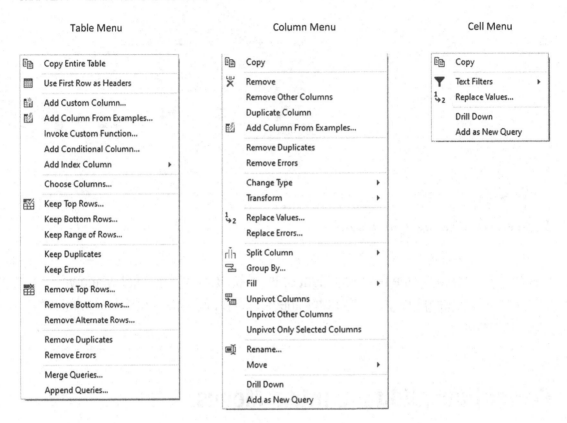

Figure 7-2. *The Power Query Editor context menus*

Because the options that are available in the context menus are explained throughout this, the previous, and the following chapters, I will not explain them all in detail here.

Note   The cell context menu will reflect the data type of the cell in the filter option. So a numeric cell will have the option "Number filters."

Using the First Row as Headers

Power Query is very good at guessing if it needs to take the first record of a source dataset and have it function as the column headers. This is fundamental for two reasons:

- You avoid leaving the columns named Column1, Column2, and so on. Leaving them named generically like this would make it needlessly difficult for a user (or even yourself) to understand the data.

- You avoid having a text element (which should be the column title) in a column of figures, which can cause problems later on. This is because a whole column needs to have the same data type for another data type to be applied. Having a header text in the first row prevents this for numeric and date/time data types, for instance. This could be because the header is a text, whereas the remainder of the column contains numbers or dates.

Yet there could be—albeit rare—occasions when Power Query guesses incorrectly and assumes that the first record in a dataset is data when it is really the header information. So instead of headers, you have a set of generic column titles such as Column1, Column2, and so forth. Fortunately, correcting this and using the first row as headers is a simple task:

1. Click Use First Row as Headers in the Transform ribbon of the Power Query window.

After a few seconds, the first record disappears and the column titles become the elements that were in the first record. The Applied Steps list on the right now contains a Promoted Headers element, indicating which process has taken place. This step is highlighted.

Note   Power Query is often able to apply this step automatically when the source is a database. It can often correctly guess when the source is a file. However, it cannot always guess accurately, so sometimes you have to intervene. You can see if Power Query has had to guess that the first row contained headers if it has added a Promoted Headers step to the Applied Steps list.

In the rare event that Power Query gets this operation wrong and presumes that a first row is column titles when it is not, you can reset the titles to be the first row by clicking the tiny triangle to the right of the Use First Row as Headers button. This displays a short menu where you can click the Use Headers as First Row option. The Applied Steps list on the right now contains a Demoted Headers element and the column titles are Column1, Column2, and so forth. You can subsequently rename the columns as you see fit.

Changing Data Type

A truly fundamental aspect of data modification is ensuring that the data is of the appropriate type; that is, if you have a column of numbers that are to be calculated at some point, then the column should be a numeric column. If it contains dates, then it should be set to one of the date or time data types. I realize that this can seem arduous and even superfluous; however, *if you want to be sure that your data can be sliced and diced correctly further down the line*, then setting the right data types at the outset is *vital*. An added bonus is that if you validate the data types early on in the process of loading data, you can see from the start if the data has any potential issues—dates that cannot be read as dates, for instance. This allows you to decide what to do with poor or unreliable data early in your work with a dataset.

The good news here is that for many data sources, Power Query applies an appropriate data type. Specifically, if you have loaded data from a database, then Power Query will recognize the source data type for each column and apply a suitable Power Query data type as the database has supplied the necessary information for Power Query to apply the correct data type. Unfortunately, things can get a little more painful with file sources, specifically CSV, text, and (occasionally) Excel files, as well as some XML files. In the case of these file types, Power Query often tries to guess the data type, but there are times when it does not succeed. If it has made a stab at deducing data types, then you see a Changed Type step in the Applied Steps list. Consequently, if you are obtaining your data from these sources, then you could well be obliged to apply data types to many of the columns manually.

Note   In some cases, numbers are not meant to be interpreted as numerical data. For instance, a French postal code is five numbers, but it will never be calculated in any way. So it is good practice to let Power Query know this by changing the data type to text in cases when a numeric data type is inappropriate.

Do the following to change the data type for a column or a group of columns:

1. Load the C:\DataMashupWithExcelSamples\Chapter07Example1.xlsx sample file.

2. Display the Queries & Connections pane by clicking Queries & Connections in the Data ribbon (unless this pane is already visible).

3. Double-click the BaseData query in the Queries & Connections pane to switch to the Query Editor.

4. Click inside the column whose data type you wish to change. If you want to modify several columns, then Ctrl-click the requisite column titles. In this example, you could select the CostPrice and TotalDiscount columns.

5. Click the Data Type button in the Transform ribbon. A popup menu of potential data types will appear.

6. Select an appropriate data type. If you have selected the CostPrice and TotalDiscount columns, then Whole Number is the type to choose.

After a few seconds, the data type will be applied. Changed Type will appear in the Applied Steps list. The data types that you can apply are outlined in Table 7-1.

Table 7-1. *Data Types in Power Query*

Data Type	Description
Decimal Number	Converts the data to a decimal number
Fixed Decimal Number	Converts the data to a decimal number with a fixed number of decimals
Whole Number	Converts the data to a whole (integer) number
Date/Time	Converts to a date and time data type
Date	Converts to a date data type
Time	Converts to a time data type
Duration	Sets the data as being a duration. These are used for date and time calculations
Text	Sets to a text data type
True/False	Sets the data type to Boolean (True or False)
Binary	Defines the data as binary, and consequently, it is not directly visible

> **Note**   The Data Type button is also available in the Home ribbon. Equally, you can right-click a column header and select Change Type to select a different data type.

Inevitably, there will be times when you try to apply a data type that simply cannot be used with a certain column of data. Converting a text column (such as Make in this sample data table) into dates will simply not work. If you do this, then Power Query will replace the column contents with Error. This is not definitive or dangerous, and all you have to do to return the data to its previous state is to delete the Changed Type step in the Applied Steps list using the technique described in the previous chapter.

Sometimes you could try and change a data type when the data type has already been changed. In this case, you will get an alert like the one shown in Figure 7-3.

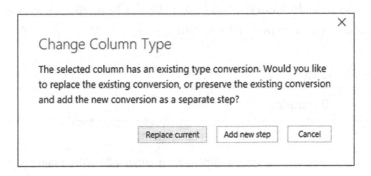

Figure 7-3. *The Change Column Type alert*

If this occurs, you can do one of two things:

- Let Power Query update the existing conversion step with the data type that you just selected.

- Add a new conversion step.

Your choice will depend on exactly what type of transformation you are applying to the underlying dataset.

It can help to alter data types at the same time for a *set* of columns where you think that this operation is necessary. There are a couple of good reasons for this approach:

- You can concentrate on getting data types right, and if you are working methodically, you are less likely to forget to set a data type.

- Applying data types for many columns (even if you are doing this in several operations, to single or multiple columns) will only add a single step to the Applied Steps list.

Note   Don't look for any data formatting options in Power Query; there aren't any. This is deliberate since this tool is designed to structure, load, and cleanse data, but *not* to present it. You carry out the formatting in the Excel as you are used to doing.

Detecting Data Types

Applying the correct data type to dozens of columns can be more than a little time-consuming. Fortunately, Power Query now contains an option to apply data types automatically to a whole table. Assuming that you still are in the BaseData query in the file C:\DataMashupWithExcelSamples\Chapter07Example1.xlsx:

1.   In the Transform ribbon, click the Detect Data Type button.

2.   Changed Type will appear in the Applied Steps list. Most of the columns will have the correct data type applied.

This technique does not always give perfect results, and there will be times when you want to override the choice of data type that Power Query has applied. Yet it is nonetheless a welcome addition to the data preparation toolset that can save you considerable time when preparing a dataset.

Data Type Indicators

It would be singularly unproductive to have to guess which column was set to which data type. So Power Query comes to your aid by indicating, visually, the corresponding data type for each column. If you look closely to the left of each individual column header, you will see a tiny icon. Each icon specifies the column's data type. The meaning of each icon is given in Table 7-2.

Table 7-2. *Data Type Icons in Power Query Editor*

Data Type Icon	Description
ABC 123	Any data type from among the possible data types
1²₃	Whole Number
1.2	Decimal Number
$	Fixed Decimal Number
%	Percentage
Aᴮc	Text
×√	True/False
📅	Date/Time
🗓	Date
🕐	Time
🌐	Date/Time/Timezone
🕕	Duration
🗒	Binary

Switching Data Types

Another quick way to alter the data type for a column is to click the data type icon to the left of the column title and select the required data type from the context menu that you can see in Figure 7-4.

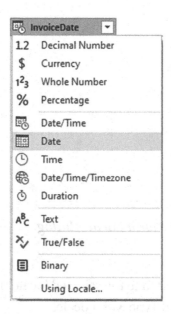

Figure 7-4. *The data type context menu*

Data Type Using Locale

When you are converting data types, you can also choose to use the current locale to specify date, time, and number formats. This means that users opening Power Query from Excel in another country will see date, time, and number formats adapted to the local formatting conventions. To do this:

1. Open the Query Editor (from inside the source file
    C:\DataMashupWithExcelSamples\Chapter07Example1.pbix).

2. Click the data type icon to the left of the column title.

3. Select Using Locale from the popup menu. The Change Type with
    Locale dialog will appear.

4. Choose the new data type to apply from the list of available data
    types.

5. Select the required locale from the list of worldwide locales. The
    dialog will look like Figure 7-5.

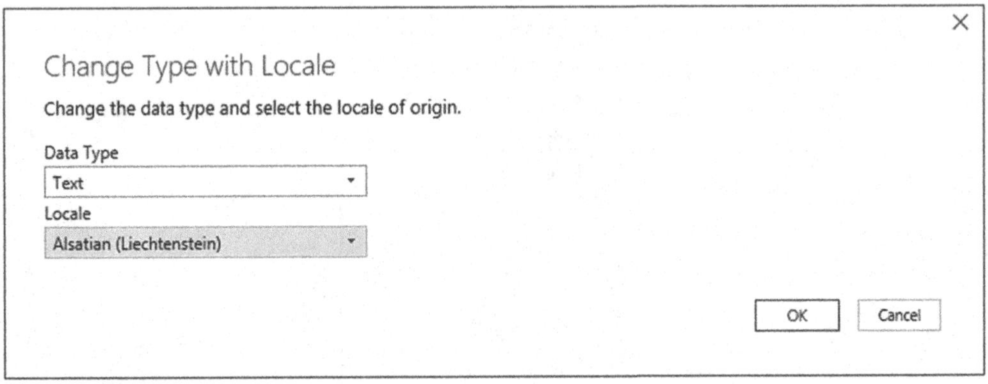

Figure 7-5. *The Change Type with Locale dialog*

> 6. Click OK.

The data type will be converted to the selected locale. The Applied Steps list will contain a step entitled Changed Type with Locale.

Replacing Values

Some data that you load will need certain values to be replaced by others in a kind of global search-and-replace operation—just as you would in a Microsoft Word document. For instance, perhaps you need to standardize spellings where a make of car (to use the current sample dataset as an example) has been entered incorrectly. To carry out this particular data cleansing operation (and presuming that you have already opened the Query Editor in the file Chapter07Sample1.xlsx), do the following:

1. Click the title of the column that contains the data that you want to replace. The column will become selected. In this example, I used the Model column.

2. In the Home ribbon, click the Replace Values button. The Replace Values dialog will appear.

3. In the Value To Find box, enter the text or number that you want to replace. I used **Ghost** in this example.

4. In the Replace With box, enter the text or number that you want to replace. I used **Fantôme** in this example, as shown in Figure 7-6.

5. Click OK. The data is replaced in the entire column. Replaced
    Values is added to the Applied Steps list.

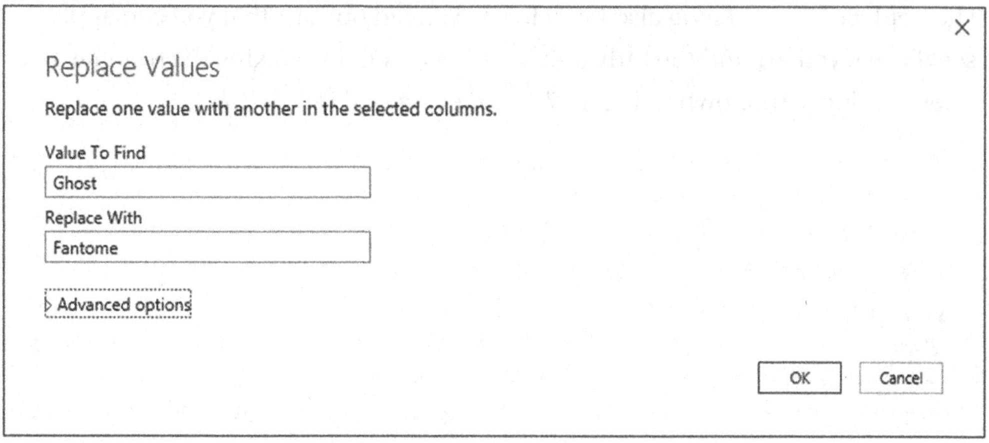

Figure 7-6. *The Replace Values dialog*

I only have a few comments about this technique:

- The Replace Values process searches for every occurrence of the text
  that you are looking for in each record of the selected columns. It
  does not look for the entire contents of the cell unless you specifically
  request this by checking the Match entire cell contents check box in
  the Advanced options.

- If you click a cell containing the contents that you want to replace
  (rather than the column title, as we just did), before starting the
  process, Power Query automatically places the cell contents in the
  Replace Values dialog as the value to find.

- You can only replace text in columns that contain text elements. This
  does not work with columns that are set as a numeric or date data
  type. Indeed, you will see a yellow alert triangle in the Replace Values
  dialog if you enter values that do not match the data type of the
  selected column(s).

- If you really have to replace parts of a date or figures in a numeric
  column with other dates or numbers, then you can

    - Convert the column to a text data type

199

- Carry out the replace operation

- Convert the column back to the original data type

The Replace Values dialog also has a few advanced options that you can apply. You can see these if you expand the "Advanced options" item by clicking the triangle to its left. These options are shown in Figure 7-7 and explained in Table 7-3.

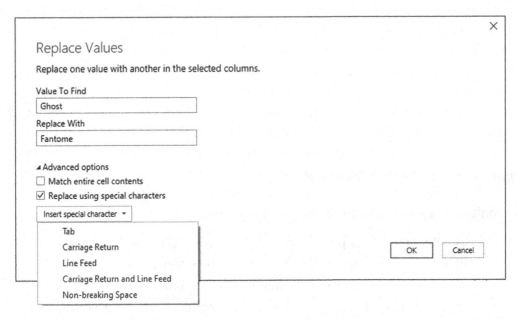

Figure 7-7. *Advanced replace options*

Table 7-3. *Advanced Replace Options*

Option	Description
Match entire cell contents	Only replaces the search value if it makes up the entire contents of the column for a row
Replace using special characters	Replaces the search value with a nonprinting character
Tab	Replaces the search value with a tab character
Carriage Return	Replaces the search value with a carriage return character
Line Feed	Replaces the search value with a line feed character
Carriage Return and Line Feed	Replaces the search value with a carriage return and line feed

Note   Replacing words that are subsets of other words is dangerous. When replacing any data, make sure that you don't damage elements other than the one you intend to change.

As a final and purely spurious comment, I must add that I would never suggest rebranding a Rolls Royce, as it would be close to automotive sacrilege.

Transforming Column Contents

Power Query has a powerful toolbox of automated data transformations that allow you to standardize the contents of a column in several ways. These include

- Setting the capitalization of text columns

- Rounding numeric data or applying math functions

- Extracting date elements such as the year, month, or day (among others) from a date column

Power Query is very strict about applying transformations to appropriate types of data. This is because *transforms are totally dependent on the data type of the selected column*. This is yet another confirmation that applying the requisite data type is an operation that should be carried out early in any data transformation process—and certainly *before* transforming the column contents. Remember, you will only be able to select a numeric transformation if the column is a numeric data type, and you will only be able to select a date transformation if the column is a date data type. Equally, the text-based transformations can only be applied to columns that are of the text data type.

Text Transformation

Let's look at a simple transformation operation in action. As an example, I will get Power Query to convert the Make column into uppercase characters.

1.   Still using the Query Editor opened from the file Chapter07Example1.xlsx, click anywhere in the column whose contents you wish to transform (Make, in this example).

2. In the Transform ribbon, click the Format button. A popup menu will appear.

3. Select UPPERCASE, as shown in Figure 7-8.

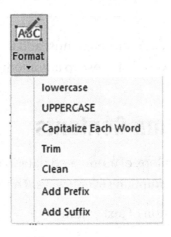

Figure 7-8. *The Format menu*

The contents of the entire column will be converted to uppercase. Uppercased Text will be added to the Applied Steps list.

As you can see from the menu for the Format button, you have seven possible options when formatting (or transforming) text. These options are explained in Table 7-4.

Table 7-4. *Text Transformations*

Transformation	Description	Applied Steps Definition
Lowercase	Converts all the text to lowercase	Lowercased Text
Uppercase	Converts all the text to uppercase	Uppercased Text
Capitalize Each Word	Converts the first letter of each word to a capital	Capitalized Each Word
Trim	Removes all spaces before and after the text	Trimmed Text
Clean	Removes any nonprintable characters	Cleaned Text
Add Prefix	Adds text at the start of the column contents	Added Prefix
Add Suffix	Adds text at the end of the column contents	Added Suffix

Note   I realize that Power Query calls text transformations formatting. Nonetheless, these options are part of the overall data transformation options.

Adding a Prefix or a Suffix

You can also add a prefix or a suffix to all the data in a column. This is as easy as the following:

1.   Click inside the column where you want to add a prefix.

2.   In the Transform ribbon, select Format ➤ Add Prefix. The Prefix dialog will be displayed, as you can see in Figure 7-9.

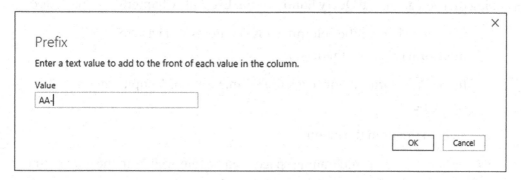

Figure 7-9.   *Adding a prefix to a text*

3.   Enter the prefix to add in the Value field.

4.   Click OK.

The prefix that you designated will be placed at the start of every record in the dataset for the selected field.

Note   If you add a prefix or a suffix to a numeric or date/time column, then the column data type will automatically be converted to text.

Removing Leading and Trailing Spaces

There will inevitably be occasions when you inherit data that has extra spaces before, after, or before *and* after the data itself. This can be insidious, as it can cause

- Data duplication, because a value with a trailing space is *not* considered identical to the same text without the spaces that follow

- Sort issues, because a leading space causes an element to appear at the *top* of a sorted list

- Grouping errors, because elements with spaces are not part of the same group as elements without spaces

Fortunately, Power Query has a ruthlessly efficient solution to this problem. So, assuming that you are in the Query Editor for the Excel file Chapter07Sample1.xlsx:

1. Click anywhere in the column whose contents you wish to transform (Make, in this case).

2. In the Transform ribbon, click the Format button. A popup menu will appear.

3. Select Trim from the menu.

All superfluous leading and trailing spaces will be removed from the data in the column. This can help when sorting, grouping, and deduplicating records.

Removing Nonprinting Characters

Some source data can contain somewhat insidious elements called nonprinting characters. These can, even if they are nearly always invisible to humans, cause problems in certain circumstances.

If you suspect that your source data contains nonprinting characters, you can remove them simply like this:

1. Click inside the column (or select the columns) that you know to contain (or that you suspect contain) nonprinting characters.

2. Click Format➤ Clean.

Power Query will add Cleaned Text to the list of Applied Steps.

Number Transformations

Just as you can transform the contents of text-based columns, you can also apply transformations to numeric values. As an example, suppose that you want to round up all the figures in a column to the nearest whole number in the Query Editor.

1. Open the Query Editor for the Excel file Chapter07Sample1.xlsx (unless already open, of course).

2. Click anywhere in the column whose contents you wish to transform (TotalDiscount, in this case).

3. In the Transform ribbon, click the Rounding button. A popup menu will appear, showing all the available options. You can see this in Figure 7-10.

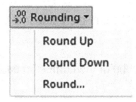

Figure 7-10. *Rounding options*

4. Select Round Up.

The values in the entire column will be rounded up to the nearest whole number. Rounded Up will be added to the Applied Steps list.

The other possible numeric transformations that are available are described in Table 7-5. Because these numeric transformations use several buttons, or sequences of menu options, in the Transform ribbon, I have indicated which button to use to get the desired result.

Table 7-5. *Number Transformations*

Transformation	Description	Applied Steps Definition
Rounding ➤ Round Up	Rounds each number to the specified number of decimal places	Rounded Up
Rounding ➤ Round Down	Rounds each number down	Rounded Down
Round...	Rounds each number to the number of decimals that you specify. If you specify a negative number, you round to a given decimal	Rounded Off
Scientific ➤ Absolute Value	Makes the number absolute (positive)	Absolute Value
Scientific ➤ Power ➤ Square	Returns the square of the number in each cell	Calculated Square
Scientific ➤ Power ➤ Cube	Returns the cube of the number in each cell	Calculated Cube Value
Scientific ➤ Power ➤ Power	Raises each number to the power that you specify	Calculated Power
Scientific ➤ Square Root	Returns the square root of the number in each cell	Calculated Square Root
Scientific ➤ Exponent	Returns the exponent of the number in each cell	Calculated Exponent
Scientific ➤ Logarithm ➤ Base 10	Returns the base 10 logarithm of the number in each cell	Calculated Base 10 Logarithm
Scientific ➤ Logarithm ➤ Natural	Returns the natural logarithm of the number in each cell	Calculated Natural Logarithm
Scientific ➤ Factorial	Gives the factorial of numbers in the column	Calculated Factorial
Trigonometry ➤ Sine	Gives the sine of the numbers in the column	Calculated Sine

(*continued*)

Table 7-5. (*continued*)

Transformation	Description	Applied Steps Definition
Trigonometry ➤ Cosine	Gives the cosine of the numbers in the column	Calculated Cosine
Trigonometry ➤ Tangent	Gives the tangent of the numbers in the column	Calculated Tangent
Trigonometry ➤ ArcSine	Gives the arcsine of the numbers in the column	Calculated ArcSine
Trigonometry ➤ ArcCosine	Gives the arccosine of the numbers in the column	Calculated ArcCosine
Trigonometry ➤ ArcTangent	Gives the arctangent of the numbers in the column	Calculated ArcTangent

Note   Power Query will not even let you try to apply numeric transformation to texts or dates. The relevant buttons remain grayed out if you click inside a column of letters or dates.

Calculating Numbers

Power Query can also apply simple arithmetic to the figures in a column. Suppose, for instance, that you want to multiply all the sale prices by 110% as part of your forecasts. This is how you can do just that in the Query Editor for the Excel file Chapter07Sample1. xlsx:

1. Click inside any column of numbers. In this example, I used the column SalePrice.

2. Click the Standard button in the Transform ribbon. The menu will appear as you can see in Figure 7-11.

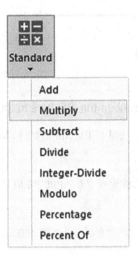

Figure 7-11. *Applying a calculation to a column*

3.   Click Multiply. The Multiply dialog will appear.

4.   Enter **1.1** in the Value box. The dialog will look like the one shown in Figure 7-12.

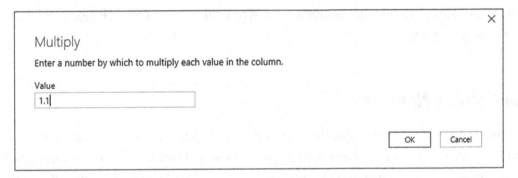

Figure 7-12. *Applying a calculation to a column*

5.   Click OK.

All the numbers in the selected column will be multiplied by 1.1. In other words, they are now 110% of the original value. Table 7-6 describes the possible math operations that you can carry out in Power Query.

Table 7-6. *Applying Basic Calculations*

Transformation	Description	Applied Steps Definition
Add	Adds a selected value to the numbers in a column	Added to Column
Multiply	Multiplies the numbers in a column by a selected value	Multiplied Column
Subtract	Subtracts a selected value from the numbers in a column	Subtracted from Column
Divide	Divides the numbers in a column by a selected value	Divided Column
Integer-Divide	Divides the numbers in a column by a selected value and removes any remainder	Integer-Divided Column
Modulo	Divides the numbers in a column by a selected value and leaves only the remainder	Calculated Modulo
Percentage	Applies the selected percentage to the column	Calculated Percentage
Percent Of	Expresses the value in the column as a percent of the value that you enter	Calculated Percent Of

Note   You can also carry out many types of calculations in Excel and avoid carrying out calculations in the Query Editor. Indeed, many Excel purists seem to prefer that anything resembling a calculation should take place inside the spreadsheet rather than at the Query stage. I will let you decide which approach you prefer.

Finally, it is important to remember that you are altering the data when you carry out this kind of operation. In the real world, you might be safer duplicating a column before profoundly altering the data it contains. This allows you to keep the initial data available, albeit at the cost of increasing both the load time and the size of the resulting Excel file.

Date Transformations

Transforming dates follows similar principles to transforming text and numbers. As an example, here is how to isolate the month from a date in the Query Editor for the Excel file Chapter07Sample1.xlsx:

1. Click inside the InvoiceDate column.

2. In the Transform ribbon, click the Date button. The menu will appear.

3. Click Year. The submenu will appear.

4. Select Year. The year part of the date will replace all the dates in the InvoiceDate column.

The other date transformations that are possible are given in Table 7-7.

Table 7-7. *Date Transformations*

Transformation	Description	Applied Steps Definition
Age	Calculates the date and time difference (in days and hours) between the original date and the current local time	Calculated Age
Date Only	Converts the data to a date without the time element	Calculated Date
Year ➤ Year	Extracts the year from the date	Calculated Year
Year ➤ Start of Year	Returns the first day of the year for the date	Calculated Start of Year
Year ➤ End of Year	Returns the last day of the year for the date	Calculated End of Year
Month ➤ Month	Extracts the number of the month from the date	Calculated Month
Month ➤ Start of Month	Returns the first day of the month for the date	Calculated Start of Month
Month ➤ End of Month	Returns the last day of the month for the date	Calculated End of Month

(continued)

Table 7-7. (*continued*)

Transformation	Description	Applied Steps Definition
Month ➤ Days in Month	Returns the number of days in the month for the date	Calculated Days in Month
Month ➤ Name of Month	Returns the name of the month for the date	Calculated Name of Month
Day ➤ Day	Extracts the day from the date	Calculated Day
Day ➤ Day of Week	Returns the weekday as a number (Monday is 1, Tuesday is 2, etc.)	Calculated Day of Week
Day ➤ Day of Year	Calculates the number of days since the start of the year for the date	Calculated Day of Year
Day ➤ Start of Day	Transforms the value to the start of the day for a date and time	Calculated Start of Day
Day ➤ End of Day	Transforms the value to the end of the day for a date and time	Calculated End of Day
Day ➤ Name of Day	Returns the weekday as a day of week	Calculated Name of Day
Quarter ➤ Quarter	Returns the calendar quarter of the year for the date	Calculated Quarter
Quarter ➤ Start of Quarter	Returns the first date of the calendar quarter of the year for the date	Calculated Start of Quarter
Quarter ➤ End of Quarter	Returns the last date of the calendar quarter of the year for the date	Calculated End of Quarter
Week ➤ Week of Year	Calculates the number of weeks since the start of the year for the date	Calculated Week of Year
Week ➤ Week of Month	Calculates the number of weeks since the start of the month for the date	Calculated Week of Month
Week ➤ Start of Week	Returns the date for the first day of the week (Monday) for the date	Calculated Start of Week
Week ➤ End of Week	Returns the date for the last day of the week (Sunday) for the date	Calculated End of Week

Time Transformations

You can also transform date/time or time values into their component parts using Power Query. This is extremely similar to how you apply date transformations, but in the interest of completeness, the following explains how to do this once the Query Editor is open for the Excel file Chapter07Sample1.xlsx:

1. Click inside the InvoiceDate column.

2. In the Transform ribbon, click the Time button. The menu will appear.

3. Click Hour. The hour part of the time will replace all the values in the InvoiceDate column.

Note   Time transformations can only be applied to columns of the date/time or time data types.

The range of time transformations is given in Table 7-8.

Table 7-8. *Time Transformations*

Transformation	Description	Applied Steps Definition
Time Only	Isolates the time part of a date and time	Extracted Time
Local Time	Converts the date/time to local time from date/time and timezone values	Extracted Local Time
Parse	Extracts the date and/or date/time elements from a text	Parsed DateTime
Hour ➤ Hour	Isolates the hour from a date/time or date value	Extracted Hour
Hour ➤ Start of Hour	Returns the start of the hour from a date/time or time value	Calculated Start of Hour
Hour ➤ End of Hour	Returns the end of the hour from a date/time or time value	Calculated End of Hour
Minute	Isolates the minute from a date/time or time value	Extracted Minute
Second	Isolates the second from a date/time or time value	Extracted Second
Earliest	Returns the earliest time from a date/time or time value	Calculated Earliest
Latest	Returns the latest time from a date/time or time value	Calculated Latest

Note   In the real world, you could well want to leave a source column intact and apply number or date transformations to a copy of the column. To do this, simply apply the same transformation technique, only use the buttons in the *Add Column* ribbon instead of those in the Transform ribbon.

Duration

If you have values in a column that can be interpreted as a duration (in days, hours, minutes, and seconds), then Power Query can extract the component parts of the duration as a data transformation. For this to work, however, the column *must* be set to the duration data type. This means that the contents of the column have to be interpreted as a duration by Power Query. Any values that are incompatible with this data type will be set to error values.

So, you are probably asking, what exactly does a duration look like? A duration is expressed as

- Days

- Hours

- Minutes

- Seconds

More specifically, a duration must be expressed in the form days. hours:minutes:seconds. So, for instance, a duration could be 11.23:5:45. This represents 11 days, 23 hours, 5 minutes, and 45 seconds.

There are a few caveats when dealing with durations:

- The figure for days is followed by a period—the other separators are colons.

- You cannot have the duration in hours greater than 23.

- You cannot have the duration in minutes or seconds greater than 60.

If you have duration data in a column in Power Query, you can extract its component parts like this:

1. Open a new, blank Excel file.

2. Click Data ➤ Get Data ➤ From File ➤ From Workbook and select the file C:\DataMashupWithExcelSamples\Durations.xlsx.

3. Click the worksheet Sheet1 and then click Transform Data to open the Query Editor. You will note that Power Query automatically adds a step that changes the data type of the DurationOnForecourt column to duration as it recognizes the data format.

4. Click inside the column DurationOnForecourt.

5. In the Transform ribbon, click the Duration button. The menu will appear.

6. Click Hours. The hour part of the time will replace all the values in the InvoiceDate column.

The range of duration transformations is given in Table 7-9.

Table 7-9. *Duration Transformations*

Transformation	Description	Applied Steps Definition
Days	Isolates the day element from a duration value	Extracted Days
Hours	Isolates the hour element from a duration value	Extracted Hours
Minutes	Isolates the minutes element from a duration value	Extracted Minutes
Seconds	Isolates the seconds element from a duration value	Extracted Seconds
Total Days	Displays the duration value as the number of days and a fraction representing hours, minutes, and seconds	Calculated Total Days
Total Hours	Displays the duration value as the number of hours and a fraction representing minutes and seconds	Calculated Total Hours

(continued)

Table 7-9. (*continued*)

Transformation	Description	Applied Steps Definition
Total Minutes	Displays the duration value as the number of minutes and a fraction representing seconds	Calculated Total Minutes
Total Seconds	Displays the duration value as the number of seconds and a fraction representing milliseconds	Calculated Total Seconds
Multiply	Multiplies the duration (and all its component parts) by a value that you enter	Multiplied Column
Divide	Divides the duration (and all its component parts) by a value that you enter	Divided Column
Statistics ➤ Sum	Returns the total for all the duration elements in the column	Calculated Sum
Statistics ➤ Minimum	Returns the minimum value of all the duration elements in the column	Calculated Minimum
Statistics ➤ Maximum	Returns the maximum value of all the duration elements in the column	Calculated Maximum
Statistics ➤ Median	Returns the median value for all the duration elements in the column	Calculated Median
Statistics ➤ Average	Returns the average for all the duration elements in the column	Calculated Average

Note   If you multiply or divide a duration, Power Query displays a dialog so that you can enter the value to multiply or divide the duration by.

Filling Down Empty Cells

Imagine a data source where the data has come into Power Query from a matrix-style structure. The result is that some columns only contain a single example of an element and then a series of empty cells until the next element in the list. If this is difficult to imagine, then take a look at the sample file CarMakeAndModelMatrix.xlsx shown in Figure 7-13.

Make	Marque	Sales
Aston Martin	DB4	391000
	DB7	500740
	DB9	915070
	DBS	230000
	Rapide	225000
	Vanquish	746500
	Vantage	320850
	Zagato	178500
Bentley	Arnage	44000
	Azure	239250
	Continental	991250
	Turbo R	347500
Jaguar	XJ12	303500
	XJ6	602000
	XK	1092250
MGB	GT	315000
Rolls Royce	Camargue	810300
	Phantom	178500
	Silver Ghost	649500
	Silver Seraph	288500
	Silver Shadow	308500
	Wraith	178500

Figure 7-13. *A matrix data table in Excel*

All these blank cells are a problem since you need a full data table without any blank cells in the dataset to analyze data in both Excel worksheets and the data model. Or rather, the blank cells would be an issue if Power Query did not have a really cool way of overcoming this particular difficulty. Do the following to solve this problem:

1. Open a new Excel file.

2. In the Data ribbon, click Get Data ➤ From File ➤ From Workbook.

3. In the Get Data dialog, select Excel. Then click Connect and navigate to C:\DataMashupWithExcelSamples\ CarMakeAndModelMatrix.xlsx.

4. Click Import, select Sheet1, and click Transform Data. This will open the Power Query Editor.

5. Select the column that contains the empty cells.

6. In the Transform ribbon, click Fill. The menu will appear.

7. Select Down. The blank cells will be replaced by the value in the first non-empty cell above. Filled Down will be added to the Applied Steps list.

The table will now look like Figure 7-14.

A^B_C Make	A^B_C Marque	1^2_3 Sales
Aston Martin	DB4	391000
Bentley	DB7	500740
Bentley	DB9	915070
Bentley	DBS	230000
Bentley	Rapide	225000
Bentley	Vanquish	746500
Bentley	Vantage	320850
Bentley	Zagato	178500
Bentley	Arnage	44000
Jaguar	Azure	239250
Jaguar	Continental	991250
Jaguar	Turbo R	347500
Jaguar	XJ12	303500
MGB	XJ6	602000
MGB	XK	1092250
MGB	GT	315000
Rolls Royce	Camargue	810300
Triumph	Phantom	178500
Triumph	Silver Ghost	649500
Triumph	Silver Seraph	288500
Triumph	Silver Shadow	308500
Triumph	Wraith	178500
Triumph	TR4	140500
TVR	TR5	98250
TVR	TR7	47750
TVR	Cerbera	89250
null	Tuscan	112250

Figure 7-14. *A data table with empty cells replaced by the correct data*

Note   This technique is built to handle a fairly specific problem and only really works if the imported data is grouped by the column containing the missing elements.

Although rare, you can also use this technique to fill empty cells with the value from below. If you need to do this, just select Fill ➤ Up from the Transform ribbon. In either case, you need to be aware that the technique is applied to the entire column.

Extracting Part of a Column's Contents

There could well be times when the contents of a source column contain more data than you actually need. In cases like this, Power Query can help you by extracting only part of a column. This technique works like this:

1. Load the C:\DataMashupWithExcelSamples\Chapter07Example1. xlsx sample file.

2. Display the Queries & Connections pane by clicking Queries & Connections in the Data ribbon.

3. Double-click the BaseData query to switch to the Query Editor.

4. Click inside the InvoiceNumber column. As you can see, the invoice number is composed of multiple elements, each separated by a hyphen.

5. In the Transform ribbon, click Extract ➤ Text Before Delimiter. The Text Before Delimiter dialog will be displayed.

6. Enter a hyphen (or a minus sign) in the Delimiter field. The dialog will look like Figure 7-15.

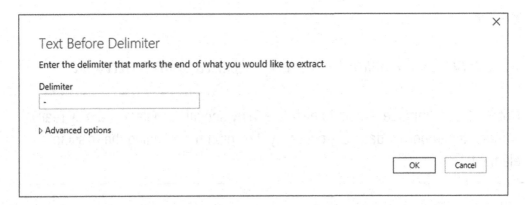

Figure 7-15. *The Text Before Delimiter dialog*

7. Click OK. The contents of the field will be replaced by the characters before the hyphen. A step named Extracted Text Before Delimiter will be added to the Applied Steps list.

The Extract function allows you to choose from a variety of ways in which you can extract a subset of data from a column. The currently available options are explained in Table 7-10.

Table 7-10. *Extract Transformations*

Transformation	Description	Applied Steps Definition
Length	Displays the length in characters of the contents of the field	Extracted Length
First Characters	Displays a specified number of characters from the left of the field	Extracted First Characters
Last Characters	Displays a specified number of characters from the right of the field	Extracted Last Characters
Range	Displays a specified number of characters between a specified start and end position (in characters, from the left of the field)	Extracted Range
Text Before Delimiter	Displays all the text occurring before a specified character	Extracted Text Before Delimiter
Text After Delimiter	Displays all the text occurring after a specified character	Extracted Text After Delimiter
Text Between Delimiters	Displays all the text occurring between two specified characters	Extracted Text Between Delimiters

Advanced Extract Options

Three of the Extract options (Text Before Delimiter, Text After Delimiter, and Text Between Delimiters) let you apply some advanced options that allow you to push the envelope even further when extracting data from a column. These techniques are explained in the following two sections.

Text Before and After Delimiter

If you are extracting data from the middle of a column and you are using a delimiter to isolate the text you want to keep, then you have a couple of additional options available.

You can access these options from the dialog that you saw in Figure 7-15 by clicking Advanced options. The dialog will then look like the one shown in Figure 7-16.

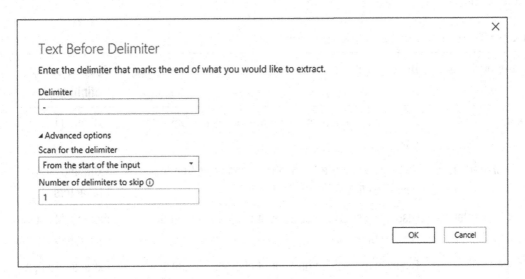

Figure 7-16. *The Advanced options of the Text Before and Text After Delimiter dialogs*

The two options that you now have are

- *Scan for the delimiter:* This option lets you choose between working forward from the start of the contents of the column and working backward from the end of the contents of the column to locate the delimiter you are searching for.

- *Number of delimiters to skip:* Here you can specify that it is the *n*th occurrence of a delimiter that interests you.

Text Between Delimiters

The Advanced options of the Text Between Delimiters dialog essentially lets you apply the same options that you saw previously, only for both the initial delimiter and the final delimiter. In Figure 7-17 you can see this in the Text Between Delimiters dialog.

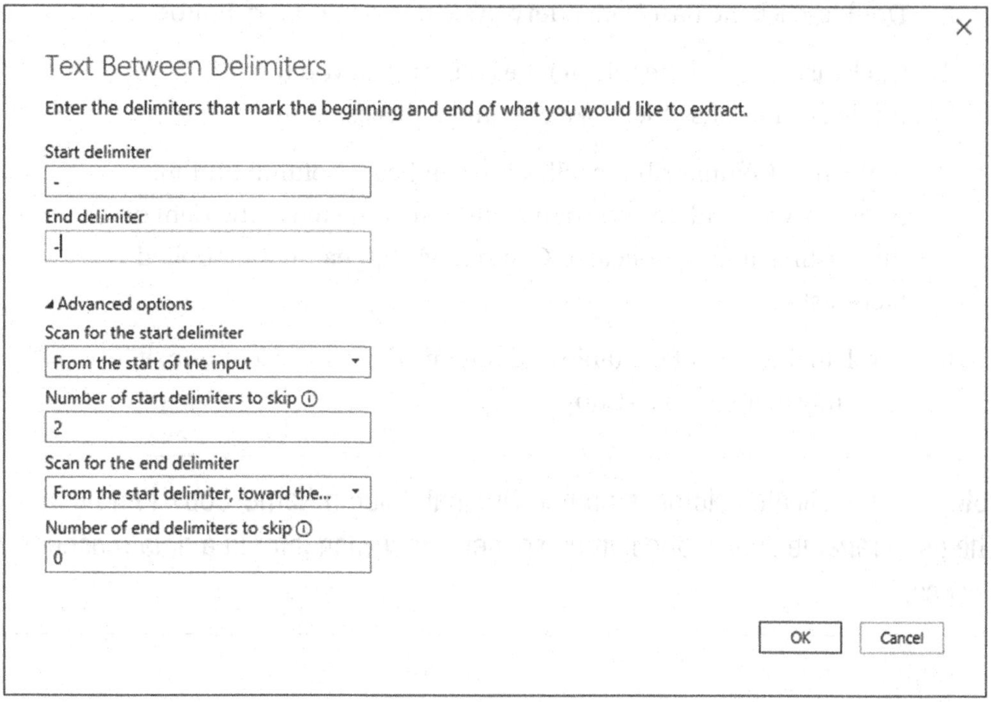

Figure 7-17. *The Advanced options of the Text Between Delimiters dialog*

Note   The Extract button can be found in both the Transform and New Column ribbons. If you carry out this operation from the Transform ribbon, then the contents of the existing column will be replaced. If you use the button in the Add Column ribbon, then a new column containing the extracted text will be added at the right of any existing columns.

Duplicating Columns

Sometimes you just need a simple copy of a column, with nothing added and nothing taken away. This is where the Duplicate Column button comes into play.

1. Load the C:\DataMashupWithExcelSamples\Chapter07 Example1.xlsx sample file.

2. Switch to the Data ribbon and click Queries & Connections to display the Queries & Connections pane (unless it is already visible).

3. Double-click the BaseData query to switch to the Query Editor.

4. Click inside (or on the title of) the column that you want to duplicate. I will use the Make column in this example.

5. In the Add Column ribbon, click the Duplicate Column button. After a few seconds, a copy of the column is created at the right of the existing table. Duplicated Column will appear in the Applied Steps list.

6. Scroll to the right of the table and rename the existing column; it is currently named Make-Copy.

Note   The duplicate column is named Original Column Name-Copy. I find that it helps to rename copies of columns sooner rather than later in a data mashup process.

Splitting Columns

Sometimes a source column contains data that you really need to break up into smaller pieces across two or more columns. The following are classic cases where this happens:

- A column contains a list of elements, separated by a specific character (known as a *delimiter*).

- A column contains a list of elements, but the elements can be divided at specific places in the column.

- A column contains a concatenated text that needs to be split into its composite elements (a bank account number or a Social Security number is an example of this).

The following short sections explain how to handle such eventualities.

Splitting Column by a Delimiter

Here is another requirement that you may encounter occasionally. The data that has been imported has a column that needs to be further split into multiple columns, and you want this to happen automatically. Imagine a text file where columns are separated by semicolons, and these subdivisions each contain a column that holds a comma-separated list of elements. Once you have imported the file, you then need to further separate the contents of this column that uses a different delimiter.

Here is what you can do to split the data from one column over several columns:

1. Open a new Excel file.

2. In the Data ribbon, click Get Data ➤ From File ➤ From Workbook.

3. Select the C:\DataMashupWithExcelSamples\DataToParse.xlsx sample file in the Query Editor.

4. Click the ClientList workbook.

5. Click Transform Data to open the Query Editor.

6. In the Transform ribbon, click Use First Row as Headers.

7. Click inside the ClientList column. You can see that this column contains several data elements, each separated by a semicolon.

8. In the Transform ribbon, click Split Column ➤ By Delimiter. The Split Column by Delimiter dialog appears.

9. Select Semicolon from the list of available options in the "Select or enter delimiter" popup (although the Query Editor could well have detected this already).

10. Click "Each occurrence of the delimiter" as the location to split the text column. The dialog should look like Figure 7-18.

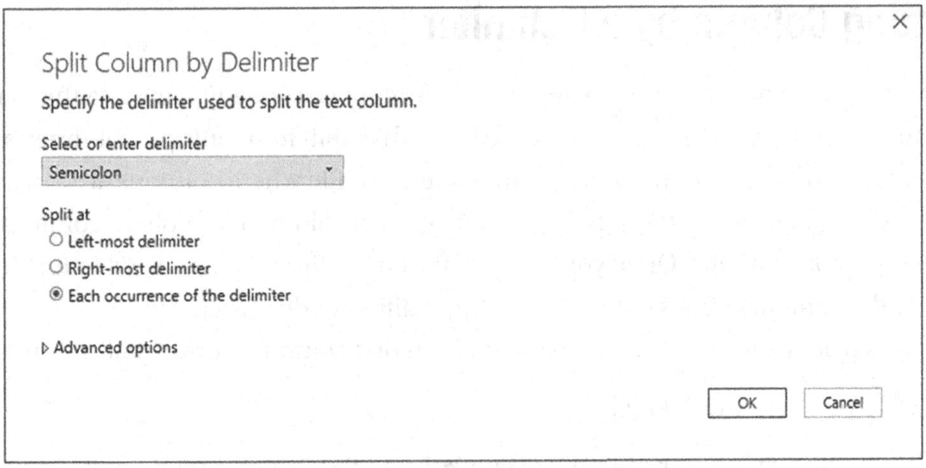

Figure 7-18. *Splitting a column using a delimiter*

11. Click OK. Split Column by Delimiter will appear in the Applied
     Steps list.

The initial column is replaced and all the new columns are named ClientList.1,
ClientList.2, and so forth. As many additional columns as there are delimiters are
created; each is named (*Column.n*) and is sequentially numbered. The result of this
operation looks like Figure 7-19.

	ABC ClientList.1	ABC ClientList.2	ABC ClientList.3	ABC ClientList.4
1	Aldo Motors	Uttoxeter	Staffs	ST17 99RZ
2	Honest John	London		NSW1 1A
3	Bright Orange	Birmingham	NULL	B1 50AZ
4	Cut'n'Shut	Manchester	NULL	M1 5AZ
5	Wheels'R'Us	London	NULL	SE1 4YY
6	Les Arnaqueurs	Paris	NULL	75010
7	Crippen & Co	Glasgow	NULL	G1 8GH
8	Rocky Riding	New York	New York	NULL
9	Voitures Diplomatiques S.A.	Geneva	NULL	NULL
10	Karz	Stuttgart	NULL	NULL
11	Costa Del Speed	Madrid	NULL	NULL
12	Olde Englande	Shrewsbury	NULL	SY10 9AX
13	Impressive Wheels	Liverpool	NULL	L5 9ZZ

Figure 7-19. *The results of splitting a column*

This particular process has several options, and their consequences can be fairly far-reaching as far as the data is concerned. Table 7-11 contains a description of the available options.

Table 7-11. *Delimiter Split Options*

Option	Description
Colon	Uses the colon (:) as the delimiter
Comma	Uses the comma (,) as the delimiter
Equals Sign	Uses the equals sign (=) as the delimiter
Semi-Colon	Uses the semicolon (;) as the delimiter
Space	Uses the space ( ) as the delimiter
Tab	Uses the tab character as the delimiter
Custom	Lets you enter a custom delimiter
At the Left-Most Delimiter	Splits the column once only at the first occurrence of the delimiter
At the Right-Most Delimiter	Splits the column once only at the last occurrence of the delimiter
At Each Occurrence of the Delimiter	Splits the column into as many columns as there are delimiters
Split into Columns	This leaves the number of rows as it is in the dataset and creates new columns for each new element resulting from the split operation
Split into Rows	Creates a new row for each new element resulting from the split operation and duplicates the existing record as many times as there are split elements

Advanced Options for Delimiter Split

There are a small number of advanced options that are available when splitting text by delimiters. These are displayed when you click the Advanced options element in the Split Column by Delimiter dialog and are explained in Table 7-12.

Table 7-12. *Delimiter Split Options*

Advanced options ➤ Number of Columns to Split Into	Allows you to set a maximum number of columns into which the data is split in chunks of the given number of characters. Any extra columns are placed in the rightmost column
Advanced options ➤ Quote Character	Separators inside a text that is contained in double quotes are not used to split the text into columns. Setting this option to "none" will split elements inside quotes
Split using special characters	Enables the Insert Special Character button. You can then click this button and select the special character to split data on. The choice is between Tab, Carriage Return, Line-Feed, Carriage Return and Line-Feed, and Non-breaking Space

Splitting Columns by Number of Characters

Another variant on this theme is when text in each column is a fixed number of characters and needs to be broken down into constituent parts at specific intervals. Suppose, for instance, that you have a field where each group of (a certain number of) characters has a specific meaning, and you want to break it into multiple columns. Alternatively, suppose you want to extract the leftmost or rightmost n characters and leave the rest. A bank account or Social Security number is an example of this. This is where splitting a column by the number of characters can come in useful. As the principle is very similar to the process that we just saw, I will not repeat the whole thing again. All you have to do is choose the "By number of characters" menu option at step 8 in the previous exercise. Options for this type of operation are given in Table 7-13.

Table 7-13. *Options When Splitting a Column by Number of Characters*

Option	Description
Number of Characters	Lets you define the number of characters of data before splitting the column
Once, As Far Left As Possible	Splits the column once only at the given number of characters in from the left (if the length of the data in the row allows this)
Once, As Far Right As Possible	Splits the column once only at the given number of characters in from the right (if the length of the data in the row allows this)
Repeatedly	Splits the column as many times as necessary to cut it into segments every defined number of characters
Advanced options ➤ Number of Columns to Split Into	Allows you to set a maximum number of columns into which the data is split in chunks of the given number of characters. Any extra columns are placed in the rightmost column
Split into Columns	This leaves the number of rows as it is in the dataset and crates new columns for each new element resulting from the split operation
Split into Rows	Creates a new row for each new element resulting from the split operation and duplicates the existing record as many times as there are split elements

There are a couple of things to note when splitting columns:

- When splitting by a delimiter, Power Query makes a good attempt at guessing the maximum number of columns into which the source column must be split. If it gets this wrong (and you can see what its guesstimate is if you expand the Advanced options box), you can override the number here.

- If you select a Custom Delimiter, Power Query displays a new box in the dialog where you can enter a specific delimiter.

- Not every record has to have the same number of delimiters. Power Query simply leaves the rightmost column(s) blank if there are fewer split elements for a row.

Note   You can only split columns if they are text data. The Split Column button remains grayed out if your intention is to try to split a date or numeric column. You can, however, convert the data type from a date, datetime, or numeric data type to a text data type before splitting a column.

Merging Columns

You may be feeling a certain sense of déjà vu when you read the title of this section. After all, we saw how to merge columns (i.e., how to fuse the data from several columns into a single, wider column) in a previous chapter, did we not?

Yes, we did indeed. However, this is not the only time in this chapter that you will see something that you have tried previously. This is because Power Query repeats several of the options that are in the Transform ribbon in the Add Column ribbon. While these functions all work in much the same way, there is one essential difference. If you select an option from the Transform ribbon, then the column(s) that you selected is *modified*. If you select a similar option from the Add Column ribbon, then the original column(s) will not be altered, but a *new column* is added containing the results of the data transformation.

Merging columns is a case in point. Now, as I went into detail as to how to execute this kind of data transformation in the previous chapter, I will not describe it all over again here. Suffice it to say, if you Ctrl-click the headings of two or more columns and then click Merge Columns in the Add Column ribbon, you will still see the data from the selected columns concatenated into a single column. However, this time the original columns *remain* in the dataset. The new column is named Merged, exactly as was the case for the first of the columns that you selected when merging columns using the Transform ribbon.

The following are other functions that can either overwrite the data in existing columns *or* display the result as a new column:

- *Format*: Trims or changes the capitalization of text

- *Extract*: Takes part of a column and creates another column from this data

- *Parse*: Adds a column containing the source column data as JSON or XML strings

- *Statistics*: Creates a new column of aggregated numeric values

- *Standard*: Creates a new column of calculated numeric values

- *Scientific*: Creates a new column by applying certain kinds of math operations to the values in a column

- *Trigonometry*: Creates a new column by applying certain kinds of trigonometric operations to the values in a column

- *Rounding*: Creates a new column by rounding the values in a column

- *Information*: Creates a new column indicating arithmetical information about the values in a column

- *Date*: Creates a new column by extracting date elements from the values in a date column

- *Time*: Creates a new column by extracting time elements from the values in a time or date/time column

- *Duration*: Creates a new column by calculating the duration between two dates or date/times.

When transforming data, the art is to decide whether you want or need to keep the original column before applying one of these functions. Yet, once again, it is not really fundamental if you later decide that you made an incorrect decision, as you can always backtrack. Alternatively, you can always decide to insert new columns as a matter of principle and delete any columns that you really do not need at a later stage in the data transformation process.

Creating Columns from Examples

Creating your own columns can be a little scary if you have not had much previous experience with Excel or Power Pivot formulas, so the Power Query development team has tried to make your life easier by adding another way to create custom columns. Instead of referring to columns by the column name (and having to handle square brackets and other peculiar characters), you can build a new column by using the actual data in a row.

The following steps show an example of how to do this:

1. Load the C:\DataMashupWithExcelSamples\Chapter07Example1. xlsx sample file.

2. Display the Queries & Connections pane if necessary by clicking Queries & Connections in the Data ribbon.

3. Double-click the BaseData query to switch to the Query Editor.

4. In the Add Column ribbon, click Column From Examples. A new kind of formula bar will appear above the data. It will look like Figure 7-20. At the same time, a new, empty column will be created at the right of the existing data.

Figure 7-20. *Creating a column from examples*

5. Double-click the new column on the right. A list of data from each field will be displayed, as shown in Figure 7-21.

Figure 7-21. *Displaying the data from a row when creating a column from examples*

6. Double-click Red to select the data from the Color column.

7. Enter a space, a hyphen, and a space, then type **Camargue** (this is the name of the model for this row).

8. Click OK in the formula bar at the top.

Power Query will add a new column containing the color, a separator, and the Model. Inserted Merged Column will be added as a new step in the Applied Steps list. In fact, what Power Query has done is to *use the column contents as a proxy for the column name*.

Note   In the popup menu for the Column from Examples button, you can choose to take all existing columns as the basis for the example or only any columns that you have previously selected.

As you can see from this short example, creating columns by example lets you use the *data from a column rather than the column name*. It also removes the need for double quotes and ampersand characters that you had to use when writing the code to create a new column in the previous section.

Tip   If you select Column From Examples ➤ From Selection, then you will only see data from the selected columns when you double-click inside the new column to see samples of data as you did in step 6 of this example.

Adding Conditional Columns

Not all additional columns are a simple extraction or concatenation of existing data. There will be times when you will want to apply some simple conditions that define the contents of a new column. This is where Power Query's Conditional Column function comes into its own.

Conditional Columns are probably best understood with the aid of a practical example. So let's suppose that you want to add a column that contains a comment on the type of buyer for Brilliant British Cars's products. Here is how you can do this:

1. Load the C:\DataMashupWithExcelSamples\Chapter07Example1.xlsx sample file.

2. Display the Queries & Connections pane (if required) by clicking Queries & Connections in the Data ribbon.

3. Double-click the BaseData query to switch to the Query Editor.

4. In the Add Column ribbon, click Conditional Column. The Add Conditional Column dialog will appear.

5. Enter **BuyerType** in the "New column name" field.

6. Select Make as the column name.

7. Leave equals as the operator.

8. Enter **Rolls Royce** as the value.

9. Enter **Posh** as the output.

10. Click Add Clause.

11. Select Make as the column name, leave equals as the operator, enter **Bentley** as the value, and add **Classy** as the output.

12. Enter **Bling** in the Else field. The dialog will look like Figure 7-22.

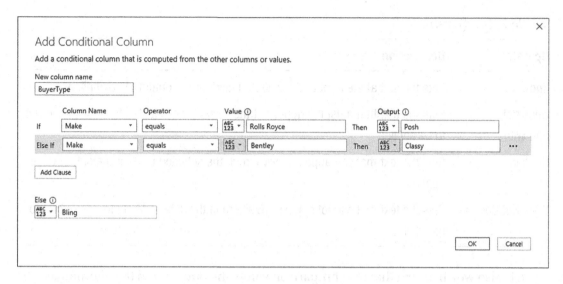

Figure 7-22. *The Add Conditional Column dialog*

13. Click OK. The new column will be added containing either Posh, Classy, or Bling, depending on the make for each record. Added Conditional Columns will appear as the new step in the Applied Steps list.

As you can see from the Add Conditional Column dialog, it has a range of options that you can tweak when defining the logic for the data matching. These options are outlined in Table 7-14.

Table 7-14. *Custom Column Operators*

Operator	Description
Equals	Sets the text that must match the contents of the selected field for the output to be applied
Does Not Equal	Sets the text that must not match the contents of the selected field for the output to be applied
Begins With	Sets the text at the left of the selected field for the output to be applied
Does Not Begin With	Sets the text that must not appear at the left of the selected field for the output to be applied

(continued)

Table 7-14. (*continued*)

Operator	Description
Ends With	Sets the text at the right of the selected field for the output to be applied
Does Not End With	Sets the text that must not appear at the right of the selected field for the output to be applied
Contains	Sets the text that can appear anywhere in the selected field for the output to be applied
Does Not Contain	Sets the text that cannot appear anywhere in the selected field for the output to be applied

It is also worth noting that the comparison value, the output, and the alternative output can be values (as was the case in this example), columns, or parameters (which you will learn about in Chapter 9). If you want to remove a rule, simply click the ellipses at the right of the required rule and select Delete.

Tip   Should you wish to alter the order of the rules in the Add Conditional Column dialog, all you have to do is click the ellipses at the right of the selected rule and select Move Up or Move Down from the popup menu.

Index Columns

An index column is a new column that numbers every record in the table sequentially. This numbering scheme applies to the table, because it is currently sorted and begins at zero. There are many situations where an index column can be useful. The following are some examples:

- Reapply a previous sort order.

- Create a unique reference for every record.

- Prepare a recordset for use as a dimension table in a Power Pivot data model. In cases like this, the index column becomes what dimensional modelers call a *surrogate key*.

This list is not intended to be exhaustive in any way; you will almost certainly find other uses as you work with Power Query. Whatever the need, here is how to add an index column inside Power Query:

1. In the Add Column ribbon, click Index Column. The new, sequentially numbered column is added at the right of the table, and Added Index is added to the Applied Steps list.

2. Scroll to the right of the table and rename the index column; it is currently named Index.

You have a fairly free hand when it comes to deciding how to begin numbering an index column. The choices are as follows:

- Start at 0 and increment by a value of 1 for each row.

- Start at 1 and increment by a value of 1 for each row.

- Start at any number and increase by any number.

As you saw when adding Index columns, the default is for Power Query to begin numbering rows at 0. However, you can choose another option by clicking the small triangle to the right of the Add Index Column button. This displays a menu with the three options outlined.

Selecting the third option, Custom, displays the dialog that you see in Figure 7-23.

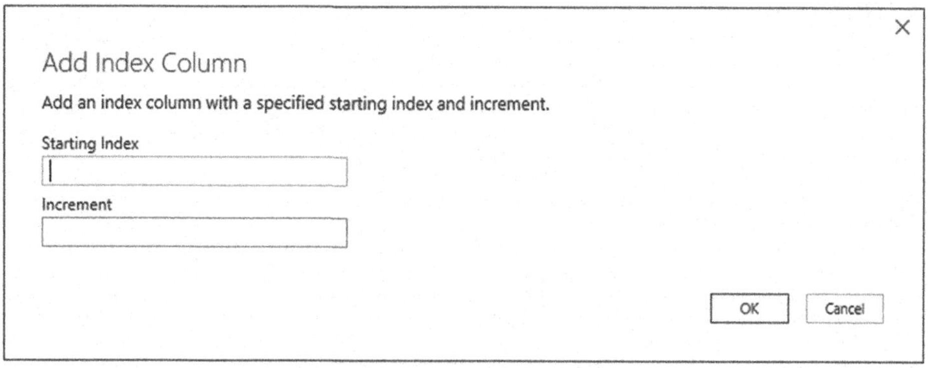

Figure 7-23. *The Add Index Column dialog*

This dialog lets you specify the start number for the first row in the dataset as well as the increment that is added for each record.

Conclusion

In this chapter, you learned some essential techniques that you can use to cleanse and structure datasets. You saw how to round numbers up and down, how to deliver conformed text presentation, and how to remove extraneous spaces and nonprinting characters from columns of data.

You also saw how to replace values inside columns, as well as ways of applying mathematical, statistical, and trigonometric functions to numbers. Other techniques covered extracting date, time, and duration elements from date/time and duration columns.

Finally, you saw a series of techniques that help you to add new columns based on the data in existing columns. These range from simple copies of an entire column or combining columns to extracting parts of a column's data or even deducing different data that is added to a new column using simple logic.

It is now time to see how you can join hitherto separate datasets into single queries and parse complex data types to add them to a dataset. You will even learn how to append multiple files in a single query and how to pivot and unpivot data. All of this will be the subject of the next chapter.

CHAPTER 8

Restructuring Data

In the previous two chapters, you saw how to hone your dataset in Power Query so that you defined only the rows and columns of data that you really need as the basis for your analysis. Then you learned how to cleanse and complete the data that they contain. In this chapter, you will learn how to build on these foundations to deliver data that is ready to be molded into a structured and usable data model.

The generic term for this kind of data preparation in Power Query is *restructuring data*. It covers the following:

- *Joining queries*: This involves taking two queries and linking them so that you display the data from both sources as a single dataset. You will learn how to extend a query with multiple columns from a second query as well as how to aggregate the data from a second query and add this to the initial dataset. You will also see how to create complex joins when merging queries.

- *Pivoting and unpivoting data*: If you need to switch data in rows to display as columns—or vice versa—then you can get the Power Query Editor to help you do exactly this. This means that you can guarantee that the data in all the tables that you are using conforms to a standardized tabular structure that is essential for Power Query to function efficiently.

- *Transposing data*: This can be required to switch columns into rows and vice versa.

© Adam Aspin 2020
A. Aspin, *Data Mashup with Microsoft Excel Using Power Query and M*,
https://doi.org/10.1007/978-1-4842-6018-0_8

These techniques can be—and probably will be—used alongside many of the techniques that you saw previously in Chapters 6 and 7. After all, one of the great strengths of Power Query is that it recognizes that data transformation is a complex business and consequently does not impose any strict way of working. Indeed, it lets you experiment freely with a multitude of data transformation options. So remember that you are at liberty to take any approach you want when transforming source data. The only thing that matters is that you use it to give you the result that you want.

The Power Query Editor View Ribbon

Until now, we have concentrated our attention on the Power Query Editor Home, Transform, and Add Column ribbons. This is for the good and simple reason that these ribbons are where nearly all the action takes place. There is, however, a fourth essential Power Query Editor ribbon—the View ribbon. The buttons that it contains are shown in Figure 8-1, and the options are explained in Table 8-1.

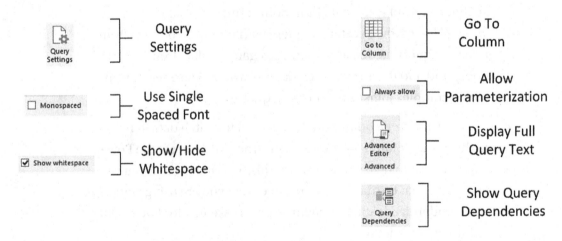

Figure 8-1. *The Power Query View ribbon*

Table 8-1. *Power Query View Ribbon Options*

Option	Description
Query Settings	Displays or hides the Query Settings pane at the right of the Power Query window. This includes the Applied Steps list
Monospaced	Displays previews in a monospaced font
Show whitespace	Displays whitespace and new line characters
Go to Column	Allows you to select a specific column
Always allow	Allows parameterization in data source and transformation dialogs. Parameterization is the subject of Chapter 11
Advanced Editor	Displays the Advanced Editor dialog containing all the code for the steps in the query
Query Dependencies	Displays the sequence of query links and dependencies

Possibly the only option that is not immediately self-explanatory is the Advanced Editor button. It displays the code for all the transformations in the query as a single block of "M" language script. You will learn more about this in Chapter 12.

Tip   Personally, I find that the Query Settings pane and the formula bar are too vital to be removed from the Power Query window when transforming data. Consequently, I tend to leave them visible. If you need the screen real estate, however, then you can always hide them for a while.

Merging Data

Until now, we have treated each individual query as if it existed in isolation. The reality, of course, is that you will frequently be required to use the output of one query in conjunction with the output of another to join data from different sources in various ways. Assuming that the results of one query share a common field (or fields) with another query, you can "join" queries into a single "flattened" data table. Power Query calls this a merge operation, and it enables you, among other things, to

- Look up data elements in another "reference" table to add lookup data. For example, you may want to add a client name where only the client reference code or number exists in your main table.

- Aggregate data from a "detail" table (such as invoice lines) and include the totals in a higher-grained table, such as a table of invoices.

Here, again, the process is not difficult. The only fundamental factor is that the two tables, or queries, that you are merging must have a shared field or fields that enable the two tables to match records coherently. Let's look at a couple of examples.

Extending a Query with Merged Data

First, let's try extending an existing query by adding linked data from a second query:

1. In a new, empty Excel file, use Power Query to connect to both the worksheets in the C:\DataMashupWithExcelSamples\SalesData. xlsx Excel file. These are Sales and Clients.

2. Do not load the data, but click the Transform data button in the Home ribbon. This will display the two separate source datasets in the Power Query Editor.

3. Click the query named Sales in the Queries pane of the Power Query window.

4. Click the Merge Queries button in the Home ribbon. The Merge dialog will appear.

5. In the upper part of the dialog—where an overview of the output from the current query is displayed—scroll to the right and click the ClientName column title. This column is highlighted.

6. In the popup under the upper table, select the Clients query. The output from this query will appear in the lower part of the dialog.

7. In the lower table, select the column title for the column—the join column—that maps to the column that you selected in step 5. This will also be the ClientName column. This column is then selected in the lower table.

8. Select Inner (only matching rows) from the Join Kind popup menu. The dialog will look like Figure 8-2.

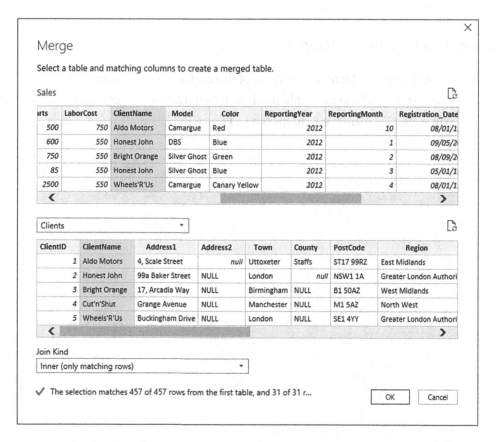

Figure 8-2. *The Merge dialog*

9. Click OK. A new column is added to the right of the existing data table. It is named Clients—representing the merged table.

10. Scroll to the right of the existing data table. The new column that has just been created from the merge step contains the word Table in every cell. This column will look something like Figure 8-3.

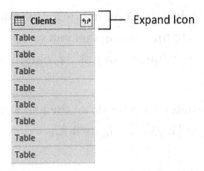

Figure 8-3. *A new, merged column*

11. Click the Expand icon to the right of the added column name. The popup list of all the available fields in this data table (or query, if you prefer) is displayed, as shown in Figure 8-4.

Figure 8-4. *The fields available in a joined query*

12. Ensure that the Expand radio button is selected.

13. Clear the selection of all the columns by unchecking the (Select All Columns) check box.

14. Select the following columns:

    a. ClientSize

    b. ClientSince

15. Uncheck Use original column name as prefix.

16. Click OK. The selected columns from the merged table are added to the main table, and the link to the reference table (the new column) is removed.

17. Rename the columns that have been added if necessary. The result should look like that in Figure 8-5.

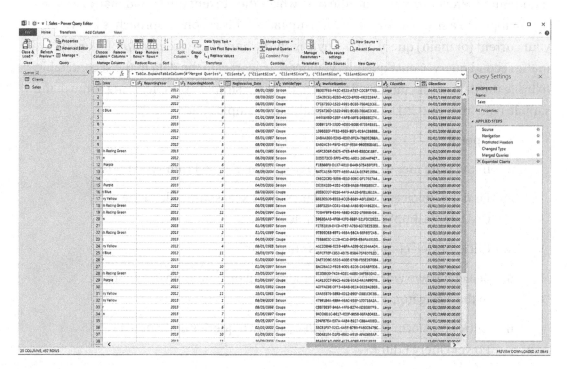

***Figure 8-5.** Merged column output*

You now have a single table of data that contains data from two linked data sources. Reprocessing the Sales query will also reprocess the dependent *clients* query and result in the latest version of the data being reloaded.

It is worth noting that it is not necessary to select from the second query any columns that you have already selected from the first query or you will simply return duplicate columns.

Note   You probably noticed that the Merge dialog indicated how many matching records there were in the two queries. This can be a useful indication that you have selected the correct column(s) to join the two queries.

Aggregating Data During a Merge Operation

If you are not just looking up reference data but need to aggregate data from a separate table and then add the results to the current query, then the process is largely similar. This second approach, however, is designed to suit another completely different requirement. Previously, you saw the case where the current query had many records that mapped to a *single* record in the lookup table. This second approach is for when your current (or main) query has a single record where there are *multiple* linked records in the second query. Consequently, you need to aggregate the data in the second table to bring the data across into the first table. Here is a simple example, using some of the sample data from the C:\DataMashupWithExcelSamples folder:

1.   Open a new Excel worksheet.

2.   In the Data menu, click Get Data ➤ From File ➤ From Workbook.

3.   Find the InvoicesAndInvoiceLines.xlsx Excel source file in the C:\DataMashupWithExcelSamples folder.

4.   Click the Select multiple items check box.

5.   Select the two worksheets it contains (Invoices and InvoiceLines) in the Navigator.

6.   Click Transform Data. This will create two queries and open the Power Query Editor.

7.   Click the query named Invoices in the Queries pane on the left.

8.   In the Home ribbon, click the Merge Queries button. The Merge dialog will open. You will see some of the data from the Invoices dataset in the upper part of the dialog.

9.   Click anywhere inside the InvoiceID column. This column is selected.

10. In the popup, select the InvoiceLines query. You will see some of the data from the InvoiceLines dataset in the lower part of the dialog.

11. Click anywhere inside the InvoiceID column for the lower table. This column is selected.

12. Select Inner (only matching rows) from the Join Kind popup menu. The dialog will look like Figure 8-6.

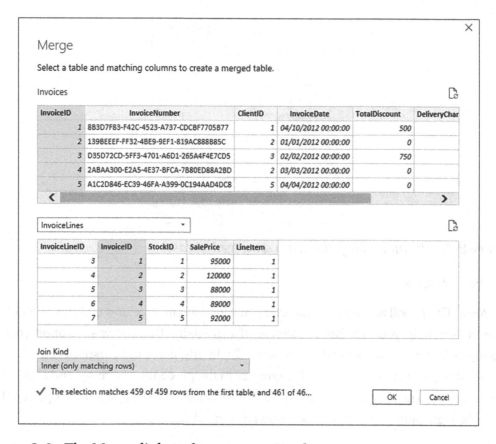

Figure 8-6. *The Merge dialog when aggregating data*

13. Click OK. The Merge dialog will close and a new column named InvoiceLines will be added at the right of the Invoices query.

14. Scroll to the right of the existing data table. You will see the new column (named InvoiceLines) that contains the word *Table* in every cell.

15. Click the Expand icon to the right of the new column title (the two arrows facing left and right). The popup list of all the available fields in the InvoiceLines query is displayed.

16. Select the Aggregate radio button.

17. Select the Sum of SalePrice field and uncheck all the others.

18. Uncheck the "Use original column name as prefix" check box. The dialog will look like Figure 8-7.

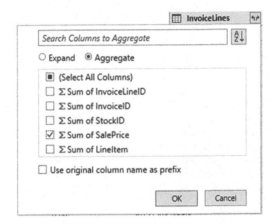

Figure 8-7. *The available fields from a merged dataset*

19. Click OK.

Power Query will add up the total sale price for each invoice and add this as a new column. Naturally, you can choose the type of aggregation that you wish to apply (before clicking OK), if the sum is not what you want. To do this, place the cursor over the column that you want to aggregate (see step 11 in the preceding exercise) and click the popup menu at the right of the field name. Power Query will suggest a set of options. The available aggregation options are explained in Table 8-2.

Table 8-2. *Merge Aggregation Options*

Option	Description
Sum	Returns the total value of the field
Average	Returns the average value of the field
Median	Returns the median value of the field
Minimum	Returns the minimum value of the field
Maximum	Returns the maximum value of the field
Count (All)	Counts all records in the dataset
Count (Not Blank)	Counts all records in the dataset that are not empty

Tip   If you loaded the data instead of editing the query in step 1, simply click the Transform Data button in the Home ribbon to switch to the Query Editor.

The merge process that you have just seen, while not complex in itself, suddenly opens up many new horizons. It means that you can now create multiple separate queries that you can then use together to expand your data in ways that allow you to prepare quite complex datasets.

Here are a couple of comments I need to make about the merge operation:

- Only queries that have been previously created in the Power Query window can be used when merging datasets. So remember to connect to all the datasets that you require before attempting a merge operation.

- Refreshing a query will cause any other queries that are merged into this query to be refreshed also. This way you will always get the most up-to-date data from all the queries in the process.

Merge as a New Query

In the two previous sections, you extended an existing query by adding data from another query. A final variation on the theme of merging queries is to create a completely new query based on the result of merging two source queries. The advantage of this approach is that it leaves the source queries intact either to reuse in yet other queries or to revert to more easily should the new merged query not give the required results.

1. Follow steps 1 through 3 from the section "Extending a Query with Merged Data."

2. In the Home ribbon, click the small triangle at the right of the Merge Queries button. You can see the available options in the popup menu in Figure 8-8.

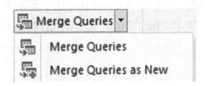

Figure 8-8. *Merging tables as a new query*

3. Select Merge Queries as New.

4. Continue with steps 5 through 17 from the section "Extending a Query with Merged Data."

This will create a new query (named Merge—but you can rename it later) and leave the initial queries intact.

This approach can be more fluid and agile than simply extending an existing query. You can rest assured that if you refresh the data, the new merged query will also be refreshed as part of the process.

Types of Join

When merging queries—either to join data or to aggregate values—you are faced with a choice when it comes to how to link the two queries. The choice of join can have a profound effect on the resulting dataset. Consequently, it is important to understand the six join types that are available. These are described in Table 8-3.

248

Table 8-3. *Join Types*

Join Type	Explanation
Left Outer	Keeps all records in the upper dataset in the Merge dialog (the dataset that was active when you began the merge operation). Any matching rows (those that share common values in the join columns) from the second dataset are kept. All other rows from the second dataset are discarded
Right Outer	Keeps all records in the lower dataset in the Merge dialog (the dataset that was not active when you began the merge operation). Any matching rows (those that share common values in the join columns) from the upper dataset are kept. All other rows from the upper dataset (the dataset that was active when you began the merge operation) are discarded
Full Outer	All rows from both queries are retained in the resulting dataset. Any records that do not share common values in the join field(s) contain blanks in certain columns
Inner	Only joins queries where there is an exact match on the column(s) that are selected for the join. Any rows from either query that do not share common values in the join column(s) are discarded
Left Anti	Keeps only rows from the upper (first) query
Right Anti	Keeps only rows from the lower (second) query

Note   When you use any of the *outer* joins, you are keeping records that do not have any corresponding records in the second query. Consequently, the resulting dataset contains empty values for some of the columns.

When you are expanding the column that is the link to a merged dataset, you have a couple of useful options that are worth knowing about:

- Use original column name as prefix
- Search columns to expand

Use the Original Column Name as the Prefix

You will probably find that some columns from joined queries can have the same names in both source datasets. It follows that you need to identify which column came from which dataset. If you leave the check box selected for the "Use original column name as prefix" merge option (which is the default), any merged columns will include the source query name to help you identify the data more accurately.

If you find that these longer column names only get in the way, you can unselect this check box. This will leave the added columns from the second query with their original names. However, because Power Query cannot accept duplicate column names, any new columns will have .1, .2, and so forth added to the column name.

Search Columns to Expand

If you are merging a query with a second query that contains a large number of columns, then it can be laborious to scroll down to locate the columns that you want to include. To narrow your search, you can enter a few characters from the name of the column that you are looking for in the Search columns to aggregate box. The more characters you type, the fewer matching columns are displayed in the Expansion popup dialog.

Joining on Multiple Columns

In the examples so far, you only joined queries on a single column. While this may be possible if you are looking at data that comes from a clearly structured source (such as a relational database), you may need to extend the principle when joining queries from diverse sources. Fortunately, Power Query allows you to join queries on *multiple* columns when the need arises.

As an example of this, the sample data contains a file that I have prepared as an example of how to join queries on more than one column. This sample file contains data from the sources that you saw in previous chapters. However, they have been modeled as a data warehouse star schema. To complete the model, you need to join a dimension named Geography to a fact table named Sales so that you can add the field GeographySK to the fact table. However, the Sales table and the Geography table share three fields (Country, Region, and Town) that must correspond for the queries to be joined. The following explains how to perform a join using multiple fields:

1. In an Excel file, in the Data ribbon, click Get Data ➤ From File ➤ From Workbook and connect to the Excel file C:\ DataMashupWithExcelSamples\StarSchema.xlsx.

2. Check the Select multiple items check box.

3. Select the two worksheets (Geography and Sales).

4. Click Transform Data to open the Query Editor.

5. Select the Sales query from the list of existing queries from the Queries pane on the left of the Power Query window.

6. In the Home ribbon, click the Merge Queries button. The Merge dialog will appear.

7. In the popup list of queries, select Geography as the second query to join to the first (upper) query.

8. Select Inner (only matching rows) from the Join Kind popup.

9. In the upper list of fields (taken from the Sales table), Ctrl-click the fields CountryName and Region, *in this order*. A small number will appear to the right of each column header indicating the order that you selected the columns.

10. In the lower list of fields (taken from the Sales table), Ctrl-click the fields CountryName and Region, *in this order*. A small number will appear to the right of each column header indicating the order that you selected the columns.

11. Verify that you have a reasonable number of matching rows in the information message at the bottom of the dialog. The dialog will look like Figure 8-9.

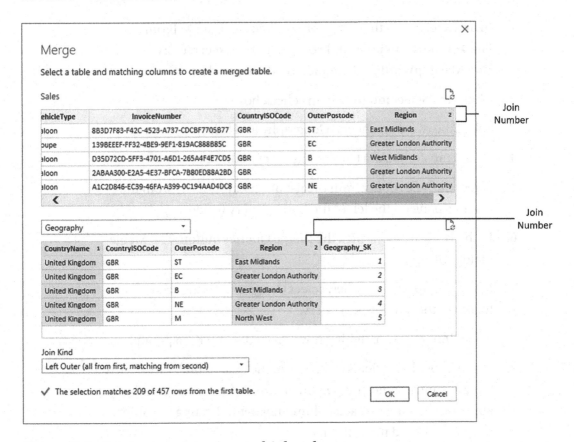

Figure 8-9. *Joining queries using multiple columns*

12.   Click OK.

You can then continue restructuring your data. In this example, that would be adding the GeographySK field to the Sales query and then removing the Country, Region, and Town fields from the Sales query, for instance.

There is no real limit to the number of columns that can be used when joining queries. It will depend entirely on the shape of the source data. However, each column used to define the join must exist in *both* datasets, and each pair of columns must be of the *same* (or a similar) data type.

Preparing Datasets for Joins

You could have to carry out a little preparatory work on real-world datasets before joining queries. More specifically, any columns that you join have to be the same basic data type. Put simply, you need to join text-based columns to other text-based columns, number columns to number columns, and date columns to date columns. If the columns are *not* the same data type, you receive a warning message when you try to join the columns in the Merge dialog.

Consequently, it is nearly always a good idea to take a look at the columns that you will use to join queries *before* you start the merge operation itself. Remember that data types do not have to be identical, just similar. So a decimal number type can map to a whole number, for instance.

You might also have to cleanse the data in the columns that are used for joins before attempting to merge queries. This could involve the following techniques that you learned in Chapter 7:

- Removing trailing or leading spaces in text-based columns

- Isolating part of a column (either in the original column or as a new column) to use in a join

- Verifying that appropriate data types are used in join columns

Correct and Incorrect Joins

Merging queries is the one data restructuring operation that is often easier in theory than in practice, unfortunately. If the source queries were based on tables in a relational or even dimensional database, then joining them could be relatively easy, as a data architect will (hopefully) have designed the database tables to allow for them to be joined. However, if you are joining two completely independent queries, then you could face several major issues:

- The columns do not map.

- The columns map, but the result is a massive table with duplicate records.

Let's take a look at these possible problems.

The Columns Do Not Map

If the columns do not map (i.e., you have joined the data but get no resulting records), then you need to take a close look at the data in the columns that you are using to establish the join. The questions you need to ask are as follows:

- Are the values in the two queries the same data type?

- Do the values really map—or are they different?

- Are you using the correct columns?

- Are you using too many columns and so specifying data that is not in both queries?

The Columns Map, but the Result Is a Massive Table with Duplicate Records

Joining queries depends on isolating *unique* data in both source queries. Sometimes a single column does not contain enough information to establish a unique reference that can uniquely identify a row in the query.

In these cases, you need to use two or more columns to join queries—or else rows will be duplicated in the result. Therefore, once again, you need to look carefully at the data and decide on the minimum number of columns that you can use to join queries correctly.

Tip   A comment at the bottom of the Merge dialog tells you how many records match between the two tables. This can be a valid and useful indicator of whether you have selected the correct join columns and an appropriate join type.

Examining Joined Data

Joining data tables is not always easy. Neither is deciding if the outcome of a merge operation will produce the result that you expect. So Power Query includes a solution to these kinds of dilemma. It can help you more clearly see what a join has done. More specifically, it can show you for each record in the first query exactly which rows are joined from the second query.

Do the following to see this in action:

1. Carry out steps 1 through 10 in the example you saw earlier (section "Joining on Multiple Columns").

2. Scroll to the right in the data table. You will see the new column named Geography (as shown in Figure 8-10).

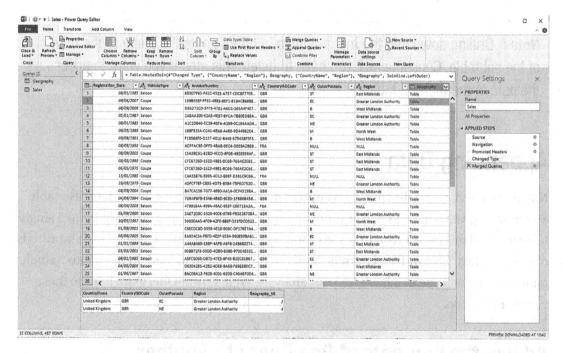

Figure 8-10. *Joined data*

3. Click to the *right* of the word *Table* in the row where you want to see the joined data. Note that you must *not* click the word *Table*. A second table will appear under the main query's data table containing the data from the second query that is joined for this particular row. Figure 8-10 shows an example of this.

This technique is as simple as it is useful. There are nonetheless a few comments that I need to make:

- You can resize the lower table (and consequently display more or less data from the second joined table) by dragging the bottom border of the top data table up or down.

255

- Clicking to the right of the word *Table* in the NewColumn column will enable the Expand and Aggregate buttons in the Transform ribbon.

- Clicking the word *Table* in the NewColumn column adds a new step to the query that replaces the source data with the linked data. You can also do this by right-clicking inside the NewColumn column and selecting Drill Down.

Note   Drilling down into the merged table in effect limits the query to the row(s) of the subtable. Consequently, you have to delete this step if you want to access all the data in the merged tables.

Appending Data

Not all source data is delivered in its entirety in a single file or as a single database table. You may be given access to two or more tables or files that have to be loaded into a single table in Excel or Power Pivot. In some cases, you might find yourself faced with hundreds of files—all text, CSV, or Excel format—and the requirement to load them all into a single table that you will use as a basis for your analysis. Well, Power Query can handle these eventualities, too.

Adding the Contents of One Query to Another

In the simplest case, you could have two data sources that are structurally identical (i.e., they have the same columns in the same order), and all that you have to do is add one to another to end up with a query that outputs the amalgamated content of the two sources. This is called *appending data*, and it is easy, provided that the two data sources have *identical* structures; this means

- They have the same number of columns.

- The columns are in the same order.

- The data types are identical for each column.

- The columns have the same names.

As long as all these conditions are met, you can append the output of queries (which Power Query also calls *Tables* and many people, including me, refer to as datasets) one into another. The queries do not have to have data that comes from identical source types, so you can append the output from a CSV file to data that comes from an Oracle database, for instance. As an example, we will take two text files and use them to create one single output:

1. Create queries to load each of the following text files into Excel worksheets. As this was explained in Chapter 2, I will not repeat the principles here. Both files are in the C:\DataMashupWithExcelSamples\MultipleIdenticalFiles folder:

    a. Colours_01.txt

    b. Colours_02.txt

2. Name the queries **Colours_01** and **Colours_02**. You can see the contents of these two queries in Figure 8-11.

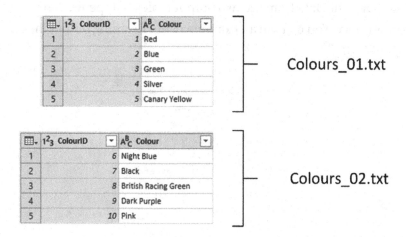

Figure 8-11. *Source data for appending*

3. Open one of the queries (I use Colours_01, but either will do) by double-clicking one of the query names in the Queries & Connections pane. This will open the Power Query Editor.

4. Click the arrow to the right of the Append Queries button in the Power Query Editor Home ribbon and select Append queries as new. The Append dialog will appear.

5. Ensure that the Two tables radio button is selected.

6. From the Select Table to Append popup, choose the query Colours_02. The dialog will look like the one in Figure 8-12.

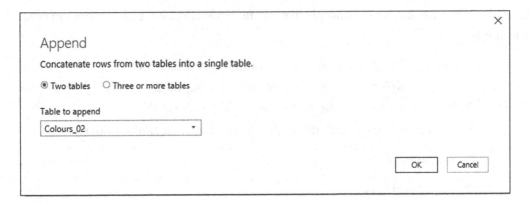

Figure 8-12. *The Append dialog*

7. Click OK. The data from the two output tables is appended in a new query. You can see an example of the resulting output in Figure 8-13.

123 ColourID	A^B_C Colour
1	1 Red
2	2 Blue
3	3 Green
4	4 Silver
5	5 Canary Yellow
6	6 Night Blue
7	7 Black
8	8 British Racing Gre...
9	9 Dark Purple
10	10 Pink

Figure 8-13. *A new query containing appended data*

You can now continue with any modifications that you need to apply. You will notice that the column names are not repeated as part of the data when the tables are appended one to the other.

One interesting aspect of this approach is that you have created a link between the two source tables and the new query. This means that when you refresh the source data, not only are the data in the tables Colours_01 and Colours_02 updated but the "derived" query that you just created is updated as well.

Appending the Contents of Multiple Queries

The Query Editor does not limit you to appending only two files at once. You can (if you really need to) append a virtually limitless number of identical files.

Moreover, you can append Excel files just as easily as you can append text or CSV files—as the following example shows:

1. Create queries to load the data in the worksheet named BaseData in the Excel file BrilliantBritishCars1.xlsx in the folder C:\ DataMashupWithExcelSamples\MultipleIdenticalExcel.

2. Repeat step 1 to load the data contained in the files BrilliantBritishCars2.xlsx and BrilliantBritishCars3.xlsx that are also in the folder C:\DataMashupWithExcelSamples\ MultipleIdenticalExcel.

3. Double-click the query named BaseData in the Queries & Connections pane on the right to open the Query Editor.

4. Click the Append Queries button.

5. Select the Three or more tables radio button in the Append dialog.

6. Ctrl-click the tables "BaseData (2)" and "BaseData (3)" in the Available table(s) list on the left of the dialog.

7. Click the Add button. You can see what the Append dialog now looks like in Figure 8-14.

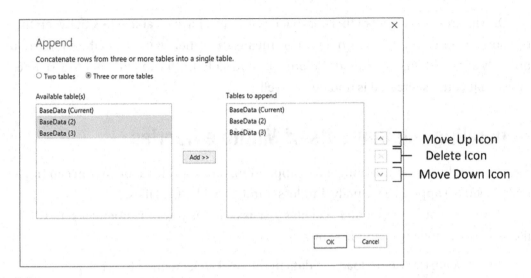

Figure 8-14. Appending multiple queries

8. Click OK. The data from the query "BaseData (2)" and "BaseData (3)" will be appended to the current query (BaseData).

Using this technique, you have "compiled" several source tables into a single output table. It is worth noting that you can

- Remove queries from the list of queries to append on the right by clicking the query (or Ctrl-clicking multiple queries) and subsequently clicking the cross icon on the right of the dialog.

- You can alter the load order of queries by clicking the query to move and then clicking the up and down chevrons on the right of the dialog.

Changing the Data Structure

Sometimes your requirements go beyond the techniques that we have seen so far when discussing data cleansing and transformation. Some data structures need more radical reworking, given the shape of the data that you have acquired. I include in this category the following:

- Unpivoting data

- Pivoting data

- Transforming rows and columns

Each of these techniques is designed to meet a specific, yet frequent, need in data loading, and all are described in the next few pages.

Unpivoting Tables

From time to time, you may need to analyze data that has been delivered in a "pivoted" or "denormalized" format. Essentially, this means that information that really should be in a single column has been broken down and placed across several columns. An example of the first few rows of a pivoted dataset is given in Figure 8-15 and can be found in the file C:\DataMashupWithExcelSamples\PivotedDataSet.xlsx.

	A	B	C	D	E	F	G	H
1	InvoiceDate	Aston Martin	Bentley	Jaguar	MGB	Rolls Royce	Triumph	TVR
2	02/01/2013	75890	25700	88200	4500	62000	8500	
3	09/01/2013	31125						
4	10/01/2013	17500						
5	02/02/2013	75890	25700	63200	8500	62000	17000	37500
6	11/02/2013	22500						
7	02/03/2013	75890	25700	88200	4500	75890	8500	
8	12/03/2013	17500						
9	13/03/2013					31125		
10	14/03/2013	17500						
11	02/04/2013	75890	25700	99500	8500	62000	17000	37500
12	15/04/2013					22500		
13	16/04/2013	17500						
14	02/05/2013	75890	62000	124500	4500	75890	8500	
15	17/05/2013	17500						
16	18/05/2013	17500						
17	19/05/2013	22500						
18	02/06/2013	62000	62000	63200	8500	62000	17000	37500
19	20/06/2013	17500						
20	02/07/2013	62000	25700	88200	4500	62000	17000	
21	21/07/2013					17500		
22	22/07/2013	22500						
23	02/08/2013	62000	62000	38200	8500	62000	17000	37500
24	02/09/2013	62000	62000	124500	4500	75890	17000	
25	23/09/2013	17500						
26	02/10/2013	62000	62000	63200	8500	75890	17000	37500
27	24/10/2013					17500		
28	02/11/2013	125000	25700	87000	4500	75890	17000	37500
29	25/11/2013	31125						
30	26/11/2013	17500						
31	27/11/2013	17500						
32	02/12/2013	125000	25700	137000	4500	62000	17000	

Figure 8-15. *A pivoted dataset*

To analyze this data correctly, we really need the makes of the cars to be switched from being column titles to becoming the contents of a specific column. Fortunately, this is not hard at all:

1.   In a new Excel file, click Get Data ➤ From File ➤ From Excel to connect to the table PivotedCosts from the C:\ DataMashupWithExcelSamples\PivotedDataSet.xlsx file into Power Query. Be sure not to load the data, but to click Transform Data from the Navigator.

2.   Ensure that the first row is set to be the table headers.

3.   In the Query Editor, select all the columns that you want to unpivot. In this example, this means all columns *except the first one* (all the makes of cars).

4.   In the Transform ribbon, click the Unpivot Columns button (or right-click any of the selected columns and choose Unpivot Columns from the context menu). The table is reorganized and the first few records look as they do in Figure 8-16. Unpivoted Columns is added to the Applied Steps list.

	InvoiceDate	Attribute	Value
1	02/01/2013	Aston Martin	75890
2	02/01/2013	Bentley	25700
3	02/01/2013	Jaguar	88200
4	02/01/2013	MGB	4500
5	02/01/2013	Rolls Royce	62000
6	02/01/2013	Triumph	8500
7	09/01/2013	Aston Martin	31125
8	10/01/2013	Aston Martin	17500
9	02/02/2013	Aston Martin	75890
10	02/02/2013	Bentley	25700
11	02/02/2013	Jaguar	63200
12	02/02/2013	MGB	8500
13	02/02/2013	Rolls Royce	62000
14	02/02/2013	Triumph	17000
15	02/02/2013	TVR	37500
16	11/02/2013	Aston Martin	22500

Figure 8-16. *An unpivoted dataset*

5. Rename the columns that Power Query has named Attribute and
    Value.

The data is now presented in a standard tabular way, and so it can be used to create a
data model (or loaded into an Excel worksheet) to serve as the basis for further analysis.

Note   The Unpivot button contains another menu option that is displayed if you
click the small triangle to the right of the Unpivot button. This is the Unpivot Other
Columns option that will switch the contents of columns into rows for all the
columns that are *not* selected when you run the transformation.

Unpivot Options

There are a couple of available options when you unpivot data using the Unpivot
Columns button popup in the Transform ribbon:

- *Unpivot Other Columns*: This will add the contents of all the other
  columns to the unpivoted output.

- *Unpivot Only Selected Columns*: This will only add the contents of any
  preselected columns to the unpivoted output.

Note   As is the case with so many of the techniques that you apply using the
Query Editor, it is really important to select the appropriate column(s) before
carrying out pivot and unpivot operations.

Pivoting Tables

On some occasions, you may have to switch data from columns to rows so that you
can use it efficiently. This kind of operation is called *pivoting data*. It is—perhaps
unsurprisingly—very similar to the unpivot process that you saw in the previous section.
The resulting data is often called a "crosstab" or "pivot table."

1. Follow steps 1 through 3 of the previous section so that you end up with the table of data that you can see in Figure 8-15.

2. Click inside the column Attribute.

3. In the Transform ribbon, click the Pivot Column button. The Pivot Column dialog will appear.

4. Select Value (the column of figures) as the values column that is aggregated by the pivot transformation.

5. Expand Advanced options and ensure that Sum is selected as the Aggregate Value Function. The Pivot Column dialog will look like Figure 8-17.

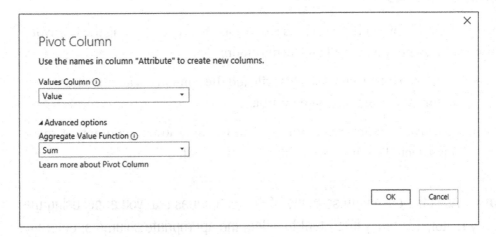

Figure 8-17. The Pivot Column dialog

6. Click OK. The table is pivoted and looks like Figure 8-18. Pivoted Column is added to the Applied Steps list.

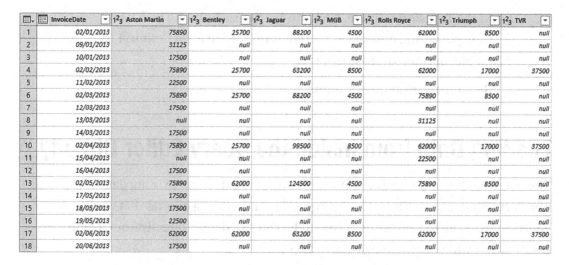

	InvoiceDate	Aston Martin	Bentley	Jaguar	MGB	Rolls Royce	Triumph	TVR
1	02/01/2013	75890	25700	88200	4500	62000	8500	null
2	09/01/2013	31125	null	null	null	null	null	null
3	10/01/2013	17500	null	null	null	null	null	null
4	02/02/2013	75890	25700	63200	8500	62000	17000	37500
5	11/02/2013	22500	null	null	null	null	null	null
6	02/03/2013	75890	25700	88200	4500	75890	8500	null
7	12/03/2013	17500	null	null	null	null	null	null
8	13/03/2013	null	null	null	null	31125	null	null
9	14/03/2013	17500	null	null	null	null	null	null
10	02/04/2013	75890	25700	99500	8500	62000	17000	37500
11	15/04/2013	null	null	null	null	22500	null	null
12	16/04/2013	17500	null	null	null	null	null	null
13	02/05/2013	75890	62000	124500	4500	75890	8500	null
14	17/05/2013	17500	null	null	null	null	null	null
15	18/05/2013	17500	null	null	null	null	null	null
16	19/05/2013	22500	null	null	null	null	null	null
17	02/06/2013	62000	62000	63200	8500	62000	17000	37500
18	20/06/2013	17500	null	null	null	null	null	null

Figure 8-18. *Pivoted data*

Note   The Advanced options section of the Pivot Column dialog lets you choose the aggregation operation that is applied to the values in the pivoted table.

Transposing Rows and Columns

On some occasions, you may have a source table where the columns need to become rows and the rows columns. Fortunately, this is a one-click transformation for Power Query. Here is how to do it:

1.   Connect to the Excel file C:\DataMashupWithExcelSamples\ DataToTranspose.xlsx in the Power Query Editor. You will need to select Sheet1. You will see a data table like the one in Figure 8-19.

	Column1	Column2	Column3	Column4	Column5	Column6
1	1	2	3	4	5	6
2	United Kingdom	France	USA	Germany	Spain	Switzerland

Figure 8-19. *A dataset needing to be transposed*

2. In the Transform ribbon, click the Transpose button. The data is transposed and appears as two columns, just like the CountryList. txt file that you saw in Chapter 2.

3. Rename the resulting columns.

Loading Data from Inside the Query Editor Directly

There will doubtless be times when you will want to extend an existing data transformation process and add a new query to any existing queries that you have already created in Power Query. Fortunately, you can do this directly from inside the Query Editor without switching back to Excel.

1. In the Query Editor, expand the Queries pane on the left (unless it is already displayed).

2. Right-click inside Queries pane.

3. Select New Query ➤ File ➤ Text/CSV. You can see this popup menu in Figure 8-20.

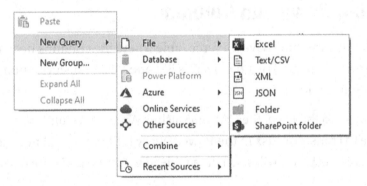

Figure 8-20. *The popup menu to add further queries directly inside the Power Query Editor*

4. Load the CSV file Countries.csv, as you learned in Chapter 2.

A new query will be added to the Queries pane in the Power Query Editor as well as in the Connections & Queries pane in Excel.

This technique, although somewhat hidden, can be particularly useful as it avoids you having to close the Query Editor to create a new query—only to return to the Query Editor to continue working. All the data source options that were available in the Excel Get Data button are present when creating new queries inside the Query Editor.

Note   As you are already inside the Query Editor, there is no Transform Data button when connecting to a new data source. You are, to all intents and purposes, already transforming the data.

Error Display

Sometimes source data may be clearly erroneous. In these cases, Power Query will flag cells that contain obvious errors. It does not presume to modify the data—after all, the data might be useful even if it is flagged as containing errors or anomalies.

However, it can help you to apply some basic data cleansing. To see how errors are displayed

1.   Open a new, blank Excel workbook.

2.   Click Data ➤ Get Data ➤ From File ➤ From Workbook.

3.   Select the Excel file SampleErrors.xlsx and click Import.

4.   Select Sheet1 and click Transform Data to display the data in the Power Query Editor.

5.   Click inside the column Price and, in the Home ribbon, set the data type to decimal number.

6.   Click Replace current in the Change Column Type dialog that appears. Two of the rows will display errors, as shown in Figure 8-21.

	ABC 123 Vehicle	ABC 123 DurationOnForecourt	1.2 Price	ABC 123 IsCorrect
1	Aston Martin DB7	92.22:15:05	10000	TRUE
2	Rolls Royce Phantom	5.01:45:00	Error	FALSE
3	Jaguar XJ6	1047:10:32:05	Error	CORRECT

Figure 8-21.   *Displaying errors*

In some datasets, the data that is flagged as being an error could be the data that you want to examine in greater detail. The point is that you can see potential errors and decide whether to remove them (as described later) or to return to the source data and correct them before reloading the data.

Removing Errors

Assuming that you do not need records that Power Query has flagged as containing an error, you can remove all such records in a single operation:

1. Click inside the column containing errors; or if you want to remove errors from several columns at once, Ctrl-click the titles of the columns that contain the errors.

2. Click the popup triangle in the Remove Rows button in the Home ribbon. The popup menu will appear.

3. Click Remove errors. Any records with errors flagged in the selected columns are deleted. Removed Errors is added to the Applied Steps list.

You have to be very careful here not to remove valid data. Only you can judge, once you have taken a look at the data, if an error in a column means that the data can be discarded safely. In all other cases, you would be best advised to look at cleansing the data or simply leaving records that contain errors in place. The range and variety of potential errors are as vast as the data itself.

Viewing Errors

If you save and close a query that contains errors, the Queries & Connections pane will indicate the number of errors for each query—as shown in Figure 8-22.

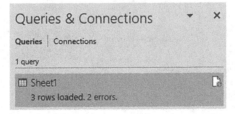

Figure 8-22. *Displaying queries with errors in the Queries & Connections pane*

Clicking the errors link (in blue in the query) will open the Query Editor and display the error records only. You can see this in Figure 8-23.

1.2 Row Number	ABC 123 Vehicle	ABC 123 DurationOnForecourt	1.2 Price	ABC 123 IsCorrect
1	2 Rolls Royce Phantom	5.01:45:00	Error	FALSE
2	3 Jaguar XJ6	1047:10:32:05	Error	CORRECT

Figure 8-23. *Displaying error records only*

Data Transformation Approaches

I quite understand that you may be bewildered at the sheer number of available transformation options. So it may help, at this point, to remember a few key principles:

- If in doubt, right-click the column that you want to transform. This will list the most common available options in the context menu.

- To alter existing data, use the Transform menu.

- To add a new column, use the New Column menu.

- Remember that you can "unwind" your modifications by deleting steps in the data transformation process.

Conclusion

This chapter showed you how to structure your source data into a valid data table from one or more potential sources. Among other things, you saw how to pivot and unpivot data, to fill rows up and down with data, as well as how to transpose rows and columns.

Possibly the most important thing that you have learned is how to join individual queries so that you can add the data from one query into another. This can involve looking up data from a separate query or carrying the aggregated results from one query into another.

Finally, you learned how to identify error records in a query.

Now it is time to push your data transformation skills to the next level and learn how to set up complex data ingestion and conversion routines. These are the subject of Chapter 9.

CHAPTER 9

Complex Data Loads

Not all data loads are a matter of simply establishing a connection and applying transformations to the source data that is, fortunately, already laid out in neatly structured tables. Sometimes you may want to "push the envelope" when loading data and prepare more complex source data structures for use in your Excel analytics. By this, I mean that the source data is not initially in a ready-to-use tabular format and that some restructuring of the data is required to prepare a clean table of data for use.

To solve these kinds of challenges, this chapter will explain to you how to

- Add multiple identical files from a source folder

- Select the identical source files to load from a source folder

- Load simple JSON structures from a source file containing JSON data

- Parse a column containing JSON data in a source file

- Parse a column containing XML data in a source file

- Load complex JSON files—and select the elements to use

- Load complex XML files—and select the elements to use

- Convert columns to lists for use in complex load routines

Finally—and purely to complete the overall overview of the Power Query Editor and its capabilities—I will mention how to

- Reuse recently used queries

- Modify the list of recently used queries

- Export data from the Power Query Editor

Any sample files used in this chapter are available for download from the Apress website as described in Appendix A.

271

© Adam Aspin 2020
A. Aspin, *Data Mashup with Microsoft Excel Using Power Query and M*,
https://doi.org/10.1007/978-1-4842-6018-0_9

Adding Multiple Files from a Source Folder

Now let's consider an interesting data ingestion challenge. You have been sent a collection of text files, possibly downloaded from an FTP site or received by email, and you have placed them all into a specific directory. However, you do not want to have to carry out the process that you saw in Chapter 2 and load files one by one if there are several hundred files—and then append all these files individually to create a final composite table of data (as you saw in Chapter 8).

Here is a much more efficient method to achieve this objective.

Note   Query Editor can only load multiple files if all the files are rigorously identical. This means ensuring that all the columns are in the same order in each file and have the same names.

---

1. Create a new Excel file.

2. In the Data ribbon, click Get Data ➤ From File ➤ From Folder. The Folder dialog is displayed.

3. Click the Browse button and navigate to the folder that contains the files to load. In this example, it is C:\ DataMashupWithExcelSamples\MultipleIdenticalFiles. You can also paste in, or enter, the folder path if you prefer. The Folder dialog will look like Figure 9-1.

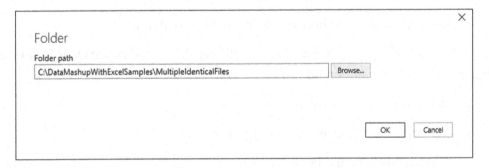

Figure 9-1. *The Folder dialog*

4. Click OK. The file list window opens. The contents of the folder
    and all subfolders are listed in tabular format, as shown in
    Figure 9-2.

Figure 9-2. *The folder contents in Power Query*

5. Click the popup arrow on the right of the Combine button and
    select Combine & Transform Data. The Combine Files dialog will
    appear, as shown in Figure 9-3. Here you can select which of the
    files in the folder is the model for the files to be imported.

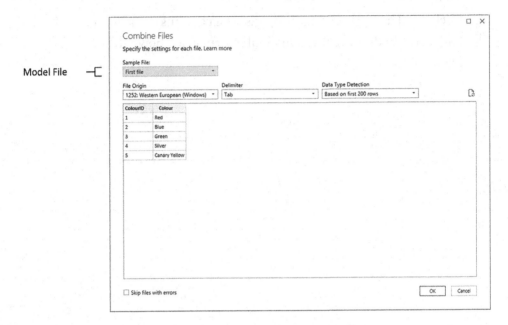

Figure 9-3. *The Combine Files dialog*

6.   Click OK. The Power Query Editor will display the imported data.
     This is shown in Figure 9-4.

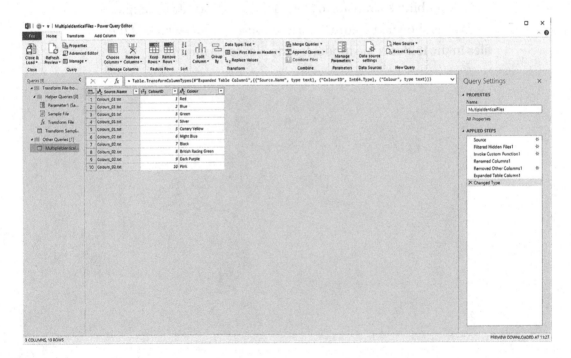

Figure 9-4. *Data loaded from a folder*

7. Click Close & Load. The data from all the source files will be loaded into the Excel data model.

As you can see, Power Query has added an extra column to the output containing the name of the file that contained each source record. You can remove this column if you wish.

Note   The other options in the Combine Files dialog are explained in Chapter 2.

Filtering Source Files in a Folder

There will be times when you want to import only a *subset* of the files from a folder. Perhaps the files are not identical or maybe you simply do not need some of the available files in the source directory. Whatever the reason, here is a way to get Power Query to do the work of trawling through the directory and *only* loading files that correspond to a file name or extension specification you have indicated, for instance. In other words, the Query Editor allows you to filter the source file set before loading the actual data. In this example, I will show you how to load multiple Excel files from a directory containing both Excel and text files.

1. Carry out steps 1 through 5 from the section "Adding Multiple Files from a Source Folder" earlier in this chapter to display the contents of the folder containing the files you wish to load. In this scenario, it is C:\DataMashupWithExcelSamples\ MultipleNonIdentical.

2. Click Transform Data. The Query Editor window will open and display the list of files in the directory and many of their attributes. You can see an example of this in Figure 9-5.

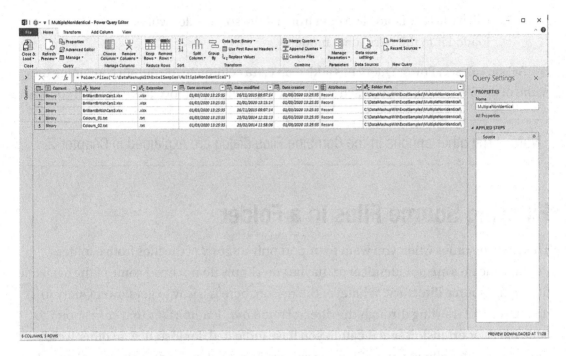

***Figure 9-5.** Displaying file information when loading multiple files*

3. As you want to load only Excel files, and avoid files of any other
type, click the filter popup menu for the column title Extension
and uncheck all elements *except* .xlsx. This is shown in Figure 9-6.

***Figure 9-6.** Filtering file types when loading multiple identical files*

4. Click OK. You will now only see the Excel files in the Query Editor.

5. Click the Expand icon (two downward-facing arrows) to the right of the first column title; this column is called Content, and every row in the column contains the word *Binary*. Power Query will display the Combine Files dialog that you saw previously in Figure 9-3.

6. Select the file from those available that you want to use as the sample file for the data load.

7. Select the BaseData worksheet as the structure to use for the load.

8. Click Skip files with errors. This time, the dialog will look like Figure 9-7.

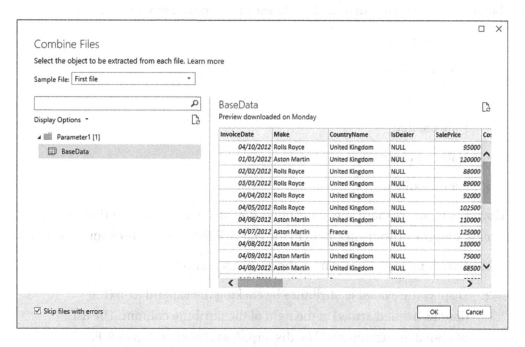

Figure 9-7. *Selecting the source data when loading multiple Excel files*

9. Click OK. Power Query Editor will load all the files and display the result.

The contents of all the source files are now loaded into the Power Query Editor and can be transformed and used like any other dataset. This might involve removing superfluous header rows (as described in the next but one section). What is more, if ever

277

you add more files to the source directory, and then click Refresh in the Home ribbon, *all* the source files that match the filter selection are reloaded, including any new files added to the specified directory since the initial load that match the filter criteria.

Note   When loading multiple Excel files, you need to be aware that the data sources (whether they are worksheets, named ranges, or tables) *must* have the same name in all the source files or the data will not be loaded.

Displaying and Filtering File Attributes

When you display the contents of a folder in the Query Editor, you see a set of file attributes that you can use to filter data. These cover basic elements such as

- File name
- File extension
- Folder path
- Date created
- Date last accessed
- Date modified

However, there are many more attributes that are available to describe files that you can access simply by displaying them in the Query Editor. Here is how you can do this:

1. Carry out steps 1 and 2 from the previous section.

2. Display the available attributes by clicking the expand icon (the double-headed arrow) at the right of the attribute column. The list of available attributes will be displayed, as shown in Figure 9-8.

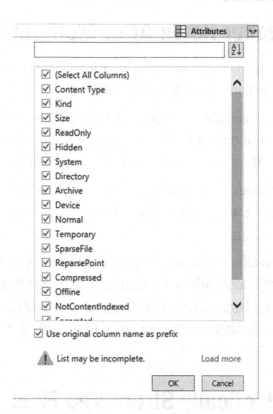

Figure 9-8. *Adding file attributes for file selection*

3. Select the attributes that you want to display from the list and click OK.

Each attribute will appear as a new column in the Query Editor. You can now filter on the columns to select files based on the expanded list of attributes.

Note   You can also filter on directories, dates, or any of the file information that is displayed. Simply apply the filtering techniques that you learned in Chapter 6.

Removing Header Rows After Multiple File Loads

If the source files contained header rows that were loaded for each source file, here is a practical way to remove them—fast—from the data:

1. If (but only if) each file contains header rows, then scroll down through the resulting table until you find a title element. In this example, it is the word *ColourID* in the ColourID column.

2. Right-click ColourID and select Text Filters ➤ Does Not Equal. All rows containing superfluous column titles are removed.

Note   If your source directory only contains the files that you want to load, then step 2 is unnecessary. Nonetheless, I always add steps like this in case files of the "wrong" type are added later, which would cause any subsequent process runs to fail. Equally, you can set filters on the file name to restrict the files that are loaded.

Combining Identically Structured Files

Power Query can also combine source files in a way that is slightly different to the technique that you saw previously in this chapter. This technique will also work with text, CSV, fixed-width, XML, or JSON files.

1. Carry out steps 1 through 5 in the section "Adding Multiple Files from a Source Folder" to display the contents of the folder containing the files you wish to load. In this scenario, it is C:\ DataMashupWithExcelSamples\MultipleIdenticalFiles.

2. Click the column named Content.

3. In the Power Query Home ribbon, click the Combine Files button. The Combine Files dialog (that you saw in Figure 9-7) will appear.

4. Click OK.

Power Query will evaluate the format of the source files and append all the source files into a single query.

> **Note**   Power Query will create a set of helper queries to carry out this operation.
> If you expand the Power Query Queries pane, you will see the new queries
> that it has added. These queries will also be displayed in the Excel Queries &
> Connections pane.

Loading and Parsing JSON Files

More and more data is now being exchanged in a format called JSON. This stands for
JavaScript Object Notation, and it is considered an efficient and lightweight way of
transferring potentially large amounts of data. A JSON file is essentially a text file that
contains data structured in a specific way.

Now, while Power Query can connect very easily to JSON data files (they are only a
kind of text file, after all), the data they contain are not always instantly comprehensible.
So you will now learn how to load the file and then see how this connection can be
tweaked to convert it into meaningful information. Transforming the source text into a
comprehensible format is often called *parsing* the data.

To connect to a JSON file and parse the data it contains into a usable table:

1. In the Data ribbon, click Get Data ➤ From File ➤ From JSON.

2. Select the file C:\DataMashupWithExcelSamples\Colors.json, and
    click Import. You will see a list of records like the one shown in
    Figure 9-9.

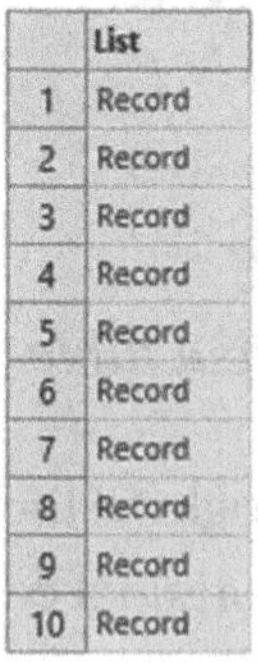

	List
1	Record
2	Record
3	Record
4	Record
5	Record
6	Record
7	Record
8	Record
9	Record
10	Record

Figure 9-9. A JSON file after initial import

3. You will see that the Query Editor has added the List Tools Transform ribbon to the menu bar. This ribbon is explained in detail in the next section. Click the To Table button in this ribbon. The To Table dialog will appear, as shown in Figure 9-10.

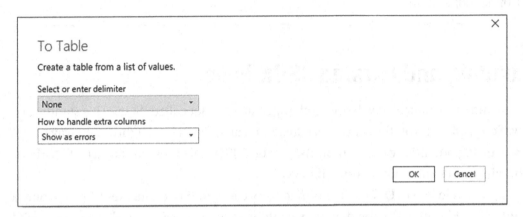

Figure 9-10. *The To Table dialog*

4. Click OK. The list of data will be converted to a table. This means that it now shows the Expand icon at the right of the column title, as you can see in Figure 9-11.

Figure 9-11. *A JSON file converted to a table*

5. Click the Expand icon to the right of the column title, and in the popup dialog, uncheck "Use original column name as prefix."

6. Click OK. The contents of the JSON file now appear as a standard dataset, as you can see in Figure 9-12.

	ABC 123 ColorID	▼	ABC 123 Color	▼
1	1		Red	
2	2		Blue	
3	3		Green	
4	4		Silver	
5	5		Canary Yellow	
6	6		Night Blue	
7	7		Black	
8	8		British Racing Green	
9	9		Dark Purple	
10	10		Pink	

Figure 9-12. *A JSON file transformed into a dataset*

Although not particularly difficult, this process may seem a little counterintuitive. However, it certainly works, and you can use it to process complex JSON files so that you can use the data they contain in Excel.

The List Tools Transform Ribbon

Power Query considers some data to be lists, not tables of data. It handles lists slightly differently and displays a specific ribbon to modify list data. The List Tools Transform ribbon is explained in Figure 9-13 and Table 9-1.

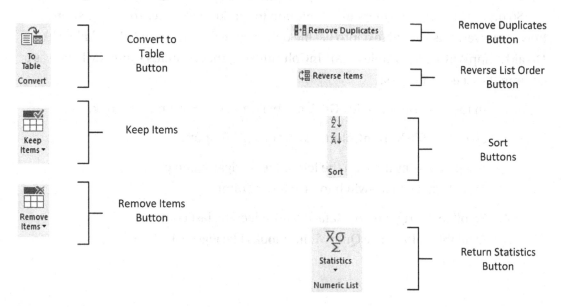

Figure 9-13. *The List Tools Transform ribbon*

Table 9-1. *The List Tools Transform Ribbon Options*

Option	Description
To Table	Converts the list to a table structure
Keep Items	Allows you to keep a number of items from the top or bottom of the list or a range of items from the list
Remove Items	Allows you to remove a number of items from the top or bottom of the list or a range of items from the list
Remove Duplicates	Removes any duplicates from the list
Reverse Items	Reverses the list order
Sort	Sorts the list lowest to highest or highest to lowest
Statistics	Returns calculated statistics about the elements in the list

Parsing XML Data from a Column

Some data sources, particularly database sources, include XML data actually inside a field. The problem here is that XML data is interpreted as plain text by Power Query when the data is loaded. If you look at the AvailableColors column that is highlighted in Figure 9-14, you can see that this is not particularly useful or even comprehensible.

So once again, Power Query has a solution to this kind of issue. To demonstrate how to convert this kind of text into usable data, you will find a sample Excel file (C:\ DataMashupWithExcelSamples\XMLInColumn.xlsx) that contains some XML data as a column. Proceed as follows:

1. In the Data ribbon, click Get Data ➤ From File ➤ From Workbook.

2. Select the file XMLInColumn.xlsx and click Import.

3. Select the Sales table on the left of the Navigator and click Transform Data to switch to the Query Editor.

4. Scroll to the right of the dataset and select the last column: AvailableColors. The Query Editor looks like Figure 9-14.

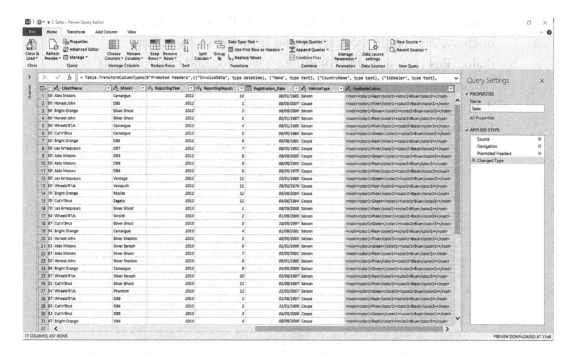

Figure 9-14. *A column containing XML*

5.   In the Add Column ribbon, click the small triangle in the Parse
     button and select XML. A new column will be added to the right. It
     will look like Figure 9-15 and will have the title XML.

A$_C^B$ AvailableColors	ABC 123 XML
\<root>\<color1>Red\</color1>\<color2>Blue\</color2>\</root>	Table
\<root>\<color1>Pink\</color1>\<color2>Black\</color2>\</root>	Table
\<root>\<color1>Green\</color1>\<color2>Blue\</color2>\</root>	Table
\<root>\<color1>Red\</color1>\<color2>Blue\</color2>\</root>	Table
\<root>\<color1>Pink\</color1>\<color2>Black\</color2>\</root>	Table
\<root>\<color1>Green\</color1>\<color2>Blue\</color2>\</root>	Table
\<root>\<color1>Red\</color1>\<color2>Blue\</color2>\</root>	Table
\<root>\<color1>Pink\</color1>\<color2>Black\</color2>\</root>	Table
\<root>\<color1>Green\</color1>\<color2>Blue\</color2>\</root>	Table
\<root>\<color1>Red\</color1>\<color2>Blue\</color2>\</root>	Table
\<root>\<color1>Pink\</color1>\<color2>Black\</color2>\</root>	Table
\<root>\<color1>Green\</color1>\<color2>Blue\</color2>\</root>	Table
\<root>\<color1>Red\</color1>\<color2>Blue\</color2>\</root>	Table
\<root>\<color1>Pink\</color1>\<color2>Black\</color2>\</root>	Table

Figure 9-15. *An XML column converted to a table column*

6. Click the Expand icon to the right of the XML column title and uncheck "Use original column name as prefix" in the popup dialog. Ensure that all the columns are selected and click OK. Two new columns (or, indeed, as many new columns as there are XML data elements) will appear at the right of the dataset. The Query Editor will look like Figure 9-16.

A^B_C AvailableColors	ABC 123 color1	ABC 123 color2
<root><color1>Red</color1><color2>Blue</color2></root>	Red	Blue
<root><color1>Pink</color1><color2>Black</color2></root>	Pink	Black
<root><color1>Green</color1><color2>Blue</color2></root>	Green	Blue
<root><color1>Red</color1><color2>Blue</color2></root>	Red	Blue
<root><color1>Pink</color1><color2>Black</color2></root>	Pink	Black
<root><color1>Green</color1><color2>Blue</color2></root>	Green	Blue
<root><color1>Red</color1><color2>Blue</color2></root>	Red	Blue
<root><color1>Pink</color1><color2>Black</color2></root>	Pink	Black
<root><color1>Green</color1><color2>Blue</color2></root>	Green	Blue
<root><color1>Red</color1><color2>Blue</color2></root>	Red	Blue
<root><color1>Pink</color1><color2>Black</color2></root>	Pink	Black
<root><color1>Green</color1><color2>Blue</color2></root>	Green	Blue
<root><color1>Red</color1><color2>Blue</color2></root>	Red	Blue
<root><color1>Pink</color1><color2>Black</color2></root>	Pink	Black
<root><color1>Green</color1><color2>Blue</color2></root>	Green	Blue
<root><color1>Red</color1><color2>Blue</color2></root>	Red	Blue

Figure 9-16. *XML data expanded into new columns*

7. Remove the column containing the initial XML data by selecting the column that contains the original XML and clicking Remove columns in the context menu.

8. Rename any new columns to give them meaningful titles.

Using this technique, you can now extract the XML data that is in source datasets and use it to extend the original source data.

Parsing JSON Data from a Column

Sometimes you may encounter data containing JSON in a field, too. The technique to extract this data from the field inside the dataset and convert it to columns is virtually identical to the approach that you saw in the previous section for XML data.

Given that the approach is so similar and is not far removed from what you saw previously when importing JSON files, I will only provide a screenshot for the final result of the process. Here you will be able to see the source JSON as well as the columns of data that were extracted from the JSON and added to the dataset.

1. Follow steps 1 through 4 from the previous example, only use the file C:\DataMashupWithExcelSamples\JSONInColumn.xlsx. Select the only worksheet in this file: Sales.

2. Scroll to the right of the dataset and select the last column: AvailableColors.

3. In the Add Column ribbon, click Parse ➤ JSON. A new column will be added to the right and will have the title JSON.

4. Click the Expand icon to the right of the JSON column title and uncheck "Use original column name as prefix" in the popup dialog. Ensure that all the columns are selected and click OK. Two new columns (or, indeed, as many new columns as there are JSON data elements) will appear at the right of the dataset. The Query Editor will look like Figure 9-17.

A^B_C AvailableColors	ABC 123 Color1	ABC 123 Color2
{"Color1":"Red", "Color2":"Blue"}	Red	Blue
{"Color1":"Red", "Color2":"Blue"}	Red	Blue
{"Color1":"Red", "Color2":"Blue"}	Red	Blue
{"Color1":"Red", "Color2":"Blue"}	Red	Blue
{"Color1":"Red", "Color2":"Blue"}	Red	Blue
{"Color1":"Red", "Color2":"Blue"}	Red	Blue
{"Color1":"Red", "Color2":"Blue"}	Red	Blue
{"Color1":"Red", "Color2":"Blue"}	Red	Blue
{"Color1":"Red", "Color2":"Blue"}	Red	Blue
{"Color1":"Red", "Color2":"Blue"}	Red	Blue
{"Color1":"Red", "Color2":"Blue"}	Red	Blue
{"Color1":"Red", "Color2":"Blue"}	Red	Blue
{"Color1":"Red", "Color2":"Blue"}	Red	Blue
{"Color1":"Red", "Color2":"Blue"}	Red	Blue
{"Color1":"Red", "Color2":"Blue"}	Red	Blue
{"Color1":"Red", "Color2":"Blue"}	Red	Blue
{"Color1":"Red", "Color2":"Blue"}	Red	Blue
{"Color1":"Red", "Color2":"Blue"}	Red	Blue
{"Color1":"Red", "Color2":"Blue"}	Red	Blue

Figure 9-17. JSON data expanded into new columns

5. Delete the column containing the initial JSON data.

6. Rename any new columns if this is necessary.

Admittedly, the structure of the JSON data in this example is extremely simple. Real-world JSON data could be much more complex. However, you now have a starting point upon which you can build when parsing JSON data that is stored in a column of a dataset.

Complex JSON Files

JSON files are not always structured as simplistically as the Colors.json file that you saw a few pages ago. Indeed, JSON files can contain many sublevels of data, structured into separated *nodes*. Each node may contain multiple data elements grouped together in a logical way. Often you will want to select "sublevels" of data from the source file—or perhaps only select some sublevel elements and not others.

This section shows you how to select the data elements that interest you from a complex JSON structure. Specifically, the sample source data file (CarSalesJSON_Complex.json) contains a "root" level which displays core data such as the invoice number, sale date, and sale price (among other elements) and three "sublevels" that contain information on

- The vehicle

- The finance data

- The customer

The challenge here will be to "flatten" the data from the Vehicle and FinanceData nodes into standard columns that can then be used for analytics.

Note   If you want to get an idea of what a complex JSON file containing several nested nodes looks like, then simply open the file C:\ DataMashupWithExcelSamples\CarSalesJSON_Complex.json in a text editor.

In this example, you will see how to select elements from one or more (but not all) of the available data in the source file.

1. In the Excel ribbon, click Get Data ➤ From File ➤ From JSON. Navigate to the folder containing the JSON file that you want to load (C:\DataMashupWithExcelSamples\CarSalesJSON_Complex.json, in this example).

2. Click Import. The Query Editor window will appear and automatically display the Record Tools Convert ribbon. You can see this in Figure 9-18.

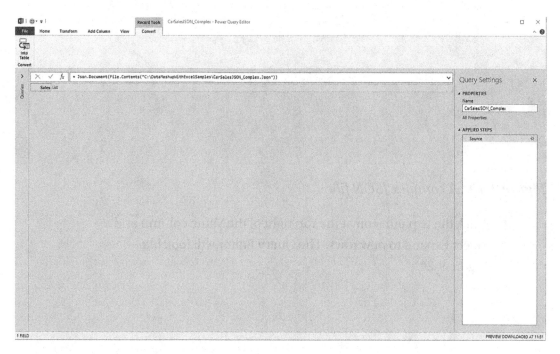

Figure 9-18. *Opening a complex JSON file*

3. Click Into Table from the Record Tools Convert ribbon. The Query Editor will look like Figure 9-19.

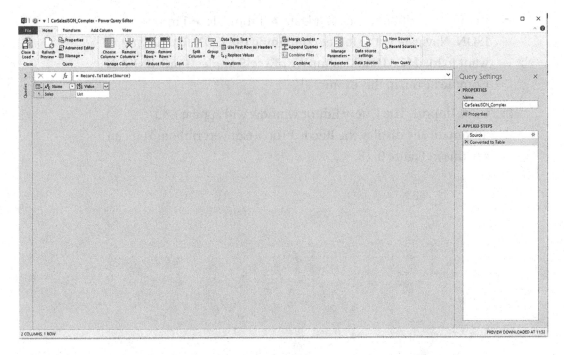

Figure 9-19. *A complex JSON file*

4. Click the Expand icon at the top right of the Value column and
    select Expand to new rows. The Query Editor will look like
    Figure 9-20.

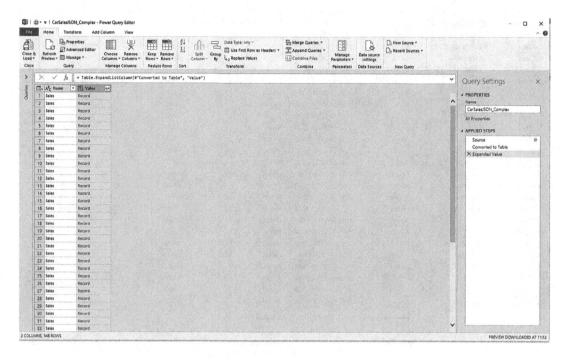

Figure 9-20. *Expanding a JSON file*

5. Click the Expand icon at the top right of the Value column and uncheck Use original column name as prefix.

6. Click OK to display all the JSON attributes. The Query Editor window will look like Figure 9-21. Each column containing the word "record" is, in fact, a JSON node that contains further sublevels of data.

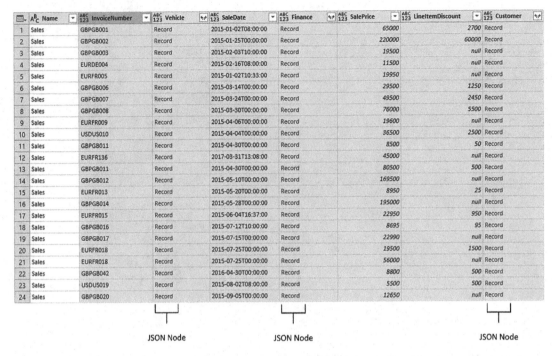

	ABC Name	ABC 123 InvoiceNumber	ABC 123 Vehicle	ABC 123 SaleDate	ABC 123 Finance	ABC 123 SalePrice	ABC 123 LineItemDiscount	ABC 123 Customer
1	Sales	GBPGB001	Record	2015-01-02T08:00:00	Record	65000	2700	Record
2	Sales	GBPGB002	Record	2015-01-25T00:00:00	Record	220000	60000	Record
3	Sales	GBPGB003	Record	2015-02-03T10:00:00	Record	19500	null	Record
4	Sales	EURDE004	Record	2015-02-16T08:00:00	Record	11500	null	Record
5	Sales	EURFR005	Record	2015-01-02T10:33:00	Record	19950	null	Record
6	Sales	GBPGB006	Record	2015-03-14T00:00:00	Record	29500	1250	Record
7	Sales	GBPGB007	Record	2015-03-24T00:00:00	Record	49500	2450	Record
8	Sales	GBPGB008	Record	2015-03-30T00:00:00	Record	76000	5500	Record
9	Sales	EURFR009	Record	2015-04-06T00:00:00	Record	19600	null	Record
10	Sales	USDUS010	Record	2015-04-04T00:00:00	Record	36500	2500	Record
11	Sales	GBPGB011	Record	2015-04-30T00:00:00	Record	8500	50	Record
12	Sales	EURFR136	Record	2017-03-31T13:08:00	Record	45000	null	Record
13	Sales	GBPGB011	Record	2015-04-30T00:00:00	Record	80500	500	Record
14	Sales	GBPGB012	Record	2015-05-10T00:00:00	Record	169500	null	Record
15	Sales	EURFR013	Record	2015-05-20T00:00:00	Record	8950	25	Record
16	Sales	GBPGB014	Record	2015-05-28T00:00:00	Record	195000	null	Record
17	Sales	EURFR015	Record	2015-06-04T16:37:00	Record	22950	950	Record
18	Sales	GBPGB016	Record	2015-07-12T10:00:00	Record	8695	95	Record
19	Sales	GBPGB017	Record	2015-07-15T00:00:00	Record	22990	null	Record
20	Sales	EURFR018	Record	2015-07-25T00:00:00	Record	19500	1500	Record
21	Sales	EURFR018	Record	2015-07-25T00:00:00	Record	56000	null	Record
22	Sales	GBPGB042	Record	2016-04-30T00:00:00	Record	8800	500	Record
23	Sales	USDUS019	Record	2015-08-02T08:00:00	Record	5500	500	Record
24	Sales	GBPGB020	Record	2015-09-05T00:00:00	Record	12650	null	Record

JSON Node   JSON Node   JSON Node

Figure 9-21. *Viewing the structure of a JSON file*

7. Select the Vehicle column and click the Expand icon at the right of the column title. The list of available elements that are "nested" at a lower level inside the source JSON will appear. You can see this in Figure 9-22.

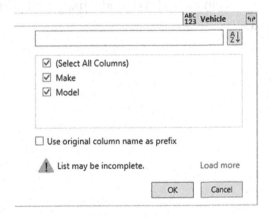

Figure 9-22. *Nested elements in a JSON file*

8. Click OK. The new columns will be added to the data table.

9. Select the Finance column and click the Expand icon at the right of the column title. The list of available elements that are "nested" at a lower level inside the source JSON for this column will appear. Select only the Cost column and click OK.

10. Remove the Customer column as we will not be using data from this column in this example. The Query Editor window will look like Figure 9-23, where all the required columns are now visible in the data table.

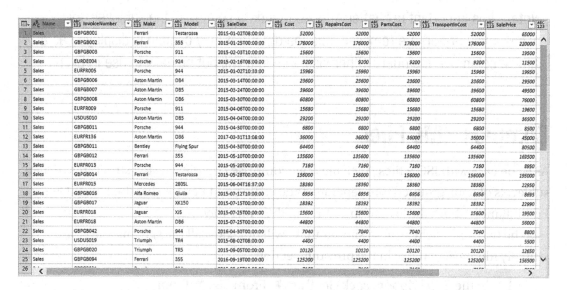

Figure 9-23. A JSON file after parsing

11. Click the Close & Load in the Power Query Home menu to return the "flattened" JSON data to an Excel worksheet.

Note It is a good idea to click the Load more link in the Expand popup menu when you are identifying the nested data in a JSON node. This will force Power Query to scan a larger number of records and return, potentially, a more complete list of nested fields.

This approach allows you to be extremely selective about the data that you load from a JSON file. You can choose to include any column at any level from the source structure. As you saw, you can select—or ignore—entire sublevels of nested data extremely easily.

This section was only a simple introduction to parsing complex JSON files. As this particular data structure can contain multiple sublevels of data, and can mix data and sublevels in each node of the JSON file, the source data structure can be extremely complex and can contain nodes within nodes within nodes. Fortunately, the techniques that you just learned can be extended to handle any level of JSON complexity and help you tame the most potentially daunting data structures.

Note   It is important to "flatten" the source data so that all the sublevels (or nodes if you prefer) are removed, and the data that they contain is displayed as a simple column in the query. Otherwise, the data will not be easy to use in Excel.

Complex XML Files

As is the case with JSON files, XML files can comprise complex nested structures of many sublevels of data, grouped into separate nodes. The good news is that the Power Query Editor handles both these data structures in the same way.

The two approaches are so similar that I will not show all the screens—they are virtually identical to those in the previous section.

1. In the Excel ribbon, click Get Data ➤ From File ➤ From XML. Navigate to the folder containing the XML file that you want to load (C:\DataMashupWithExcelSamples\ComplexXML.xml, in this example).

2. Click Import. The Navigator dialog will appear.

3. Select Sales as the source data table on the left.

4. Click Transform Data. The Query Editor will appear.

5. Select the Vehicle column and click the Expand icon at the right of the column title. The list of available elements that are "nested" at a lower level inside the source XML will appear.

6. Uncheck the Use original column name as prefix check box.

7. Click OK.

8. Click the Expand icon at the top right of the Finance column and uncheck the Use original column name as prefix check box.

9. Click Load more to display a more exhaustive list of data elements.

10. Click OK. The new columns will be added to the data table.

11. Select the Customer column and click the Expand icon at the right of the column title. The list of available elements that are "nested" at a lower level inside the source XML will appear. Select only the CustomerName column and click OK.

12. Click the Close & Load button at the top of the Power Query window.

As was the case with JSON files, this approach allows you to be extremely selective about the data that you load from an XML source file. You can choose to include any column at any level from the source structure. You can select—or ignore—entire sublevels of nested data extremely easily.

Convert a Column to a List

Sometimes you will need to use data in a list format. You will see a practical example of this in Chapter 11 when you learn how to parameterize queries. Fortunately, Power Query lets you convert a column to a list really easily:

1. Click Get Data ➤ From File ➤ From Excel and select the Excel file C:\DataMashupWithExcelSamples\BrilliantBritishCars.xlsx.

2. Click Import to display the Navigator.

3. Select the worksheet BaseData and click Transform Data to open the Query Editor.

4. Select a column to convert to a list by clicking the column header. I will use the column Make in this example.

5. In the Transform ribbon, click Convert to List. The Query Editor will show the resulting list, as you can see in Figure 9-24.

	List
1	Rolls Royce
2	Aston Martin
3	Rolls Royce
4	Rolls Royce
5	Rolls Royce
6	Rolls Royce

Figure 9-24. *The list resulting from a conversion-to-list operation*

This list can now be used in certain circumstances when carrying out more advanced data transformation processes.

Reusing Data Sources

Over the course of Chapters 2 through 5, you saw how to access data from a wide variety of sources to build a series of queries across a range of reports. The reality will probably be that you will frequently want to point to the same sources of data over and over again. In anticipation of this, the Power Query development team has found a way to make your life easier.

Excel remembers the most recent data sources that you have used and lets you reuse them quickly and easily in any report. Here is how:

1. In the Home ribbon, click the Recent Sources button. A dialog containing the most recently used data sources will appear. You can see this in Figure 9-25.

Figure 9-25. *Recently used sources*

2. Click the source that you want to reconnect to, and continue with
    the data load or connection by clicking the Connect button.

Pinning a Data Source

If you look closely at Figure 9-25, you see that the database connection
ADAM03:CarSalesData is pinned to the top of the Recent Sources dialog, reflecting a
recent database connection that I have made. This allows you to make sure that certain
data sources are always kept on hand and ready to reuse.

Do the following to pin a data source that you have recently used to the menu and
dialog of recent sources:

1. Click the Recent Sources button in the Data ribbon. The Recent
    Sources dialog will appear.

2. Hover the mouse over a recently used data source. A pin icon will
    appear at the right of the data source name.

3. Click the pin icon. The data source is pinned to the top of both the Recent Sources menu and the Recent Sources dialog. A small pin icon remains visible at the right of the data source name.

Note   To unpin a data source from the Recent Sources menu and the Recent Sources dialog, all you have to do is click the pin icon for a pinned data source. This unpins it and it reappears in the list of recently used data sources.

If you so wish, you can also apply the following options when deciding which elements you want to make appear in the Recent Sources list:

- Remove from list

- Clear unpinned items from list

Copying Data from Power Query Editor

Power Query is designed as a data destination. It does not have any data export functionality as such. You can manually copy data from the Power Query Editor, however. More precisely, you can copy any of the following:

- The data in the query

- A column of data

- A single cell

In all cases, the process is the same:

1. Click the element to copy. This can be

    a. The top-left square of the data grid

    b. A column title

    c. A single cell

2. Right-click and select Copy from the context menu.

You can then paste the data from the clipboard into the destination application.

Note   This process is somewhat limited because you cannot select a range of cells. And you must remember that you are only looking at sample data in the Query Editor. As you can simply load the data into Excel from Power Query, I explain this purely as a minor point that is of limited interest in practice.

Conclusion

This chapter pushed your data transformation knowledge with the Power Query Editor to a new level, by explaining how to deal with multiple file loads of Excel- and text-based data. You then learned ways of handling data from source files that contain complex, nested source structures—specifically JSON and XML files. You also saw how to parse JSON and XML elements from columns contained in other data sources.

Then, you learned how to reuse data sources and manage frequently used data sources to save time. Finally, you learned how to copy sample data resulting from a data transformation process into other applications.

So now the basic tour of data load and transformation with the Power Query Editor is over. It is time to move on to more advanced techniques that you can apply to accelerate and enhance, manage, and structure your data transformation processes and add a certain level of interactivity. These approaches are the subject of the following two chapters.

CHAPTER 10

Organizing and Managing Queries

Producing a robust and efficient data query is not just about finding the appropriate load and transform functions and placing them in the correct sequence. It is also about extending, maintaining, and updating the process. This can be either to correct an error once the query is being tested or to adapt a query to new requirements. This chapter will introduce you to some of the techniques that you can apply to handle the various stages of the query life cycle.

Delivering revelatory analytics can mean sourcing data from a large range and variety of queries. It may also imply that these queries have to be linked together to create a cascade of data transformations that prepares the core elements of a practical and usable data model collated from multiple sources. It follows that you will therefore need to know how to *manage* the queries that you create to use them efficiently and to keep your queries under control in real-world situations.

Managing the Transformation Process

Pretty nearly all the transformation steps that we have applied so far have been individual elements that can be applied to just about any data table. However, when you are carrying out even a simple data load and transform process, you are likely to want to step through several transformations in order to shape, cleanse, and filter the data to get the result you want. This is where the Power Query approach is so malleable, because you can apply most data transformation steps to just about any data table. The art consists of placing them in a sequence that can then be reused any time that the data changes to reprocess the new source data and deliver an up-to-date output.

© Adam Aspin 2020
A. Aspin, *Data Mashup with Microsoft Excel Using Power Query and M*,
https://doi.org/10.1007/978-1-4842-6018-0_10

The key to appreciating and managing this process is to get well acquainted with the Applied Steps list in the Query Settings pane. This list contains the details of every step that you applied, in the order in which you applied it. Each step retains the name that Power Query gave it when it was created, and each can be altered in the following ways:

- Renamed

- Deleted

- Moved (in certain cases)

The even better news is that, in many cases, steps can be modified. This way you are not stuck with the choices that you made initially, but have the opportunity of tweaking and improving individual steps in a process. This can avoid your having to rebuild an entire sequence of steps in an ETL routine simply by replacing one element in the ETL process.

In order to experiment with the various ways that you can modify queries, you are going to need some initial data. So, to start with, I suggest that you use the following Excel source file: C:\DataMashupWithExcelSamples\CarSalesDataForQueries.xlsx. This source file contains queries that connect to six source tables in another Excel file, thereby imitating a real-world scenario (where the data sources could come from multiple different sources and have different origins: database, text, etc.).

Once you have opened this file, switch to the Query Editor window by double-clicking any of the existing queries in the Queries & Connections window.

Modifying a Step

How you alter a step will depend on how the original transformation was applied. This becomes second nature after a little practice and will always involve first clicking the step that you wish to modify and then applying a different modification. If you invoke a ribbon option, such as altering the data type, for instance, then you change the data type by simply applying another data type directly from the ribbon. If you used an option that displayed a dialog (such as splitting a column, among others), then you can right-click the step in the Applied Steps list and select Edit Settings from the context menu. Alternatively, and if you prefer, you can click the "gear" icon that is displayed to the right of most (but not all) steps to display a dialog where you can adjust the step settings. This dialog will show all the options and settings that you applied initially; in it, you can make any modifications that you consider necessary.

A final possibility that makes it easy to alter the settings for a process is to edit the formula that appears in the formula bar each time you click a step. This, however, involves understanding all the complexities of each piece of the code that underpins the data transformation process. I will provide a short overview of code modification in Chapter 12.

Tip   If you can force yourself to organize the process that you are writing with Power Query, then a little forethought and planning can reap major dividends. For instance, certain tasks, such as setting data types, can be carried out in a single operation. This means that you only have to look in one place for a similar set of data transformations. Not just that, but if you need to alter a data type for a column at a later stage, I suggest that you click the Changed Type step before you make any further alterations. This way, you extend the original step, rather than creating other steps—which can make the process more confusing and needlessly voluminous.

Renaming a Step

Power Query names steps using the name of the transformation that was applied. This means that if another similar step is applied later, Power Query uses the same name with a numeric increment. As this is not always comprehensible when reviewing a sequence of transformation steps, you may prefer to give more user-friendly names to individual steps. This is done as follows:

1. Select the query (or source table or worksheet, if you prefer). I will use the Clients query in this example.

2. Right-click the step that you want to rename, Changed Type, for instance.

3. Select Rename from the context menu.

4. Type in the new name. I will use **NewDataTypes**.

5. Press Enter.

The step is renamed and the new name will appear in the Applied Steps list in the Query Settings pane. This way you can ensure that when you come back to a data transformation process days, weeks, or months later, you are able to understand more intuitively the process that you defined, as well as why you shaped the data like you did.

Note   You can use upper- or lowercase characters—or a mixture of both—when naming steps in Power Query. You can also add spaces and special characters.

Deleting a Step or a Series of Steps

Deleting a step is all too easy, but doing so can have serious consequences. This is because an ETL process is often an extremely tightly coupled series of events, where each event depends intimately on the preceding one. So deleting a step can make every subsequent step fail. Knowing which events you can delete without drastic consequences will depend on the types of process that you are developing as well as your experience with Power Query. In any case, this is what you should do if you need to delete a step:

1. Place the pointer over the process step that you want to delete.

2. Click the cross (×) icon that appears.

3. Select Delete. The Delete Step dialog *might* appear (if deleting this step might have unexpectedly negative consequences), as shown in Figure 10-1.

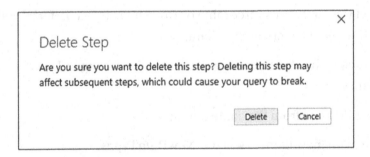

Figure 10-1. The Delete Step dialog

4. Confirm by clicking the Delete button. The step is deleted.

If—and it is highly possible—deleting this step causes issues for the rest of the process, you will see that the data table is replaced by an error message. This message will vary depending on the type of error that Power Query has encountered.

When describing this technique, I was careful to state that you *might* see the Delete Step dialog. If you are deleting the final step in a sequence of steps, then you will probably not see it, since there should not be any potentially horrendous consequences; at worst, you will have to re-create the step. If you are deleting a step in the middle of a process, then you might want to think seriously about doing so before you cause a potentially vast number of problems. Consequently, you are asked to confirm the deletion in these cases.

An alternative technique is to right-click the step that you want to delete and select Delete. You may still have to confirm the deletion.

If you realize that an error in a process step has invalidated all your work up until the end of the process, rather than deleting multiple elements one by one, click Delete Until End from the context menu at step 2 in the preceding exercise.

Discarding Changes

If, when working with Power Query, you realize at any point that you have just destroyed hours of work, then (after drawing a deep breath)

1. Click the close button (the small cross) at the top right of the Power Query Editor window. The dialog shown in Figure 10-2 will appear.

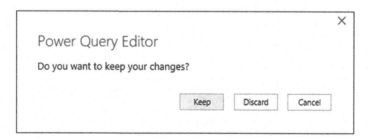

Figure 10-2. *The discard changes dialog in Power Query*

2. Click Discard to close Power Query without applying any changes.

Don't count on using an undo function as you can in other desktop applications. To lower your blood pressure, you may prefer to save a copy of a file containing an intricate data transformation process *before* deleting any steps. You can also make copies of the entire data transformation process as "M" code—as you will learn in Chapter 12.

Modifying an Existing Step

Power Query does not try and lock you into a rigid sequence of events when you create a series of applied steps to create and transform a data flow. This really becomes obvious when you discover that you need to alter a step in a process.

Suppose, for instance, that you discover that you have loaded a wrong Excel worksheet when you selected the initial data from an Excel file. You do not want to repeat the process when you can simply substitute one worksheet name for another.

Assuming that you have opened the Excel workbook CarSalesDataForQueries.xlsx and have switched to the Query Editor:

1. Select the query that you want to modify (Clients in this example).

2. Click the step to modify (in this case, it will be Navigation).

3. Click the gear (or cog) icon to the right of the step name.
    The appropriate dialog will appear. In this case, it will be the
    Navigation dialog that you can see in Figure 10-3.

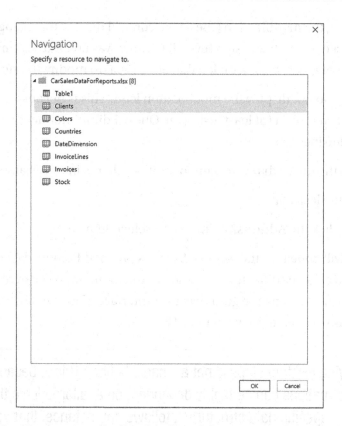

Figure 10-3. *The Navigation dialog displayed for step modification*

4.   Click the table or worksheet that you want to use instead of the current dataset (Table1 in this example).

5.   Click OK.

The Query Editor will replace one source dataset with another. It might also add extra steps to ensure that the data is adapted for use in the query.

As you saw in the previous nine chapters, Power Query offers a vast range of data ingestion and modification possibilities. So I cannot, here, describe every possible option as far as modifying an Applied Step is concerned. Nonetheless, the principle is simple:

- If the Query Editor can modify a step, the gear icon will be displayed to the right of the step name.

- Clicking the modification (the gear) icon will display the dialog that was used to create the step (even if the step was created automatically by Power Query)—or a dialog that allows you to modify the step.

Certain steps do not display the modification icon. This is because the step cannot be modified, only removed (at least, using the Query Editor interface). As an example of this, add the following step:

1. Select the query that you want to modify (Clients in this example).

2. Click the last step.

3. Right-click the Address2 column and select Remove.

A new step will appear in the Applied Steps list, named Removed Columns. This step does not have the modification icon. So, for the moment, you can remove it, but *not* modify it—at least, not using the graphical user interface. You can, however, modify the code for a step as you will learn in Chapter 12.

Note   Modifying existing steps is not a "magic bullet." This is because a series of data transformations can be highly dependent on a tailored logic that has been developed for a specific data structure. It follows, for instance, that you can only replace a data source with another one that has a virtually identical structure. However, modifying a step can avoid your having to rewrite an entire data flow sequence in many cases.

Adding a Step

You can add a step anywhere in the sequence. All you have to do is click the step that *precedes* the new step that you want to insert *before* clicking the icon in any of the ribbons that corresponds to the new step. As is the case when you delete a step, Power Query will display an alert warning you that this action *could* cause problems with the process from this new step on.

Altering Process Step Sequencing

It is possible—technically—to resequence steps in a process. However, in my experience, this is not always practical, since changing the order of steps in a process can cause as much damage as deleting a step. Nonetheless, you can always try it like this:

1. Right-click the step that you want to resequence.

2. Select Move Up or Move Down from the context menu.

I remain pessimistic that this can work miracles, but it is good to know that it is there.

Tip   Remember that before tweaking the order in which the process is applied, clicking any process step causes the table in the Power Query window to refresh to show you the state of the data up to and including the selected step. This is a very clear visual guide to the process and how the ETL process is carried out. Indeed, clicking the steps one after another will "scroll through" the changes in the data and demonstrate exactly how the while process is structured and works.

An Approach to Sequencing

Given the array of available data transformation options, you may well be wondering how best to approach a new ETL project using Power Query. I realize that all projects are different, but as a rough and ready guide, I suggest attempting to order your project like this:

1. Load the sample data into Power Query.

2. Promote or add comprehensible column headers. For example, you really do not want to be looking at step 47 of a process and wondering what Column29 is, when it could read (for instance) ClientName.

3. Remove any columns that you do not need. The smaller the dataset, the faster the processing. What is more, you will find it easier to concentrate on, and understand, the data if you are only looking at information that you really need. Any columns that have been removed can be returned to the dataset simply by deleting or editing the step that removed them.

4. Alter the data types for every column in the table. Correct data types are fundamental for many transformation steps and are essential for filtering, so it's best to get them sorted out early on.

5. Filter out any records that you do not need. Once again, the smaller the dataset, the faster the processing. This includes deduplication.

6. Parse any complex JSON or XML elements.

7. Carry out any necessary data cleansing.

8. Carry out any necessary transforms.

9. Carry out any necessary column splits or adding custom columns.

10. Add any derived columns.

11. Add any calculations or logical transformations of data.

12. Handle any error records that the ETL process has thrown up.

Once again, I must stress that this is not a definitive guide. I hope, however, that it will help you to see "the wood for the trees" when you are creating data load and transformation processes using Power Query.

Error Records

Some data transformation operations will cause errors. This can be a fact of life when mashing up source data. For instance, you could have a few rows in a large dataset where a date column contains a few records that are texts or numbers. If you convert the column to a date data type, then any values that cannot be converted will appear as error values.

Managing Queries

Once you have used Power Query for any length of time, you will probably become addicted to creating more and deeper analyses based on wider-ranging data sources. Inevitably, this will mean learning to manage the data sources that feed into your data models efficiently and productively.

Fortunately, Power Query comes replete with a small arsenal of query management tools to help you. These include

- Organizing and grouping queries into folders

- Duplicating queries

- Referencing queries

- Documenting queries

- Adding a column as a new query

Let's take a look at these functions, one by one.

Note   Query management is heavily dependent on the Queries pane. Power Query hides this pane by default, so you will need to display it by clicking the chevron at the top right of the collapsed Queries pane on the left of the data. What is more, many of the query management functions are also available directly from inside Excel in the popup menu of the Queries & Connections pane.

Organizing Queries

When you have anything from a handful to a few dozen queries that you are using in the Power Query Editor, you may want to exercise some control over how they are organized. To begin with, you can modify the order in which queries appear in the Queries pane on the left of the Power Query Editor window. This lets you override the default order, which is that the most recently added data source appears at the bottom of the list.

Do the following to change the position of a query in the list:

1. Display the Queries pane if it is not already visible.

2. Right-click the query that you want to move.

3. Select Move Up (or Move Down) from the context menu.

You have to carry out this operation a number of times to move a query up or down a number of places. So the alternative—dragging queries up and down in the list—is probably worth using as well.

Grouping Queries

You can also create custom groups to better organize the queries that you are using in an Excel file. This will not have any effect on how the queries work. Grouping queries is simply an organizational technique, and it will not change in any way the data tables that you see in report mode in Excel. You will, however, see the groups that you created reflected in the Queries & Connections pane in Excel.

Creating a New Group

Here is how to create a new group:

1. Right-click the query that you want to add to a new group. I will use the Colors query in the Query Editor—opened from the Excel file CarSalesDataForQueries.xlsx.

2. Select Move To Group ➤ New Group from the context menu. The New Group dialog will appear.

3. Enter a name for the group and (optionally) a description. I will name the group **ReferenceData**. The dialog will look something like Figure 10-4.

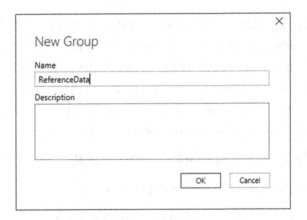

Figure 10-4. *The New Group dialog*

4. Click OK.

The new group is created and the selected query will appear in the group. The Queries pane will look something like Figure 10-5.

Figure 10-5. *The Queries pane with a new group added*

Note   By default, all other queries are added to a group named Other Queries.

If you have created dozens of queries, this technique can really help you to manage a complex data load process. As you might expect, you can expand or close a group by clicking the triangle to the left of the folder name.

Renaming Groups

You can rename any groups that you have added.

1. Right-click the group that you want to rename.

2. Select Rename from the context menu.

3. Edit or replace the name.

4. Press Enter.

Note   The Other Queries group cannot be renamed or deleted. By default, all new queries will be added to this group. You can also double-click the group to rename it directly.

Adding a Query to a Group

To move a query from its current group to another group, you can carry out the following steps:

1. Right-click the query that you want to add to another existing group.

2. Select Move To Group ➤ *Destination Group Name* from the context menu.

The selected query is moved to the chosen group. The group structure will also be visible in the Queries & Connections pane in Excel.

Duplicating Queries

If you have done a lot of work transforming data, you could well want to keep a copy of the original query before trying out any potentially risky alterations to your work. Fortunately, this is extremely simple.

1. Right-click the query that you want to copy.

2. Select Duplicate from the context menu.

The query is copied and the duplicate appears in the list of queries inside the same group as the source query. It has the same name as the original query, with a number in parentheses appended. You can always rename it in the Query Settings pane, in the Queries pane on the left of the Query Editor window, or in the Queries & Connections pane in Excel itself.

Note   You can copy and paste queries if you prefer. The advantage of this technique is that you can choose the destination group for the copied query simply by clicking the folder icon for the required group *before* pasting the copy of the query.

Referencing Queries

If you are building a complex ETL (Extract, Transform, Load) routine, you might conceivably organize your work in stages to better manage the process. To help you with this, the Power Query Editor allows you to use the output from one query as the source for another query. This enables you to break down different parts of the process (e.g., structure, filters, then cleansing) into separate queries so that you can concentrate on different aspects of the transformation in different queries.

To use the output of one query as the source data for another, you need to *reference* a query, like this:

1. Right-click the query that you want to use as the source data for a new query.

2. Select Reference from the context menu. A new query is created in the list of queries in the Queries pane.

3. Right-click the new query, select Rename, and give it a meaningful name.

Unless you rename the query, the new query has the same name as the original query, with a number in parentheses appended. If you click the new query, you see exactly the same data in the referenced query as you can see if you click the final step in the source query.

From now on, any modifications that you make in the referenced (source) query produce an effect on the data that is used as the source for the second query. In other words, you have created a sequence of queries in a data ingestion process.

In practice, I suspect, you will not want to use two copies of the same query to create reports. Indeed, if a query is being used as an "intermediate" query, the data that it contains might not even be fully usable. So you could want to *prevent the intermediate query from outputting data to Excel*. To do this:

1. In the Data ribbon, click Get Data ➤ From File ➤ From Workbook.

2. Select the file BrilliantBritishCars.xlsx and click Import.

3. In the Navigator dialog, select the source table BaseData.

4. Click the popup menu at the right of the Load button and select Load To. The Import Data dialog will be displayed.

5. Click Only create connection.

6. Click OK.

The source query will appear in the Queries & Connections pane, but will be flagged as Connection only.

Tip   You cannot hide queries in the Queries & Connections pane in Excel—but you can place reference queries in a custom group to isolate them visually.

You may be wondering why you would want to create "intermediate" queries. Some ideas are

- You want to isolate complex data transformations into more manageable subsets. You may, for instance, want one intermediate query that transforms the data while a subsequent query cleanses the data.

- You could want to apply a common set of initial transformations that then feed into two separate data preparation paths—a detailed view of the data and an aggregated view.

Note   The way to convert an existing query to a connection only—ready for use as a reference query—is to delete the worksheet (or Power Pivot sheet) containing the output data.

Documenting Queries

In a complex ETL process, it is easy to get confused—or simply forget—which query does what. Consequently, I always advise documenting queries by adding a meaningful description.

1. Right-click the query that you want to annotate.

2. Select Properties from the context menu. The Query Properties dialog will appear.

3. Add a description. The result could be like the dialog shown in Figure 10-6.

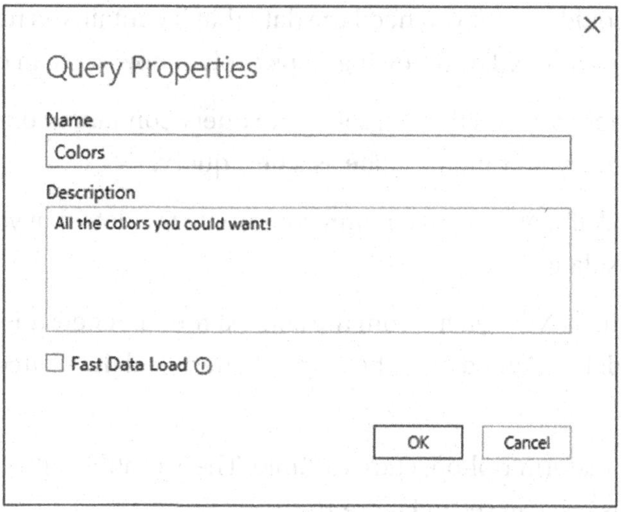

Figure 10-6. *Adding a description to a query*

4. Click OK.

The description that you added is now visible as a tooltip if you hover the cursor over the query name in the list of queries in the Queries pane of the Query Editor. You will also see the description in the Peek window for this query if you hover the mouse pointer over the query in the Queries & Connections pane in Excel.

Note   Clicking Fast Data Load will attempt to load the data faster—but Power Query could remain unresponsive for some time while the data is loaded.

Adding a Column as a New Query

There are occasions when you might want to extract a column of data and use it as a separate query. It could be that you need the data that it contains as reference data for another query, for example. The following steps explain how you can do this:

1. In the Queries list on the left, select the query containing the column that you want to isolate as a new query.

2. Right-click the title of the column containing the data that you want to isolate.

3. Select Add as New Query from the context menu. A new query is created. It is named after the original query and the source column.

4. In the Transform ribbon, click To Table. The To Table dialog will appear, as you can see in Figure 10-7.

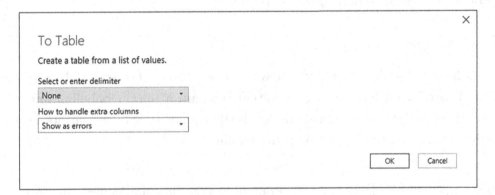

Figure 10-7. The To Table dialog

5. Click OK. The new query will become a table of data and will have the name of the column that you selected.

6. Rename the query, if you judge this necessary.

You can now use this query in your data model and as part of a linked set of query processes.

Note   A query created in this way is *completely disconnected* from the source query from where the data was taken. Put another way, any refresh of the source data will have *no* effect on the new query that you created from a column.

Managing Queries from the Queries & Connections Pane

You are not obliged to switch to the Query Editor to carry out many of the query management tasks that you discovered in this chapter. You can perform several operations directly from the Queries & Connections pane.

For example:

1. Open the Excel file Chapter10Sample.xlsx, and display the Queries & Connections pane.

2. Right-click one of the queries. The popup menu will appear, as shown in Figure 10-8.

Figure 10-8. *The Queries & Connections pane popup menu*

3. Click the menu option that you want.

As you can see, not all the query management options are available. However, you can use this context menu to

- Create, delete, and modify groups of queries or queries

- Move queries between groups and inside groups

- Expand and collapse groups

- Alter group properties

- Copy and paste queries and groups

- Duplicate and reference queries

- Merge and append queries

- Alter query and group properties

- Refresh queries

- Show the Peek window for a query

Note   The contents of the context menu will vary depending on whether you have right-clicked a group or an individual query.

Conclusion

In this chapter, you saw how to manage and extend the contents of the queries that you can create using Power Query. Specifically, you saw how to modify individual steps in a data load and transformation process. This ranged from renaming steps to changing the order of steps in a process—or even altering the specification of what a step actually does.

Then you saw how to manage whole queries. You learned how to rename and group queries as well as how to chain queries so that the output from one query became the source of data for another query.

Finally, you learned how to reference—or link—queries to isolate parts of a data ingestion process or to break down a complex process into manageable parts.

It is now time to learn how to add interactivity to your processes using parameters in Power Query. You will discover this in the next chapter.

CHAPTER 11

Parameterizing Queries

Not all data flows are rigid and predictable. There will, inevitably, be cases where you also want to shape the data ingestion process depending on aspects of the source data. This can mean parameterizing your queries to allow user interaction or adjusting the data flow dynamically. Adding parameters to queries enables you to define and apply specific criteria to certain aspects of query processing.

All the files used in examples in this chapter are available for download from the Apress website as described in Appendix A.

As parameters are entirely managed inside the Query Editor, you will need to have the Query Editor open to carry out any of the examples in this chapter.

Parameterizing Queries

At their heart, parameters are a technique that enables you to

- Select a value that can be used in one or more queries to alter the query flow by injecting a required element into a query step. This could be a file source or a filter value, for instance.

- Restrict the selection of potential parameter values to a predefined list of options for a user to choose from.

There are currently three basic ways a user can select a parameter before running a query that will apply the chosen parameter. A parameter can be

- A single value that you or the user enters

- A selection of a value from a list of possible values that you enter manually

- A selection of a value from a list of possible values that you create using existing queries

© Adam Aspin 2020
A. Aspin, *Data Mashup with Microsoft Excel Using Power Query and M*,
https://doi.org/10.1007/978-1-4842-6018-0_11

It follows that using parameters is a two-step process:

- Create a parameter.

- Apply it to a query.

A parameter is really nothing more than a specialized type of query. As it is a query, you can

- Load it into the data model (although this is rarely required)

- Reference it from another query

- Build and modify it just like any other query

This chapter will explain how you can create and apply parameters. This will include showing you some of the ways that you can apply parameters in the Query Editor to filter or transform the data.

Creating a Simple Parameter

At its simplest, a parameter is a value that you store so that you can use it later to assist you in your data transformation. Here is how you can store a parameter containing a "True" value ready for use in filtering subsequent datasets:

1. Open the Excel file C:\DataMashupWithExcelSamples\ CarSalesDataForQueries.xlsx (unless it is already open, of course).

2. Display the Queries & Connections pane (unless it is already visible). Double-click any of the queries in the Queries & Connections pane to open the Query Editor.

3. In the Query Editor Home ribbon, click the small triangle at the bottom of the Manage Parameters button, then select New Parameter from the available menu options. The Parameters dialog will appear.

4. Enter **DealerParameter** as the parameter name and **Filter dealer types** as the description.

5. Ensure that the Required check box is selected.

6. Choose True/False from the popup list of types.

7. Enter True as the Current Value from the popup list. The dialog
    will look like the one in Figure 11-1.

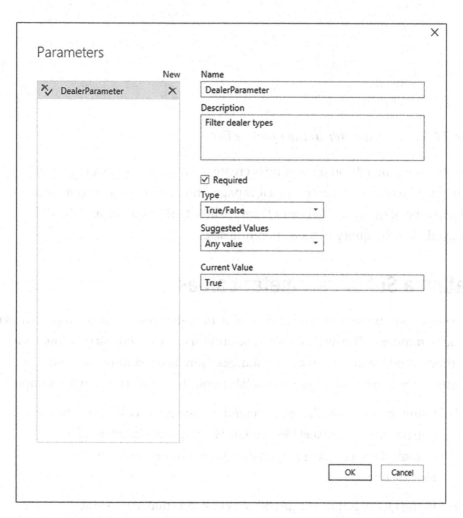

Figure 11-1. *The Parameters dialog*

8. Click OK. The new parameter will appear in the Queries list on the
    left. You can see this in Figure 11-2.

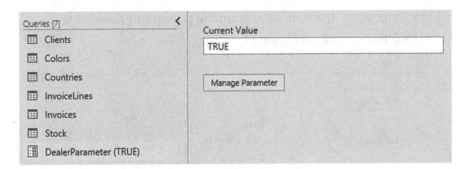

Figure 11-2. *A parameter in the Queries list*

For the moment, all you have done is create a parameter and store a value in it. You will see how to use this parameter in a few pages' time. As you can see, a parameter is stored as a type of query in the Power Query Editor Queries pane, and the default value is displayed after the query name in parentheses.

Creating a Set of Parameter Values

While a single parameter can always be useful, in reality you are likely to need lists of potential parameters. This will allow you or other users to choose a parameter value from a predefined list in certain circumstances. Here is an example of creating a parameter containing a subset of the available country names used in the sample data:

1.   Using the Excel file that you created in the previous section (the one based on the Excel file C:\DataMashupWithExcelSamples\ CarSalesOverview.xlsx), open the Query Editor—unless it is already open.

2.   In the Query Editor Home ribbon, click the small triangle at the bottom of the Manage Parameters button, then select New Parameter from the available menu options. The Parameters dialog will be displayed.

3.   Enter **CountriesParameter** as the parameter name.

4.   Ensure that the Required check box is selected.

5.   Choose Text from the popup list of types.

6.   In the Suggested Values popup list, select List of values.

7. Enter the following three values in the grid that has now appeared:

    a. France

    b. Spain

    c. Germany

8. Select France as the Default Value from the popup list.

9. Select Spain as the Current Value from the popup list. The dialog will look like the one shown in Figure 11-3.

Figure 11-3. *The Parameters dialog for a set of options*

10. Click OK. The new parameter will appear in the Queries list on the left.

325

Once again, all you have done is create the parameter. You will see how it can be applied in a couple of pages' time.

Note   As you can see, any current value that you have chosen will appear in the Queries pane in parentheses to the right of the parameter name. This is to help you remember which value is current—and is possibly being used to shape a data flow process.

Creating a Query-Based Parameter

Typing lists of values that you can use to choose a parameter is not only laborious, it is also potentially error-prone. So you can use the data from existing queries to create the series of available elements that you use in a parameter instead of manually entering lists of values. Moreover, any lists that you enter manually are completely static. So you will have to remember to update them if the user requirements change. Parameter lists are, by contrast, dynamic. That is, they update automatically if the source data changes.

As an example of this, suppose that you want a parameter that contains all the available makes of car that the company sells:

1. Using the Excel file C:\DataMashupWithExcelSamples\ CarSalesDataForQueries.xlsx, open the Query Editor by double-clicking on any of the queries in the Queries & Connections pane.

2. Select the query Stock in the Queries list.

3. Right-click the title of the column named Model, and select Add as New Query. A new query named Model will appear in the Queries list. This query contains the contents of the column you selected.

4. In the newly created query, click Remove Duplicates in the Transform ribbon. The List column will only display unique values.

5. Rename the newly created query **ModelList**.

6. In the Query Editor Home ribbon, click the small triangle at the bottom of the Manage Parameters button, then select New Parameter from the available menu options. The Parameters dialog will be displayed.

7.   Enter **ModelsParameter** as the parameter name.

8.   Ensure that the Required check box is selected.

9.   Choose Text from the popup list of types.

10.   In the Suggested Values popup list, select Query.

11.   Select ModelList as the query containing a list of values to use from the popup list of available lists.

12.   Enter DB7 as the Current Value. The Parameters dialog should look like the one in Figure 11-4.

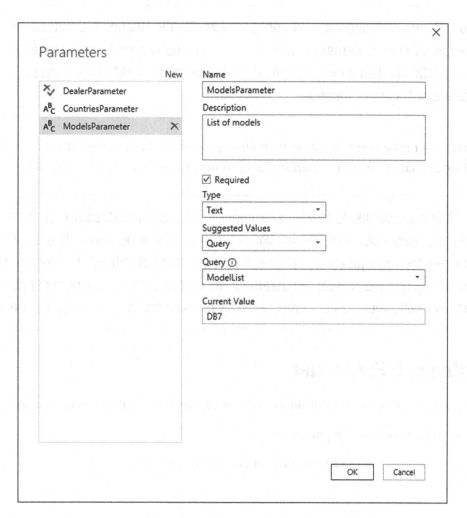

Figure 11-4. *The Parameters dialog for a list of options*

13. Click OK. The new parameter will appear in the Queries list on the left.

You should now be able to see all three parameters that you have created in the Queries pane, as shown in Figure 11-5.

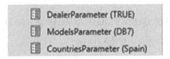

Figure 11-5. *Parameters in the Queries list*

Note   Parameters and lists will appear in Excel in the Queries & Connections pane. Lists will also normally load to a new Excel worksheet. Unless you define these as "Connection only" you will need to remember—and to warn users—that these are not "classic" queries.

Once your parameters have been created, you can quit the Query Editor by clicking the Close & Load button. Your parameters can now be used to shape a data flow process.

Tip   It is also possible to create parameters "on the fly" (i.e., directly from inside a dialog that uses a parameter) when you want to use them. However, I find it better practice—and more practical—to prepare parameters beforehand. This forces you to think through the reasons for the parameter as well as the potential range of its use. It can also avoid your making errors when trying to do two different things at once.

Modifying a Parameter

Fortunately, parameters are not set in stone once they are created. You can easily modify

- The structure of a parameter

- The selected parameter element (the current value)

Modifying the Structure of a Parameter

Should you need to modify the way that a parameter is constructed, one way is to do the following:

1. In the Query Editor Home ribbon, click Manage Parameters. The Parameters dialog will be displayed as seen in the previous sections.

2. In the left pane of the dialog, click the parameter that you want to modify. The parameter definition will appear on the right.

3. Carry out any required modifications.

4. Click OK.

Alternatively, you can do this:

1. Click the parameter in the Queries pane on the left of the Query Editor.

2. Click the Manage Parameters button. The Parameters dialog will appear.

3. Carry out any required modifications.

4. Click OK.

You can also, if you prefer, right-click a parameter in the Queries pane and select Manage from the popup menu to display the Parameters dialog.

Applying a Parameter When Filtering Records

Now that you have seen how parameters are created, it is time to see them in action. As a first example of applying a parameter, you will see how to use a parameter to filter a query:

1. Open the file C:\DataMashupWithExcelSamples\ ParametersExample.xlsx. This file contains the three parameters created previously.

2. Double-click the Countries query in the Queries & Connections pane to open the Power Query Editor and select the Countries dataset. You may need to display the Queries & Connections pane by clicking Data ➤ Queries & Connections.

3. Click the popup menu for the CountryName column on the right of the field name.

4. Select Text Filters ➤ Equals. The Filter Rows dialog will appear.

5. Leave Equals as the first choice.

6. Click the central popup (between equals and enter or select a value) and select Parameter from the list. You can see this in Figure 11-6.

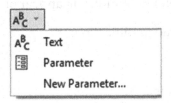

Figure 11-6. *Selecting a parameter for a filter*

7. Select CountriesParameter for the third popup. The dialog will look like the one shown in Figure 11-7.

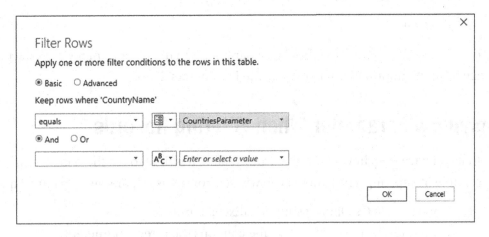

Figure 11-7. *Applying a parameter for a filter*

8. Click OK. The current parameter value (the country that you selected) will be applied, and the dataset will be filtered using the current parameter value.

Note   To remove a parameter from a filter, simply delete the relevant step in the Applied Steps list.

Modifying the Current Value of a Parameter

You could be forgiven for wondering if it is worth setting up a parameter merely to filter a dataset. However, this whole approach becomes more interesting if you modify the current parameter value and then refresh the data to apply the new parameter. Here is an example of this:

1. In the Query Editor Home ribbon, click the small triangle to display the menu for the Manage Parameters button.

2. Select Edit Parameters. The Enter Parameters dialog will appear.

3. From the popup list of values for the CountriesParameter, select one of the available values (and not the value that was previously selected). The dialog should look like the one shown in Figure 11-8.

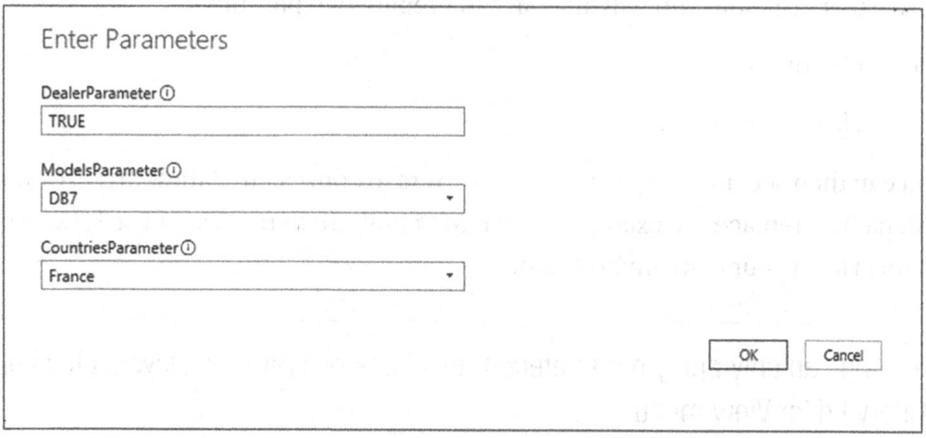

Enter Parameters

DealerParameter ⓘ
TRUE

ModelsParameter ⓘ
DB7

CountriesParameter ⓘ
France

OK   Cancel

Figure 11-8. *Modifying the current value of a parameter*

4. Click OK.

5. In the Query Editor Home ribbon, click Refresh Preview. The data will be refreshed and the new parameter values applied to the filters that use these parameters.

This approach becomes particularly useful if you have many combinations of filter values to test. In essence, you can apply a series of filters to several columns (or create complex filters) using several parameters and then test the results of different combinations of parameters on a dataset using the Enter Parameters dialog. This technique avoids having to alter multiple filters manually—and repeatedly. As an added bonus, you can restrict the user (or yourself) to specific lists of parameter choices by defining the lists of available parameter options. You can see this for the popup lists that appear when you select the CountriesParameter popup or the ModelsParameter popup.

Applying a Parameter to a Data Source

In some corporate environments, there are many database servers that are available, and possibly even more databases. You may find it difficult to remember all of these—and so may the users that you are preparing reports for using Power Query in Excel.

One solution that can make a corporate environment easier to navigate is to prepare parameters that contain the lists of available servers and databases. These parameters can then be used—and updated—to guide users in their choice of SQL Server, Oracle, or other database data sources.

To see this in action, you will first have to prepare two parameters:

- A list of servers

- A list of databases

You can then see how to use these parameters to connect to data sources. Of course, you will have to replace the example server and database names that I use here in step 6 with names from your own environment.

Note   You can only apply parameters if the check box Always allow is checked in the Query Editor View menu.

---

1. Open a new Excel file.

2. Click Get Data ➤ From Database ➤ From SQL Server Database.

3. Enter your server and database, and connect to the database.

4. Select a data table—or tables.

5. Click Transform Data to open the Query Editor.

6. Create a new parameter using the following elements:

   a. *Name*: Servers

   b. *Type*: Text

   c. *Suggested Values*: List of Values

   d. *Values in the list*: ADAM03 and ADAM03\SQL2017 (or your database server)

   e. *Default Value*: ADAM03\SQL2017 (or your database server)

   f. *Current Value*: ADAM03\SQL2017 (or your database server)

7. Select the query that you created to connect to the source data.

8. In the Applied Steps list, click the cog icon to the right of the first step, named Source.

9. On the Server line, click the popup for the server and choose Parameter. Select the Server parameter. The SQL Server database dialog will look like the one shown in Figure 11-9.

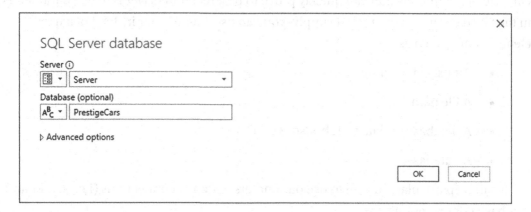

Figure 11-9. *Using a parameter to select the server and database*

10. Choose the data connectivity mode and any advanced options that you want to set.

11. Click OK. The server connection process and dialogs will appear, and you will then see the Navigator dialog displaying the tables and views for the current server and database values in the two parameters.

You could have defined and applied a database parameter as well. However, as the approach is virtually identical, I will leave you to attempt this unaided.

Other Uses for Parameters

These examples only cover a few of the cases where parameters can be applied in Power Query. Indeed, the range of circumstances where a parameter can be applied is increasing with each release of the product. So look out for all the dialogs that give you the option of using a parameter.

Using Parameters in the Data Source Step

One use of parameters that can quickly prove to be a real time-saver is to use parameters in the Source step of a query. Put simply, you can use a parameter instead of a fixed element name such as

- An Excel file name

- A file path

- A database or data warehouse server

- A database

It can be particularly useful to use parameters to define connections (i.e., server and database references), as this

- Provides a central reference point for connection information

- Avoids you having to type connection details for similar queries from the same server—and minimizes the risk of introducing typos

- Makes it easier to switch between development, test, and production servers

To illustrate this, and assuming that you have created the parameter "Servers" from the previous section, try the following:

1. Create a connection to a SQL Server database (as described in Chapter 3).

2. Click the Transform Data button in the Home ribbon.

3. In the Query Editor, select the query created by the database connection.

4. Click the first of the Applied Steps on the right. This step should be named "Source."

5. In the formula bar, replace the code that looks something like this:

    ```
    = Sql.Database("ADAMO3\SQL2017", "PrestigeCars")
    ```

6. With this

    ```
    = Sql.Database(Servers, "PrestigeCars")
    ```

7. Confirm your modifications by clicking the check box in the formula bar—or by pressing Enter. You will almost certainly have to confirm your database credentials.

Note   You need to be aware that hard-coded server and database names must be contained in double quotes, whereas parameters must *not* be enclosed in quotes. Also note that the M language used in the formula bar is case-sensitive. So you need to enter parameter names *exactly* as they were created. You will learn more about the M language in Chapter 12.

Applying a Parameter to a SQL Query

If you are using a relational database, such as Oracle or SQL Server, as a data source (and if you are reasonably up to speed with the flavor of SQL that the source database uses), you can query a database using SQL and then apply Power Query parameters to the source query.

Let's see this in action:

1. Open a new Excel file, open the Query Editor, and create the parameter named CountriesParameter that you saw a few pages ago.

2. Click Close & Load to close the Query Editor.

3. In the Excel Report screen, click SQL Server Database.

4. Enter the server and database that you are using. (If you are using the examples from the Apress website, then it will be your server and the database CarSalesData.)

5. Click Advanced options and enter the following SQL statement:

```
SELECT   *
FROM     CarSalesData.Data.CarSalesData
WHERE    CountryName = 'Germany'
```

6. Click OK and confirm any dialogs about data access and permissions.

7. Click Edit to connect to the data and open the Query Editor.

8. There should only be one Applied Step for the data connection. Expand the formula bar and tweak the formula so that it looks like this:

```
= Sql.Database("ADAMO3\SQLSERVER2016", "CarSalesData",
[Query="SELECT   * FROM CarSalesData.Data.CarSalesData WHERE
CountryName = '"& CountriesParameter &"'"])
```

9. Click the tick icon in the formula bar to confirm your changes. The data will change to display the data for France (the current parameter value) rather than Germany (the initial value in the SQL).

You can now alter the parameter value and refresh the data. This will place the current parameter inside the SQL WHERE clause and only get the data for the current parameter.

In case this seems a little succinct, let's look at the code used by Power Query *before* you made the change in step 8. The M language read:

```
= Sql.Database("ADAMO3\SQLSERVER2016", "CarSAlesDAta", [Query="SELECT   *
FROM    CarSalesData.Data.CarSalesData WHERE   CountryName = 'France'"])
```

The change was to replace

France

with

"& CountriesParameter &"

What you did was to replace the hard-coded criterion "France" with the parameter reference. Indeed, much as you would in Excel, you added double quotes and ampersands to the formula to allow the code to include an extraneous text element.

This was an extremely simple example, but I hope that it opens the door to some fairly advanced use of parameters in database connections.

Note   Updating data once a parameter has changed might require accepting data changes and new permissions.

Query Icons

As you could see previously in Figure 11-9, there are three query icons. These are explained in Table 11-1.

Table 11-1. *Query Icons*

Icon	Query Type	Description
▦	Query	The icon for a standard query
▯	List	The icon for a list
▤	Parameter	The icon for a parameter

Conclusion

In this chapter, you saw how to add parameters to queries and how to interact with queries in a controlled fashion. This lets you make queries—and so the entire ETL process—more flexible and interactive.

CHAPTER 12

The M Language

Data ingestion and modification are not only interface-driven in Power Query. In fact, the entire process is underpinned and powered by a highly specific programming language. Called "M," this language underlies everything that you have learned to do in the last 11 chapters.

Most users—most of the time—are unlikely to need to use the M language directly at all. This is because the Power Query Editor interface that you have learned so much about thus far in this book is both comprehensive and extremely intuitive. Yet there may be times when you will need to

- Add some additional functionality that is not immediately accessible through the graphical interface

- Add programming logic such as generating sequences of dates or numbers

- Create or manipulate your own lists, records, or tables programmatically

- Create your own built-in functions to extend or enhance those that are built in to the M language

- Use the Advanced Editor to modify code

- Add comments to your data ingestion processes

Before introducing you to these concepts, I need to add a few caveats:

- The "M" language that underpins Power Query queries is not for the faint of heart. The language can seem abstruse at first sight.

- The documentation is extremely technical and not wildly comprehensible for the uninitiated.

© Adam Aspin 2020
A. Aspin, *Data Mashup with Microsoft Excel Using Power Query and M*,
https://doi.org/10.1007/978-1-4842-6018-0_12

- The learning curve can be steep, even for experienced programmers.

- The "M" language is very different from VBA, which many Excel power users know well.

- Tweaking a step manually can cause havoc to a carefully wrought data load and transform process.

Moreover, the "M" language is so vast that it requires an entire book. Consequently, I have deliberately chosen to provide only the most superficial (and I hope, helpful) of introductions here. For greater detail, I suggest that you consult the Microsoft documentation. This is currently available at the following URLs:

- `https://msdn.microsoft.com/en-us/library/mt779182.aspx`

- `https://msdn.microsoft.com/en-us/library/mt807488.aspx`

In this chapter, I am not going to presume that the reader has any in-depth programming knowledge. I will provide a few comparisons with standard programming concepts to assist any readers that have programmed in VBA, C#, or Java. However, rest assured, the intention is to open up new horizons for passionate Power Query users rather than spiral off into a complex technical universe.

All of this is probably best understood by building on your existing knowledge and explaining how (simply by using the Power Query graphical interface) you have been writing M code already. Then you can extend this knowledge by learning how to tweak existing code, and finally you will see how to write M code unaided.

What Is the M Language?

I should, nonetheless, begin with a few technical stakes in the ground to explain what the Power Query Formula Language (or M as everyone calls the language now) is and what it can—and cannot—do.

M is a *functional* language. It is certainly not designed to perform general-purpose programming. Indeed, battle-hardened programmers will search in vain for coding structures and techniques that are core to other languages.

At the risk of offending programming purists, I prefer to introduce M to beginners as being a functional language in three ways:

- It exists to perform a simple function which is to load and transform data.

- It is built on a compendium of over 700 built-in functions, each of which is designed to carry out a specific piece of data load and/or transformation logic.

- It exists as a series of functions, each of which computes a set of input values to a single output value.

To complete the whirlwind introduction, you also need to know that

- M is *case-sensitive*, so you need to be very careful when typing in function keywords and variable names.

- M is *strongly typed*—which means that you must respect the core types of data elements used and convert them to the appropriate type where necessary. M will not do this for you automatically.

- M is built on a set of keywords, operators, and punctuators.

I don't want to get too technical at this juncture. Nonetheless, I hope that a high-level overview will prepare you for some of the approaches that you will learn later in this chapter.

M and the Power Query Editor

The good news about M is that you can already write it. By this I mean that every example that you followed in the previous 11 chapters wrote one or more lines of M code for you. Indeed, each step in a data load and transformation process that you generated when using the Power Query Editor created M code for you—automatically.

This means several (very positive) things:

- You do not necessarily have to begin writing M code from a blank slate. Often you can use the Query Editor interface to carry out most of the work—and then tweak the automatically generated code to add the final custom elements that you require.

- You do not have to learn over 700 functions to deliver M code as the Query Editor can find and write many of the appropriate instructions for you.

- The Query Editor interface is tightly linked to the way that M code is written. So understanding how to use the interface helps you in understanding what M code is and how it works. Indeed, there is a one-to-one relationship between many Power Query interface elements and the underlying M function.

Modifying the Code for a Step

If you feel that you want to delve into the inner reaches of Power Query, you can modify steps in a query by editing the code that is created automatically every time that you add or modify a query step.

To get a quick idea of what can be done:

1. Open a new Excel file.

2. In the Data ribbon, select Get Data ➤ From File ➤ From Worksheet.

3. Select the Excel file C:\DataMashupWithExcelSamples\ BrilliantBritishCars.xlsx.

4. Select the source table named BaseData.

5. Click Transform Data to open the Query Editor.

6. Select the column IsDealer and remove it.

7. Click the Remove Columns step in the BaseData query. You will see the "M" code in the formula bar. It will look like that shown in Figure 12-1.

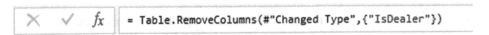

Figure 12-1. "M" code for an applied step

8. In the formula bar, edit the M code to replace IsDealer with
   ReportingYear.

9. Press Enter or click the tick icon (check mark) in the formula bar
   to confirm your changes.

The step and subsequent data will be updated to reflect your changes.

The modification that you carried out in step 8 effectively means that you are adding
back the IsDealer column and removing the ReportingYear column instead. You could
have done this using the interface (by clicking the gear cog icon in the Applied Steps list
for this step), but the whole point is to understand that both options are available and
that the Power Query interface is only generating and modifying M code. So you can
modify this code directly, if you prefer. Indeed, modifying M code is often faster than
making a series of interface-based maneuvers.

If you are an Excel power user (as many Power Query aficionados are), then you can
be forgiven for thinking that this is similar to Excel Macro development. Indeed, it is in
some respects:

- The core code can be recorded (VBA for Excel, M for Power Query).

- The resulting code can then be modified.

This is, of course, an overtly simplistic comparison. The two approaches may be
similar, but the two languages are vastly different. Yet if this helps as a metaphor to
encourage you to move to M development, then so be it.

There are, inevitably, a series of caveats when modifying the M code for a query step
in the formula bar. These include (but are far from restricted to)

- Any error will not only cause the step to fail, it will cause the whole
  data load and transformation process to fail from the current step
  onward.

- You need to remember that M is case-sensitive—and even the
  slightest error of capitalization can cause the entire process to fail.

- The use of quotes to define literal elements (such as column names)
  must be respected.

- M makes lavish use of both parentheses and braces. It can take some
  practice and understanding of the underlying logic to appreciate
  their use fully in various contexts.

Fortunately, M will provide fairly clear error messages if (or when) errors creep in. If you enter an erroneous field name, for instance, you could see a message like the one in Figure 12-2.

 Expression.Error: The column 'Reporting Year' of the table wasn't found.
Details:
    Reporting Year

Figure 12-2. *An "M" error message*

I do not want you to feel that modifying M code is difficult or dangerous, however. So, to extend the example given earlier, this is what the M code would look like if you extended it to remove two columns, and not just one:

```
= Table.RemoveColumns(#"Changed Type",{"ReportingYear", "IsDealer"})
```

Note   More generally, it is often best to look at the code for existing steps—or create "dummy" code using a sample dataset in parallel—to get an idea of what the M code for a particular function looks like. This will then indicate how best to modify the code.

M Expressions

To give you a clearer understanding of what each M "step" contains, Figure 12-3 shows the core structure of a step. However, only the Power Query interface calls this a step. M actually calls this an *expression*. So that is the term I will use from now on.

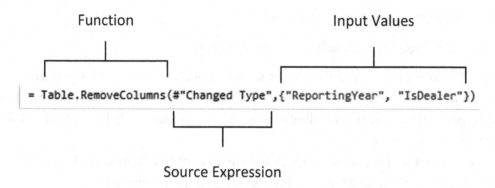

Figure 12-3. *An M expression*

There are several fundamental points that you need to be aware of here:

- Each M *expression* is made up of *functions*. These can be any of the built-in functions (such as the Table.RemoveColumns) used here—or functions that you have defined (which is explained a little later in this chapter). They can also be calculations or simple logic.

- As you learned in the course of this book so far, data mashup is essentially a series of individual actions (or *steps* as the Power Query interface calls them). These actions are linked in a "chain" where each expression is built on—and refers to—a preceding expression. In Figure 12-3, this specific expression refers to the output of the #"Changed Type" expression which preceded it.

- M expressions can become extremely complex and include multiple functions—rather like complex Excel formulas. As functions can be nested, this can lead to quite complex expressions.

Writing M by Adding Custom Columns

Another way to write certain types of M code is to add custom columns. Although these are known as *custom columns* in Power Query, they are also known more generically as *derived columns* or *calculated columns*. Although they can do many things, their essential role is to carry out any or all of the following (and this list is far from exhaustive):

- Concatenate (or join, if you prefer) existing columns

- Add calculations to the data table

- Extract a specific part of a column

- Add flags to the table based on existing data

The best way to understand these columns is probably to see them in action. You can then extend these principles in your own processes. This can, however, be an excellent starting point to learn basic M coding—albeit limited to a narrowly focused area of data wrangling in M.

Initially, let's perform a column join and create a column named Vehicle, which concatenates the Make and Model columns with a space in between.

1. Open a blank Excel file.

2. Connect to the C:\DataMashupWithExcelSamples\ BrilliantBritishCars.xlsx data source.

3. Click Transform to open the Power Query Editor.

4. In the Add Column ribbon, click Custom Column. The Add Custom Column dialog is displayed.

5. Click the Make column in the column list on the right, then click the Insert button; =[Make] will appear in the Custom column formula box at the left of the dialog.

6. Enter & " " & in the Custom column formula box after =[Make]. Note the space between the pair of double quotes.

7. Click the Model column in the column list on the right, and then click the Insert button.

8. Click inside the New column name box and enter a name for the column. I call it CarType. The dialog will look like Figure 12-4.

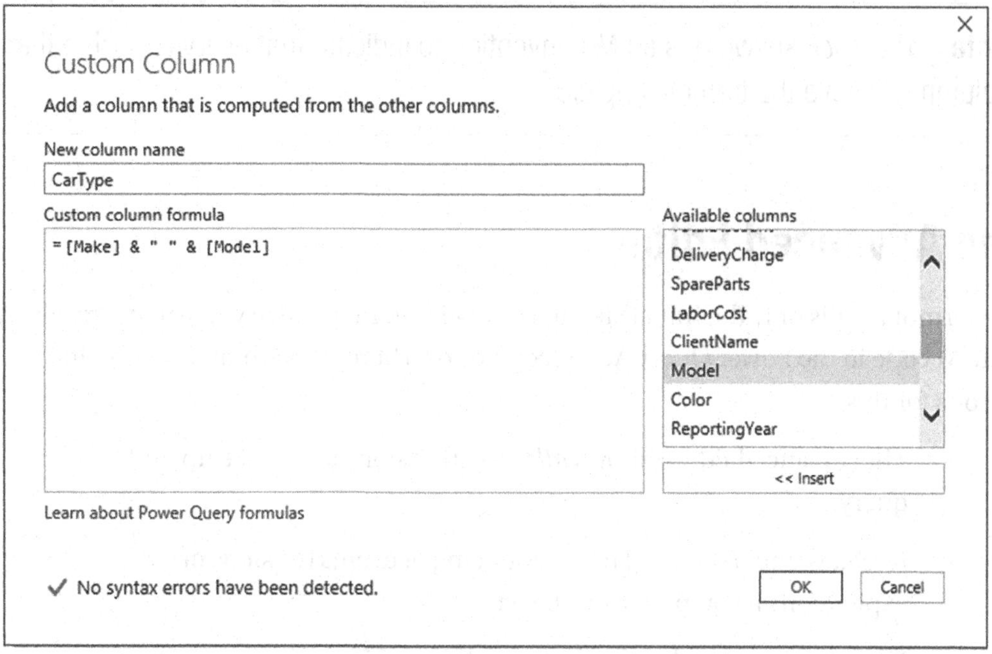

Figure 12-4. *The Custom Column dialog*

9. Click OK. The new column is added to the right of the data table;
   it contains the results of the formula. Inserted Column appears
   in the Applied Steps list. The formula bar contains the following
   formula:

```
= Table.AddColumn(#"Changed Type", "CarType", each [Make] & " " & [Model])
```

You can always double-click a column to insert it into the Custom column formula
box if you prefer. To remove a column, simply delete the column name (including the
square brackets) in the Custom column formula box.

Tip   You must always enclose a column name in square brackets.

You can see that this line of M code follows the principles that you have already seen.
It uses an M formula (Table.AddColumn) that refers to a previous expression (#"Changed
Type") and then applies the code that carries out the expression requirements—in this
case adding a new column that contains basic M code.

> **Note** The *each* keyword is an M convention to indicate that every record in the column will have the formula applied.

The Advanced Editor

The formula bar is only the initial step to coding in M. In practice you will nearly always write M code in the Power Query Advanced Editor. There are several fundamental reasons for this:

- The Advanced Editor shows *all* the expressions that make up an M query.

- It makes understanding the sequencing of events (or steps or expressions if you prefer) much easier.

- It has a syntax checker that helps isolate and identify syntax errors.

> **Note** The Advanced Editor, unfortunately, does not yet have IntelliSense built-in. This means that you cannot see M function popup as you type.

Expressions in the Advanced Editor

The M expressions that you can see individually in the formula bar do not exist in a vacuum. Quite the contrary, they are always part of a coherent sequence of data load, cleansing, and transformation events. This is probably best appreciated if you now take a look at the whole block of M code that was created when you loaded a table from an Excel file previously.

To see the M code, you need to open the Advanced Editor.

1. In the Home ribbon, click the Advanced Editor button. The Advanced Editor window will open, as shown in Figure 12-5. You can also see the Applied Steps list from the Power Query Editor to help you understand how each step is, in fact, an M expression.

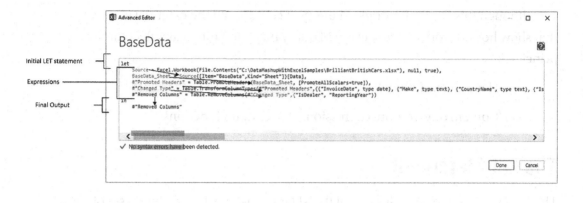

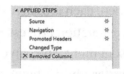

Figure 12-5. *Syntax checking in the Advanced Editor*

This dialog contains the entire structure of the connection and transformation process that you created. It contains the following core elements:

- A sequence of expressions (which are steps)

- A *let* expression that acts as an outer container for a sequence of data transformation expressions

- An *in* expression that returns the output of the entire query

If you look at Figure 12-5, you can see several important things about the sequence of expressions that are inside the Let...In block:

- Each expression is named—and you can see its name in the Applied Steps list.

- Each expression refers to another expression (nearly always the previous expression) except for the first one.

- All but the final expression are terminated by a comma.

- An expression can run over several lines of code. It is the final comma that ends the expression in all but the last expression.

- The final expression becomes the output of the query.

349

Although this is a fairly simple M query, it contains all the essential elements that show how M works. Nearly every M query that you build will reflect these core principles:

- Have a Let...In block

- Contain one or more expressions that contain functions

The Let Statement

The *let* statement is a core element of the M language. It exists to allow a set of values to be evaluated individually where each is assigned to a variable name. These variables form a structured sequence of evaluation processes that are then used in the output expression that follows the *in* statement. You can consider it to be a "unit of processing" in many respects. Let statements can be nested to add greater flexibility.

In most let statements, the sequence of variables will be ordered from top to bottom (as you can see in Figures 12-5 and 12-6) where each named expression refers to, and builds on, the previous one. This is the way that the Query Editor presents named expressions as steps and is generally the easiest way to write M scripts that are easy to understand. However, it is not, technically, necessary to order the expressions like this as the expressions can be in any order.

Modifying M in the Advanced Editor

As with all things Power Query related, the Advanced Editor is best appreciated through an example. You saw in Chapter 3 how to create and modify connections to data sources. You can also modify connections directly in the "M" language. This assumes that you know and understand the database that you are working with.

1. Add a new query that connects to a SQL Server database. I am using a SQL instance and database on my PC.

2. Select this query in the Queries list on the left.

3. In the Home ribbon, click the Advanced Editor button. The Advanced Editor dialog will appear, as shown in Figure 12-6.

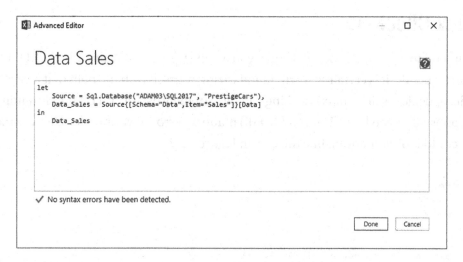

Figure 12-6. *The Advanced Editor dialog to alter a database connection*

4. Alter any of the following elements:

    a. The server name in the Source line (currently "ADAM03\SQL2017").

    b. The database name in the second line (currently Name="PrestigeCars").

    c. The schema name in the third line (currently Schema="Data").

    d. The table name in the third line (currently Item="Sales").

5. Click Done to confirm any changes and close the Advanced Editor.

This approach really is working without a safety net, and I am showing you this more to raise awareness than to suggest that you must always code M in this fashion. However, it does open the door to some far-reaching possibilities if you wish to continue learning all about the "M" language.

Note   You can, of course, click Cancel to ignore any changes that you have made to the M code in the Advanced Editor. The Query Editor will ask you to confirm that you really want to discard your modifications.

Syntax Checking

If you intend to write and modify M code, you are likely to be using the Advanced Editor—a lot. Consequently, it is certainly worth familiarizing yourself with the help that it can provide. Specifically, its syntax checking can be extremely useful and is entirely automatic.

Suppose that you have (heaven forbid!) made an error in your code. The Advanced Editor could look something like the one in Figure 12-7.

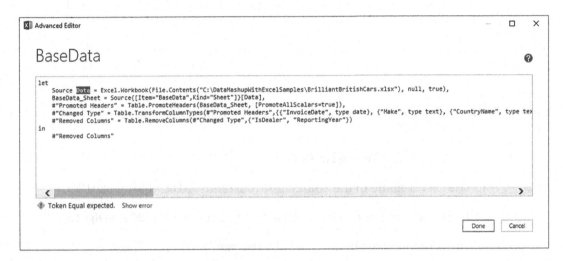

Figure 12-7. *Syntax checking in the Advanced Editor*

As you can see, in this case the Advanced Editor no longer displays a check box under the code and the reassuring message "No syntax errors have been detected." Instead you see an error message. Clicking the Show error link will highlight the source of the error by displaying it on a blue background.

Basic M Functions

The M language is vast—far too vast for anything other than a cursory overview in a single chapter. Nonetheless, to give some structure to the overview, it is worth knowing that there are a few key categories of M functions that you might find useful when beginning to use M.

The following list is not exhaustive by any means, but can, hopefully, serve as a starting point for your journey into M functions. The elementary categories are

- Text functions

- Date functions

- Time functions

- DateTime functions

- Logical functions

- Number functions

I am focusing on these categories as they are probably the most easily comprehensible in both their application and their use. Once you have seen some of these functions, we can move on to other functions from the range of those available.

Most of the more elementary M functions can be applied in ways that will probably remind you of their Excel counterparts. For instance, if you want to extend the formula that you used to concatenate the Make and Model columns so that you are only extracting the leftmost three characters from the Make, you can use code like this:

```
= Table.AddColumn(#"Changed Type", "CarType", each Text.Start([Make], 3) &
" " & [Model])
```

The result is shown in Figure 12-8.

Figure 12-8. *Applying a first text function*

As you can see, wrapping the Make column inside this particular text function has added an extra layer of data transformation to the expression.

Text Functions

Rather than take you step by step through every possible example of text functions, I prefer to show you some of the more useful text functions (at least, in my experience). These code snippets are given in Table 12-1, where you will doubtless recognize many of the functions that you have been accessing up until now through the Power Query user interface. Indeed, you may have used equivalent Excel functions when writing formulas in spreadsheets.

Table 12-1. *Text Function Examples*

Output	Code Snippet	Description
Left	Text.Start([Make],3)	Returns the first three characters from the Make column
Right	Text.End([Make],3)	Returns the last three characters from the Make column
Up to a specific character	Text.Start([Make],Text. PositionOf([Make]," "))	Returns the leftmost characters up to the first space
Up to a delimiter	Text.BeforeDelimiter([In voiceNumber], "-" ,"2")	Returns the text before the third hyphen
Text length	Text.Length([Make])	Finds the length of a text
Extract a substring	Text.Range([Make], 2, 3)	Extracts a specific number of characters from a text—starting at a specified position
Remove a subtext	Text.RemoveRange([Make], 2, 3)	Removes a specific number of characters from a text—starting at a specified position
Replace a text	Text.Replace([Make], "o", "a")	Replaces all the o characters with an a in the text or column
Trim spaces	Text.Trim([Make])	Removes leading and trailing spaces in the text or column
Convert to uppercase	Text.Upper([Make])	Converts the text or column to uppercase

(continued)

Table 12-1. (*continued*)

Output	Code Snippet	Description
Convert to lowercase	`Text.Lower([Make])`	Converts the text or column to lowercase
Add initial capitals	`Text.Proper([Make])`	Adds initial capitals to each word of the text or column

Note   You have probably noticed if you looked closely at these functions that any numeric parameters are zero based. So, to define the third hyphen when splitting text in a column, you would use *2*, not *3*.

There are, as you might expect, many more text functions available in M. However, the aim is not to drown the reader in technicalities, but to make you aware of both the way that M works and what is possible.

You may well wonder why you carry out operations like this in Power Query when you can do virtually the same thing in Excel formulas. Well, it is true that there is some overlap; so you have the choice of which to use. However, remember that there is no need to copy formulas down over a column in M, as the formula will apply, by definition, to an entire column.

Overall, you can perform certain operations at multiple stages in the data preparation and analysis process. It all depends on how you are using the data and with what tool you are carrying out the analyses.

Table 12-1 is only a subset of the available text functions in M. If you want to see the complete list, it is on the Microsoft website at `https://docs.microsoft.com/en-us/powerquery-m/text-functions`.

Number Functions

To extend your knowledge, Table 12-2 shows a few of the available number functions in M. Here I have concentrated on showing you some of the numeric type conversions as well as the core calculation functions.

Table 12-2. *Number Function Examples*

Output	Code Snippet	Description
Returns an 8-bit integer	Int8.From("25")	Converts the text or number to an 8-bit integer
Returns a 16-bit integer	Int16.From("2500")	Converts the text or number to a 16-bit integer
Returns a 32-bit integer	Int32.From("250000")	Converts the text or number to a 32-bit integer
Returns a 64-bit integer	Int64. From("2500000000")	Converts the text or number to a 64-bit integer
Returns a decimal number	Decimal.From("2500")	Converts the text or number to a decimal
Returns a Double number value from the given value	Double.From("2500")	Converts the text or number to a floating-point number
Takes a text as the source and converts to a numeric value	Number.FromText("2500")	Converts the text to a number
Rounds a number	Number.Round(5000, 0)	Rounds the number up or down to the number of decimals (or tens, hundreds, etc. for negative parameters)
Rounds a number up	Number.RoundUp (5020, -2)	Rounds the number up to the number of decimals (or tens, hundreds, etc. for negative parameters)
Rounds a number down	Number. RoundDown(100.01235, 2)	Rounds the number down to the number of decimals (or tens, hundreds, etc. for negative parameters)
Removes the sign	Number.Abs(-50)	Returns the absolute value of the number

(continued)

Table 12-2. (*continued*)

Output	Code Snippet	Description
Raises to a power	`Number.Power(10, 4)`	Returns the value of the first parameter to the power of the second
Modulo	`Number.Mod(5, 2)`	Returns the remainder resulting from the integer division of number by divisor
Indicates the sign of a number	`Number.Sign(-1)`	Returns 1 if the number is a positive number, -1 if it is a negative number, and 0 if it is zero
Gives the square root	`Number.Sqrt(4)`	Returns the square root of the number

---

Note   If you are an Excel user, you can probably see a distinct similarity with how you build formulas in Excel (in pivot tables in Power Pivot) except that here (as in Power Pivot) you use column names rather than cell references.

Table 12-2 is only a minor subset of the vast range of number functions that are available in M. If you want to see the complete list, it is on the Microsoft website at `https://docs.microsoft.com/en-us/powerquery-m/number-functions`.

Date Functions

M has many date functions. Table 12-3 contains a potentially useful sample of some of the available functions.

Table 12-3 is only a subset of the available date functions in M. If you want to see the complete list, it is on the Microsoft website at `https://docs.microsoft.com/en-us/powerquery-m/date-functions`.

Table 12-3. *Date Function Examples*

Output	Code Snippet	Description
Day	Date.Day(Date. FromText("25/07/2020"))	Returns the number of the day of the week from a date
Month	Date.Month(Date. FromText("25/07/2020"))	Returns the number of the month from a date
Year	Date.Year(Date. FromText("25/07/2020"))	Returns the week from a date
Day of week	Date.DayOfWeek(Date. FromText("25/07/2020"))	Returns the day of the week from a date
Name of weekday	Date.DayOfWeekName(Date. FromText("25/07/2020"))	Returns the weekday name from a date
First day of month	Date.StartOfMonth(Date. FromText("25/07/2020"))	Returns the first day of the month from a date
Last day of month	Date.EndOfMonth(Date. FromText("25/07/2020"))	Returns the last day of the month from a date
First day of year	Date.StartOfYear(Date. FromText("25/07/2020"))	Returns the first day of the year from a date
Last day of year	Date.EndOfYear(Date. FromText("25/07/2020"))	Returns the last day of the year from a date
Day of year	Date.DayOfYear(Date. FromText("25/07/2020"))	Returns the day of the year from a date
Week of year	Date.WeekOfYear(Date. FromText("25/07/2020"))	Returns the week of the year from a date
Quarter	Date.QuarterOfYear(Date. FromText("25/07/2020"))	Returns the number of the quarter from a date
First day of quarter	Date.StartOfQuarter(Date. FromText("25/07/2020"))	Returns the first day of the quarter from a date
Last day of quarter	Date.EndOfQuarter(Date. FromText("25/07/2020"))	Returns the last day of the quarter from a date

Time Functions

M also has many time functions. Table 12-4 contains a potentially useful sample of the available functions.

Table 12-4. *Time Function Examples*

Output	Code Snippet	Description
Hour	Time.Hour(#time(14, 30, 00))	Returns the hour from a time
Minute	Time.Minute(#time(14, 30, 00))	Returns the minute from a time
Second	Time.Second(#time(14, 30, 00))	Returns the second from a time
Time from fraction	Time.From(0.5)	Returns the time from a fraction of the day

Table 12-4 is only a subset of the available time functions in M. If you want to see the complete list, it is on the Microsoft website at https://docs.microsoft.com/en-us/powerquery-m/time-functions.

Equally, as they are so similar to the date and time functions, I have not shown here the datetime functions and the datetimezone functions. These are also available on the Microsoft website.

Duration Functions

M can also extract durations—in days, hours, minutes, and seconds. Table 12-5 shows some of the basic duration functions.

Table 12-5. *Duration Function Examples*

Output	Code Snippet	Description
Days	Duration.Days(#duration(10, 15, 55, 20))	Duration in days
Hours	Duration.Hours(#duration(10, 15, 55, 20))	Duration in hours
Minutes	Duration.Minutes(#duration(10, 15, 55, 20))	Duration in minutes
Seconds	Duration.Seconds(#duration(10, 15, 55, 20))	Duration in seconds

Table 12-5 is nearly all the available duration functions in M. If you want to see the remaining few functions, they are on the Microsoft website at `https://docs.microsoft.com/en-us/powerquery-m/duration-functions`.

M Concepts

The time has now come to "remove the stabilizers" from the bicycle and learn how to cycle unaided. This means, firstly, becoming acquainted with several M structural concepts.

This means moving on from the "starter" functions that you can use to modify the contents of the data to creating and modifying data structures themselves. M is essentially focused on loading and presenting tabular data structures, so tables of data are an essential data structure. However, there are other data structures that it can manipulate—and that you have seen in passing in previous chapters. In this chapter, then, we will look at the three core data structures. Collectively, these are classified as *structured* values—as opposed to the *primitive* values such as text, number, or date and time. Some of these are

- Lists

- Records

- Tables

However, before delving into these structured data elements, you need to understand two fundamental aspects of the M language. These are

- Data types

- M values (also referred to as variables or identifiers)

So, without further ado, let's start your journey into M.

M Data Types

If you are creating your own lists, records, and tables, then it will help to know the basics about data types in M.

When beginning to use M, you need to remember that primitive data values must always be one of the following types:

- Number
- Text
- Date
- Time
- DateTime
- DateTimeZone
- Duration
- Logical (Boolean if you prefer)
- Binary
- Null

There are other types such as function, any, or anynonnull, but we will not be covering them in this chapter.

All data types expect to be entered in a specific way. Indeed, you must enter data in the way shown in Table 12-6 to avoid errors in your M code.

Table 12-6. *Data Type Entry*

Data Type	Code Snippet	Comments
Number	100 0.12345 2.4125E8	Do not use formatting such as thousand separators or monetary symbols
Text	"Calidra Power Query Training"	Always enclose in double quotes. Use two double quotes to enter the actual quotes text

(continued)

Table 12-6. (*continued*)

Data Type	Code Snippet	Comments
Date	#date(2020,12,25)	Dates must be year, month, and day in the #date() function
Time	#time(15,55,20)	Times must be hour, minute, and second in the #time() function
DateTime	#datetime(2020,12,25, 15,55,20)	Datetimes must be year, month, day, hour, minute, and second in the #datetime() function
DateTimeZone	#datetimezone(2020,12,25, 15,55,20,-5,-30)	Datetimezones must be year, month, day, hour, minute, second, day offset, and hour offset in the #datetimezone() function
Duration	#duration(0,1,0,0)	Days, hours, minutes, and seconds comma-separated inside the #duration() function
Logical	true	True or false in lowercase

M Values

Before diving deeper into actual coding, you really need to know a few fundamentals concerning M values:

- Values are the output of expressions.

- Values are also variables.

- The names of values are case-sensitive.

- If the value name contains spaces or restricted characters, they must be wrapped in #"" (pound sign followed by double quotes).

This fourth bullet point clearly begs the question "what is a restricted character?" The simple answer—that avoids memorizing lists of glyphs—is "anything not alphanumeric."

> **Note**   The Power Query Editor interface makes the steps (which are the values returned by an expression) more readable by adding spaces wherever possible. Consequently, these values always appear in the M code as #"Step Name".

Defining Your Own Variables in M

As the values returned by any expression are also variables, it follows that defining your own variables in M is breathtakingly simple. All you have to do is to enter a variable name (with the pound sign and in quotes if it contains spaces or restricted characters), an equals sign, and the variable definition.

As a really simple example, take a look at Figure 12-9. This M script defines the three parameters required for the List.Numbers() function that you will see in Table 12-7 and then uses the variables inside the function.

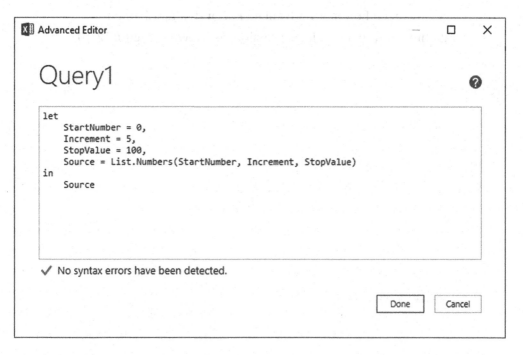

Figure 12-9. *User variables in M*

There are only a few things to remember when defining your own variables:

- They respect the same naming convention as output values in M.

- A variable can be referenced inside the subexpression where it is defined and any expressions that contain the subexpression.

- A variable can be a simple value or a calculation that returns a value.

Writing M Queries

Before actually writing M, you need to know how and where to write your code. Suppose that you need an environment to practice the examples in the remainder of this chapter:

1. Open a new, blank Excel file.

2. In the Data ribbon, click Get Data ➤ From Other Sources ➤ Blank Query. The Power Query Editor will open.

3. Click Advanced Editor. An Advanced Editor dialog will open containing only an outer let expression, as shown in Figure 12-10.

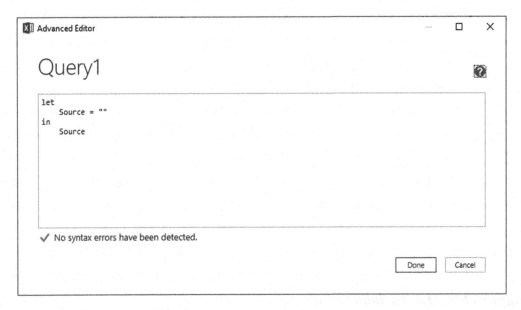

Figure 12-10. *Preparing the Advanced Editor to write M code*

Note   Technically, a let clause is not required in M. You can simply enter an expression. However, I prefer to write M "by the book"—at least to begin with.

Lists

You met M lists in Chapter 11 when creating popup lists for query-based parameters (showing, once again, that everything in the Query Editor is based on M). Lists are nothing more than a series of values.

Lists have specific uses in M and can be used directly in a data model. However, they are more generally used as intermediate steps in more complex data transformation processes. If you have a programming background, you might find it helpful to consider lists as being something akin to arrays.

Creating Lists Manually

A list is simply a comma-separated set of values enclosed in braces—such as

{1,2,3}

Once integrated into the structure of an M query, it could look like the example shown in Figure 12-11.

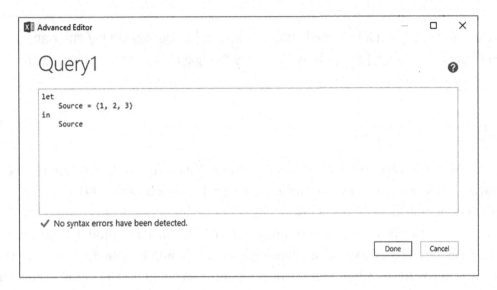

Figure 12-11. *A list in the Advanced Editor*

Once created—either as an intermediate step in a query or as the final output of the query—the list can be used by anything that requires a list as its input. Indeed, if you click the Done button for the example shown earlier, the Power Query Editor will display this piece of M code as a functioning list—exactly like the one that you created in Chapter 11. So you can now create custom lists for parameters (for instance) quickly and easily.

There is some technical information that you need to know about lists:

- Lists are unlimited in size.

- Lists can contain data of the same type (i.e., all elements are numeric values, dates, or texts, for instance)—or the data can be of different types.

- Lists can be empty—that is, composed of a pair of empty braces.

- Lists can be entered horizontally or vertically. That is, the list shown earlier could have been typed in as

```
Source = {
          1,
          2,
          3
        }
```

Generating lists is really easy; knowing when to use lists is the hard part.

Generating Sequences Using Lists

Lists have many uses in M, but there is one area where they shine, and that is generating sequences of numbers, dates, or texts. Rather than laboriously explain each approach individually, I have collated a set of examples of M code snippets for list generation in Table 12-7.

Table 12-7. *List Generation*

Code Snippet	Description
{1..100}	An uninterrupted sequence of numbers from 1 to 100, inclusive
{1..100, 201..400}	An uninterrupted sequence of numbers from 1 to 100, then from 201 to 400
List.Numbers(0, 100, 5)	Starting at zero increments by 5 until 100 is reached
{"A".."Z"}	The uppercase letters A through Z
List.Dates(#date(2020, 1, 1), 366, #duration(1, 0, 0, 0))	Each individual day for the year 2020—starting on 1st January 2020, 366 days (expressed as a duration in days) are added
List.Times(#time(1, 0, 0), 24, #duration(0, 1, 0, 0))	Each hour in the day starting with 1 AM

Accessing Values from a List

If you move to more advanced M coding, you may well want to refer to a value from a list in your M script. At its simplest, this is done using *positional references*. Here is a short piece of M code that does just this:

```
let
    MyList = {"George","Bill","George W.", "Barack", "Donald"},
    source = MyList{3}
in
    source
```

The output of this code snippet is the *fourth* element in the list—making the point that lists in M are *zero based*. That is, the first element in a list is the element 0.

List Functions

There are many dozens of list functions available in M. Far too many to go through in detail here. So, to give you an idea of some of the possible ways that you can manipulate lists, take a look at Table 12-8. All of them use the very simple list of that you can see earlier.

Table 12-8. *List Functions*

Output	Code Snippet	Description
First value	`List.First(MyList)`	Returns the first element in a list
Last value	`List.Last(MyList)`	Returns the last element in a list
Sort list values	`List.Sort(MyList)`	Sorts the values in a list
Extract range	`List.Range(MyList, 4)`	Extracts a range of values from a list
Return value(s)	`List.Select(MyList , each _ ="Adam")`	Returns the elements from a list that match a criterion
Generate a list	`List.Generate()`	Creates a list of sequential values
Aggregate values	`List.Sum(MyList)`	Aggregate the numeric values in a list
Replace values	`List.ReplaceMatchingItems (MyList, {"Joe", "Fred"})`	Replaces a range of values in a list
Convert to list	`Table.Column(MyList)`	Returns a column from a table as a list

Table 12-8 is only a small subset of the available list functions in M. If you want to see the full range of functions, it is on the Microsoft website at `https://docs.microsoft.com/en-us/powerquery-m/list-functions`.

Records

If lists can be considered as columns of data that you can use in your M code, *records* are rows of data. You might well find yourself needing to define records when creating more complex data transformation routines in M.

At its simplest, here is a sample record created in M:

```
let
    Source = [Surname = "Aspin", FirstName = "Adam"]
in
    Source
```

If you need to access the data in one element of a record, you append the record variable name with the field name in square brackets, like this:

```
let
    Source = [Surname = "Aspin", FirstName = "Adam"],
    Output = Source[Surname]
in
    Output
```

There are a few record functions that you may find useful. These are outlined in Table 12-9.

Table 12-9. *Record Functions*

Output	Code Snippet	Description
Add field	Record.AddField()	Adds a field to a record
Remove field	Record.RemoveFields()	Removes a field from a record
Rename field	Record.RenameFields()	Renames a field in a record
Output field	Record.Field()	Returns the value of the specified field in the record
Count	Record.FieldCount()	Returns the number of fields in a record

Table 12-9 is only a subset of the available record functions in M. If you want to see the complete list, it is on the Microsoft website at https://docs.microsoft.com/en-us/powerquery-m/record-functions.

Tables

The final structured data type that you could well employ in M code is the *table* type. As you might expect in a language that exists to load, cleanse, and shape tabular data, the table data type is fundamental to M.

If you decide to create your own tables manually in M, then you will need to include, at a minimum, the following structural elements:

- The #table() function

- A set of column/field headers where each field name is enclosed in double quotes and the set of field names is wrapped in braces

- Individual rows of data, each enclosed in braces and comma-separated, where the collection of rows is also wrapped in braces

A very simple example of a hand-coded table could look like this:

```
#table(
        {"Surname", "FirstName"},
        {
            {"Johnson","Vladimir"},
            {"Putin","Emmanuel"},
            {"Macron","Angela"},
            {"Merkel","Boris"}
        }
    )
```

However, the weakness with this approach is that there are no type definitions for the fields. Consequently, a much more robust approach would be to extend the table like this:

```
#table(
        type table
                [
                    #"Surname" = text,
                    #"FirstName" = text
                ],
            {
                {"Johnson","Vladimir"},
```

```
            {"Putin","Emmanuel"},
            {"Macron","Angela"},
            {"Merkel","Boris"}
        }
    )
```

Note   The data type keywords that you specify to define the required data type were outlined earlier in this chapter.

There are many table functions available in M. I have outlined a few of the more useful ones in Table 12-10.

Table 12-10. *Table Functions*

Output	Code Snippet	Description
Merge tables	Table.Combine()	Merges tables of similar or different structures
Number of records	Table.RowCount()	Returns the number of records in a table
First	Table.First()	Returns the first record in a table
Last	Table.Last()	Returns the last record in a table
Find rows	Table.FindText()	Returns the rows in the table that contain the required text
Insert rows	Table.InsertRows()	Inserts rows in a table
Output rows	Table.Range()	Outputs selected rows
Delete rows	Table.DeleteRows()	Deletes rows in a table
Select columns	Table.SelectColumns()	Outputs selected columns

Table 12-10 is, as you can probably imagine, only a tiny subset of the available table functions in M. If you want to see the complete list, it is on the Microsoft website at https://docs.microsoft.com/en-us/powerquery-m/table-functions.

Other Function Areas

As I mentioned previously, M is a vast subject that could fill an entire (and very large) book. We have taken a rapid overview of some of the core concepts and functions, but there is much that remains to be learned if you wish to master M. If you are really interested in learning more, then I suggest that you search the Microsoft documentation for the elements outlined in Table 12-11 to further your knowledge.

Table 12-11. *Other Function Areas*

Function Area	Description
Accessing data functions	Access data and return table values
Binary functions	Access binary data
Combiner functions	Used by other library functions that merge values to apply row-by-row logic
DateTime functions	Functions applied to datetime data
DateTimeZone functions	Functions applied to datetime data with time zone information
Expression functions	M code that was used for expressions
Line functions	Converts data to lists of values
Replacer	Used by other functions in the library to replace a given value in a structure
Splitter	Splits values into subelements
Type	Returns M types
Uri	Handles URLs and URIs
Value	Handles M values

Custom Functions in M

M also allows you to write custom functions that can carry out highly specific tasks repeatedly.

As an example of a very simple custom function, try adding the following code snippet to a new, blank query:

```
let DiscountAnalysis =
                (Discount as number) =>
                                if Discount < 10 then
                                "Poor" else "Excellent"

in DiscountAnalysis
```

When you close the Advanced Editor, you will see that this query has been recognized as being an M function and appears as such in the list of queries. You can see this in Figure 12-12 (where I have renamed it to "DiscountAnalysis").

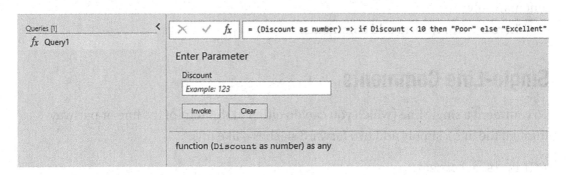

Figure 12-12. *User-defined functions in M*

You can now invoke the function at any time interactively by entering a value as the discount and clicking the Invoke button. You can also use this function inside other M functions. Indeed, this is probably why you created a custom function in the first place.

If you want to see a more advanced function, take a look at the following code snippet, which pads out a date to add leading zeroes to the day and month if these are required:

```
let
    FormatDate = (InDate as date) =>
let
    Source = Text.PadStart(Text.From(Date.Month(InDate)),2,"0")
    & "/" & Text.PadStart(Text.From(Date.Day(InDate)),2,"0")
    & "/" &Text.From(Date.Year(InDate))
```

```
in
        Source
in
        FormatDate
```

Adding Comments to M Code

Complex M code can be extremely dense. So you will likely need ways of remembering why you created a process when you return to it weeks or months later.

One simple way to make your own life easier is to add comments to M code. You can do this both for code that you have written and queries that have been generated automatically.

There are two ways to add comments.

Single-Line Comments

To comment a single line (which you can do either at the start of the line or partway through the line), simply add two forward slashes—like this:

```
//This is a comment
```

Everything from the two slashes until the end of the line will be considered to be a comment and will not be evaluated by M.

Multiline Comments

Multiline comments can cover several lines—or even part of a line. They cover all the text that is enclosed in /* ... */.

```
/* This is a comment
Over
Several lines */
```

Everything inside the /* ...*/ will be considered to be a comment and will not be evaluated by M.

Conclusion

This final chapter completes this book on loading and transforming source data for analysis in Excel. In this chapter, you learned the basics of the M language that underpins everything that you learned in this book up until now.

You began by seeing how you can use the Power Query Editor interface to assist you in writing short snippets of M code. Then you moved on to discovering the fundamental M concepts such as expressions, variables, and values. Finally, you learned about data types in M and the more complex data types such as lists and tables that underlie complex data transformations. This involved learning to use the Advanced Editor to write and debug your code.

In this chapter and the 11 previous chapters, you have seen essentially a three-stage process: first, you find the data, then you load it into Power Query, and from there, you cleanse and modify it. The techniques that you can use are simple but powerful and can range from changing a data type to merging multiple data tables. Now that your data is prepared and ready for use, you can add it to the Power Pivot/Excel data model or directly into an Excel spreadsheet and start using it to deliver real-world analytics.

I hope that you have enjoyed reading this book, and that it will help you to master the art of finding, transforming, and loading external data into Excel using Power Query and M.

APPENDIX A

Sample Data

If you wish to follow the examples used in this book—and I hope you will—you will need some sample data to work with. All the files referenced in this book are available for download and can easily be installed on your local PC. This appendix explains where to obtain the sample files, how to install them, and what they are used for.

Downloading the Sample Data

The sample files used in this book are currently available on the Apress site. You can access them as follows:

1. In your web browser, navigate to the following URL: `www.apress.com/9781484260173`.

2. Click the button Download Source Code. This will take you to the GitHub page for the source code for this book.

3. Click Clone or Download ➤ Download Zip and download the file DataMashupWithExcelSamples.zip.

You will then need to extract the files and directories from the zip file. How you do this will depend on which software you are using to handle zipped files. If you are not using any third-party software, then one way to do this is

1. Create a directory named C:\DataMashupWithExcelSamples.

2. In the Windows Explorer navigation pane, click the file DataMashupWithExcelSamples.zip.

3. Select all the files and folders that it contains.

4. Copy them to the folder that you created in step 1.

377

© Adam Aspin 2020
A. Aspin, *Data Mashup with Microsoft Excel Using Power Query and M*,
https://doi.org/10.1007/978-1-4842-6018-0

Index

379

© Adam Aspin 2020
A. Aspin, *Data Mashup with Microsoft Excel Using Power Query and M*,
https://doi.org/10.1007/978-1-4842-6018-0

Printed in the United States
By Bookmasters